The Process of Reading

The Process of Reading

A Cognitive Analysis
of Fluent Reading and Learning to Read

D. C. Mitchell
University of Exeter, Devon, England

JOHN WILEY & SONS
Chichester · New York · Brisbane · Toronto · Singapore

Library of Congress Cataloging in Publication Data:

Mitchell, D. C. (Don C.)
   The process of reading.

   Bibliography: p.
   Includes indexes.
   1. Reading.   I. Title.
LB1050.M56   428.4   81-21912
                               AACR2
ISBN 0 471 10199 0

British Library Cataloguing in Publication Data:

Mitchell, D. C.
   The process of reading; a cognitive analysis
   of fluent reading and learning to read.
   1. Reading, Psychology of
   I. Title
   428.4′01′9   BF456.RZ

ISBN 0 471 10199 0

Photosetting by Thomson Press (India) Limited, New Delhi
and printed in the United States of America.

For Etta and my father

Contents

Preface

In the past decade or two there has been a dramatic increase in the amount of research on reading. We have now reached a stage where several hundred new and relevant papers are being published every year. As the amount of work has increased investigators have tended to specialize in more and more detailed aspects of the process and it has become increasingly difficult for anyone interested in reading to keep himself adequately informed about a broad range of developments in the field. Obviously, there is a case for trying to summarize and integrate parts of this research. The part I have concentrated on concerns the cognitive skills that underlie reading.

There are two recognized ways of reviewing a field like this. One is to assemble a group of experts and give each person responsibility for presenting his or her own individual topic. The other is for one or two authors to cover the whole field without outside assistance. The first approach is easily the more common: it demands less of a commitment from any individual contributor and it has the clear advantage that every aspect of the subject is dealt with by a specialist. However, there are certain drawbacks as well. In particular, the subject-matter of the book tends to be divided up into relatively isolated subsections, and all too often the individual topics are covered without any systematic consideration of the interactions and relationships between them. This kind of deficiency could be particularly important in any attempt to describe a complex and integrated skill like reading, and for this reason, among others, I decided to adopt the second approach. Perhaps the most obvious result of this is that in addition to an analysis of the various subskills of reading there is a relatively strong emphasis throughout the book on the way in which the individual subprocesses work together to achieve their common purpose.

The book is intended for anyone interested in the skills that underlie reading and learning to read. This almost certainly includes educationists, educational researchers and people responsible for designing reading curricula. It should also include experimental psychologists and students interested in cognitive psychology and psycholinguistics. It is not really intended to be an 'easy read' for those who might want a quick overview of the subject and some of my readers might feel that there is an excessive concentration on empirical evidence and on detailed methodological issues. The emphasis on empirical work is partly a reaction to some of the earlier literature on reading. In the past, too much attention has been paid to speculative and unsubstantiated theories. Indeed, such theories have sometimes even been offered as part of the rationale xii

for certain widespread types of teaching practice. Applications of this kind are premature and they might even have damaging consequences for the learners. If a theory is to serve a practical purpose it must amount to something more than an elegant and intuitively plausible account of the behaviour under consideration. It should be subjected to empirical tests to ensure that it genuinely corresponds to the way in which real readers perform. If it fails to do this, then it is no more than an imaginative piece of fiction. With this in mind, I have tended to pay careful attention to empirical evidence and to ignore untested theories even when they are consistent with my own views. On the few occasions that I have departed from this guiding principle I have tried to indicate that the ideas are speculative to avoid giving any misleading impression about their true status.

So much for ideology. It only remains for me to thank some of the people who contributed in one way or another to the development and completion of the book. First, I am grateful to Ken Strongman and to Max Coltheart for their help and influence in getting the project off the ground. I am also indebted to David Green for his full and stimulating contribution to the ideas that emerged when we were collaborating on an SSRC-funded project on 'semantic processes during reading' between 1974 and 1977. Some of these ideas form the basis of the work covered in Chapters 4 and 5. Next, it is a pleasure to acknowledge the contribution of a number of people including Gordon Stanley, Andrew Monk and Noel Sharkey all of whom assisted me by reading and making useful comments on preliminary drafts of one or more chapters of the book. I would also like to thank Angela Boobyer for taking on the task of typing the manuscript and for carrying it out so rapidly and efficiently, and James Gould of the Exeter University Teaching Services Unit for his careful work in preparing the illustrations. On a more domestic note my sincere thanks go to my father, J. Clyde Mitchell, for his general encouragement and advice and to my wife, Etta, for her support, encouragement and tolerance of diversion throughout the period I was working on the book. Last, but not least, I am grateful to several generations of students in my third-year undergraduate seminar on Reading. They served as a panel for my informal 'market research' on the book and their comments and criticisms succeeded in killing off many of my less viable ideas before (or less efficiently shortly *after*) they were first committed to paper.

Exeter, July 1981   DON MITCHELL

Acknowledgements

I am grateful to the following authors and publishers for permission to reproduce copyrighted material:

K. Rayner and Academic Press for my Figures 2.2 and 2.3. From Rayner, K., The perceptual span and peripheral cues in reading. *Cognitive Psychology*, 1975, **7**, 65–81.

K. S. Goodman for Figure 6.1. From a diagram accompanying Goodman, K. S., Reading: A psycholinguistic guessing game. In Singer, H., and Ruddell, R. B. (Eds.), *Theoretical Processes and models of Reading*. IRA, Delaware, 1970.

P. B. Gough, and MIT Press for Figure 6.2. From Gough, P. B. One second of reading. In Kavanagh, J. F., and Mattingly, I. G. (Eds.), *Language by Ear and Eye.*, Cambridge, Mass.: MIT Press, 1972.

D. E. Rumelhart and the International Association for the Study of Attention and Performance for Figure 6.3. From Rumelhart, D. E., Towards an interactive model of reading. In Dornic, S. (Ed.), *Attention and Performance VI*. Hillsdale, N. J.: Lawrence Erlbaum Associates, 1977.

CHAPTER 1

Introduction

1.1 WHAT IS READING?

Reading can be defined loosely as the ability to make sense of written or printed symbols. The reader uses the symbols to guide the recovery of information from his or her memory and subsequently uses this information to construct a plausible interpretation of the writer's message.

It is easy to forget how complicated this process is. Anyone reading this book will be a highly accomplished reader. For people like this, reading has become a skilled, automatic process and there is rarely any occasion for them to pause and consider what the process entails.

Consider some of the facts, though. A skilled reader may be familiar with 30 000 or more words and yet he or she is normally able to identify any one of these words within a fraction of a second. He can do this despite the fact that the constituent letters are frequently represented by different shapes from one text to another and even, in the case of handwriting, from one instance of the letter to the next. He can even identify words that have been misprinted or mis-spelt. In identifying stimuli that are subject to this amount of variation, he is capable of performing a feat which is well beyond the capacity of the most powerful computer programs available today.

Accomplished readers can cope with the fact that many words have different meanings in different contexts and they can use this knowledge to appreciate puns and other forms of word-play. They can combine the meanings of individual words to derive the meanings of sentences and more extended passages of prose. This may involve them in drawing inferences, calling upon their previous experiences in the situation under consideration, constructing images of scenes, and appreciating poetic form and nuances of meaning.

How does the fluent reader meet all the requirements of this extremely demanding task? How is the skill acquired in the first place? These are the central questions that will be addressed in the body of this book.

1.2 PSYCHOLOGY AND READING

Psychologists have studied reading skills for two main reasons. One is simply curiosity. It represents an intellectual challenge to discover how a person makes sense of printed material.

Part of the challenge lies in the very complexity of the process since, as Huey observed, 'to completely analyze what we do when we read would almost be the acme of a psychologist's achievements, for it would be to describe very many of the most intricate workings of the human mind' (Huey, 1908, p. 6).

The second motive for studying reading is a more practical one. It is to discover principles that can be used as a basis for improving techniques of teaching reading. Clearly, the main concern in this case is with the processes by which children learn the skills required for fluent reading. However, it is not easy to discover how these skills are learned unless we have a clear idea of *what* is learned. This means that we have to understand the nature of the definitions, rules and procedures which are eventually used by accomplished readers to extract the meaning of the text. Thus, it is useful to start by trying to understand the mental operations that enable a fluent reader to arrive at the meaning of text, and then proceed later to the more practical issues of learning to read.

1.3   MENTAL OPERATIONS IN FLUENT READING

How can we analyse and describe the process of reading? The most common approach is to divide the process up into a number of distinct subskills each of which has a different function and a different mode of operation. For example, many models of reading incorporate subprocesses that are responsible for 'word recognition', 'sentence comprehension' and other similar subtasks. Once the process has been analysed in this way an attempt can be made to specify the procedures by which each subprocess achieves its purpose and to describe how all of the separate units interact and work together within the whole process.

Many of the processes that would be included in a detailed description of this kind would be similar to the kinds of operation that can be carried out by a computer program. For example, it would be necessary to store and retrieve information, to compare the contents of different stores, and to manipulate information in several other ways. For this reason it will be convenient to describe the mental operations in terms of the computer analogy. In doing so we shall be adopting an approach to theorizing which is used by most current researchers in the field of cognitive psychology.

A computer program that operated like a 'normal' reader would be extraordinarily complex. For one thing, it would have to be extremely flexible since people read in different ways in different circumstances. For example, the strategy a person adopts is likely to depend on the nature of the response that he has to make to the text. Thus a person reading a novel with the aim of following the plot (and perhaps enjoying it) is likely to process the material in a different way from someone who is required to read the same text aloud. Reading strategy is also likely to be influenced by the characteristics of the reading matter. Difficult material will normally be processed differently from easy material. Furthermore, the reading process is bound to depend on the visual quality of the text and the way in which it is presented. When the quality is poor, as in bad handwriting, the reader will be forced to guess and reconstruct the text to a greater extent than he would if he were reading a clear script.

All of these potential strategies would have to be included in a comprehensive description of the reading process and, if a computer program were used to model the process, they would obviously have to be included in this program as well. Furthermore, it would be necessary to add a new subroutine to evaluate the task demands in any reading situation and select the most appropriate strategy.

There are other problems which make it difficult to develop a complete and satisfactory model of the reading process. Foremost among these is the fact that different people read in different ways. In particular, it is likely that the way in which a learner reads is quite different from the kinds of processing used by a fluent reader. One might attempt to tackle this problem by trying to provide a different description of the reading process for each kind of reader that can be identified. However, it is unlikely that a goal of this kind could be achieved within the foreseeable future and so it is necessary to accept a more modest account of the reading process.

The approach that will be adopted in this book will be to concentrate initially on one type of strategy (silent reading for meaning) and on one kind of reader (the fluent reader). The description of this reading process will be used as a basis for observations about alternative strategies, and for an extended discussion of individual differences in reading skills.

1.4   PLAN OF THE BOOK

The first part of the book deals with fluent reading. Various subprocesses of fluent reading are examined in turn. The order corresponds roughly to the order in which mental operations are carried out on new material.

First, and rather trivially, the reader must direct his eyes towards the appropriate part of the text. This is essential because we can only pick up detailed information from a small area of the visual field at a time, and so the only way of covering the text is to move the eyes and fixate on a series of different points along each line. During each fixation the stimulus material is processed visually and an internal representation of part of the page is built up. Chapter 2 deals with a number of aspects of this preliminary visual analysis of the text and it will focus, in particular, on two questions. First, what are the characteristics of the internal representation produced by the peripheral processes? For example, how much detail does it contain? Does it include visual information derived from different fixations? If so, how are the successive visual samples combined? Secondly, what are the factors that determine which portions of the page are fixated upon? For example, are the eye movements guided by the processing requirements of the 'higher' cognitive processes of reading?

The internal representation produced by these preliminary visual processes provides the raw data for the next mental operation: the identification of the individual words in the text. Chapter 3 concentrates on this process and on the retrieval of stored information about these words. It will be assumed that the reader possesses an internal dictionary which contains information about the shape, spelling, pronunciation and meaning of each of the words in his vocabulary. The problem of word recognition is to identify successive portions of the visual data base with appropriate entries in the dictionary. Various kinds of information could potentially be drawn upon to help establish this kind of link (e.g. the identity of individual letters, word-shape, rules for spelling and pronunciation, contextual information, etc.) and one purpose of the chapter will be to determine which of these sources actually play a part in the identification process in fluent reading. The second main aim will be to describe and evaluate some of the more important suggestions as to how this process is carried out.

Once the words have been identified and information has been recovered about their potential meanings and grammatical functions, the reader is in a position to try to understand the meanings of larger linguistic units such as phrases, clauses and sentences. Some of the processes that are used for this purpose are examined in Chapter 4. One aspect of the problem is to determine the grammatical relationships between the words. To do this it is necessary to make a number of decisions about each sentence: Which is the main verb? Which noun is its subject, and its object (if any)? Which adjectives qualify which nouns? How are the subordinate clauses related to the main clause? And so on. Various hypotheses about these processes will be considered, but it will only be possible to draw tentative conclusions because the experimental data bearing on these issues are open to a variety of interpretations.

The meaning of a sentence is also influenced by factors other than its grammatical structure. It depends upon the meanings of the individual words and upon rules which govern the ways in which they can be combined. Also, the significance of a sentence depends on the relationship between the sentence itself and earlier material. For example, consider the first sentence in the previous paragraph. The phrase 'the words' refers to entities in the previous paragraphs and cannot be understood properly if the appropriate links with earlier material are not established by the reader. Experiments on these contextual processes will be summarized in an attempt to determine how the links are made and how the meaning of the sentence is reformulated.

This section on the links between different sentences will complete the account of the subprocesses of reading. However, as mentioned earlier, an analysis of this kind needs to be supplemented before it can be regarded as a comprehensive description of the process. It is necessary to consider how the different processes influence one another and how they are modified as they work together. The next chapter (Chapter 5) therefore pays particular attention to the relationships between the subprocesses.

At this point we will be in a good position to summarize and draw together the main conclusions that have been reached about the process of fluent reading. Chapter 6 will tackle this indirectly by reviewing some of the more important models of the process and commenting both on their completeness and on the extent to which they are consistent with the experimental data. We shall argue that current models are inadequate in many ways and we shall present the framework of a new description which attempts to avoid the major shortcomings of the earlier models.

The description of reading that emerges will be used in Chapter 7 as a framework for considering individual differences in reading. Several different kinds of reader will be compared in turn with fluent readers. These will include acquired dyslexics and other poor readers, people who read effectively but slowly and, finally, normal children who are in the process of learning to read. In each case an attempt will be made to determine which subprocesses are responsible for the major part of the difference. The main emphasis in this chapter will be placed on the differences between learners and fluent readers and this will provide the starting point for a discussion of learning to read (in Chapter 8).

The examination of the learning process will start by considering some of the interdependencies between the acquisition of different subskills. Are there skills that cannot be developed until other, more basic skills have been acquired? If so, what are the main bottlenecks in the process of learning to read? After considering relationships in the development of different subskills we proceed to look at the acquisition of some of the more important subskills, such as the pronunciation and direct recognition of words. Finally, we cover some of the ways in which the learning process can be facilitated. Here we evaluate the benefits of presenting the reading material in appropriate linguistic or pictorial contexts and we pay particular attention to the advantages and disadvantages of phonic training programmes and programmes that use modified teaching alphabets.

CHAPTER 2

The extraction of visual information from the page

2.1 PRELIMINARIES

When we read we tend to get the impression that our eyes pick out the words by drifting continuously and smoothly along successive lines of print. In fact, as long as a century ago Javal (1878) demonstrated that this impression is a misleading one. Instead of gliding smoothly across the text, the eyes jump sharply from one position to another and they remain relatively stationary in each position for about a quarter of a second. These rapid eye movements are referred to as *saccades* or *saccadic movements* and the intervening pauses are known as *fixations*.

The basic characteristics of the patterns of eye movements in reading are well-established. The saccade itself lasts between 20 and 50 ms (Huey, 1908; Woodworth, 1938). The duration of fixations can vary markedly within a single experimental session (Rayner and McConkie, 1976) and the average pause changes as a function of reading experience (Buswell, 1922), but for fluent readers most fixations tend to last between 200 and 250 ms.

When a person is reading English most of the saccades are obviously movements from left to right, but all readers make a small proportion of movements in the opposite direction. These are known as *regressions* or *regressive eye movements* and they account for about 10 per cent and 30 per cent of all saccades for fluent readers and learners respectively (Buswell, 1922).

The distance covered during saccadic movements varies dramatically from moment to moment. Saccades as small as two character spaces (or 0.5°) and as large as 18 character space (4.5°) have been observed within a few lines of one another (Rayner and McConkie, 1976). Overall, however, the size of a forward eye movement seems to be about eight character spaces or 2°.

These basic characteristics of eye movement have obvious implications for all of the subsequent processes in reading. The pattern of fixations and saccades that occurs when a person reads a page of text obviously determines the way in which the information on the page is made available to the higher centres. For example, suppose that in reading the middle line of the following portion of text* a person fixated first on the *s* in *callous* and then on the *e* in *the*, and so on. Then for the first quarter of a second, the information available for analysis would consist of the *s* and whatever other material was visible around it.

* From *The Ebony Tower* by John Fowles.

early childhood. A master at my preparatory school had once,
   2   1   3   4   5   6   7
in the callous manner of his kind, referred to me as a shrimp,

and the sobriquet was unanimously adopted by my then friends.

For the next 30 ms (say) (i.e. the duration of the regressive movement to the second fixation in the word *the*) the information would consist of any material which is visible while the eye is in motion. After this, the raw visual data would be made up of words and letters in the vicinity of the second fixation, and so on.

The amount of information that can be extracted from the page will obviously be determined by the following three factors: (1) the amount of information that can be extracted during the saccades, (2) the amount that can be picked up during fixations and (3) the spatial distribution of the fixations on the page. In the case of this last factor the efficiency of the extraction process will depend on the degree to which the reader can guide and control his eye movements to cover the page economically.

In the next three sections we shall try to determine how much information can be extracted during a saccade and during a fixation. Later in the chapter we consider the nature of eye movement control. The conclusions drawn from this discussion should equip us to say something about the processes by which visual information is extracted from the page and converted into a form in which it can be identified.

2.2   EXTRACTION OF INFORMATION DURING A SACCADE

It is doubtful whether very much information can be picked up from the page while the eye is in motion. The main reason for this is that the visual sensitivity of the eye is substantially reduced during a saccade. This phenomenon, which is known as *saccadic suppression* (Matin, 1974; Volkmann, 1976), was first noticed by Javal and other early workers, but it was not quantified until relatively recently when Latour (1962) and Volkmann (1962) conducted experiments in which subjects were required to detect brief flashes that were presented before, during and after the saccade. The results showed that the probability of detecting a target was much lower when the eye was moving than when it was fixated. Moreover, Latour showed that the suppression effects were evident 50 ms *before* the movement began and up to 50 ms *after* it had ended. A typical set of results in an experiment of this kind is shown in Figure 2.1.

A variety of different explanations have been offered for saccadic suppression, including accounts which attribute the phenomenon to central inhibition, to inhibition caused by shearing forces, to visual masking and to smearing of the retinal image. However, these explanations will not be reviewed here since our present concern is not so much with the *causes* of suppression as with the implications it has for investigations of reading. The reader who is interested

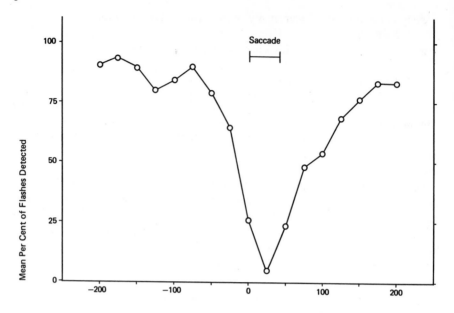

Figure 2.1 A saccadic suppression curve redrawn from data reported by Volkmann *et al.* (1968). The graph represents the average detection rates for stimuli that arrive at points ranging from 200 ms *before* to 200 ms *after* the beginning of the saccade. The average saccade duration is represented on the same scale

in the causes of the phenomenon is referred to one of the more specialized reviews of the subject (e.g. Matin, 1974; Volkmann, 1976; Riggs, 1976).

The reduction in the sensitivity of the eye during a saccade may not always be sufficient to prevent a stimulus from being detected. Indeed, Volkmann (1962) found that if the target flash is bright enough subjects are capable of detecting it on almost 100 per cent of trials. This means that we cannot rule out the possibility that some information is picked up during saccadic movements in reading. However, it seems unlikely that this information would have a strong influence on subsequent processing since the stimulus quality that is required for the successful recognition of letters and words is considerably greater than that needed for the detection of flashes.

In short, we can safely conclude that visual stimulation of the eye at about the time of the movement makes little or no contribution to the subsequent processing of the stimulus material. This implies that all of the visual information used in reading must be extracted during the fixations. In the next section we shall try to determine how much information is picked up during a single fixation.

2.3 THE USEFUL FIELD OF VISION DURING A FIXATION

The amount of information that can be picked up during a fixation depends partly on the physical and physiological limitations of the visual system and partly on constraints that are imposed after the preliminary visual analysis of the material. For the moment we shall concentrate on the first type of restriction and try to determine the area over which information can be detected and recognized when the eyes are stationary. As we shall see, the size of this area (in terms of the vertical and horizontal angles subtended at the eye) varies from situation to situation depending upon the amount of visual detail that is needed to carry out the task under consideration. This means that before we can determine the extent of 'the useful field of vision' in reading we need to make some decisions about the kinds of information that are likely to be useful in reading. We shall tackle this problem presently but first, to set the scene, it is important to consider a few basic findings concerning variations in retinal sensitivity.

Retinal sensitivity varies from point to point because the structure of the retina is not uniform. The two different kinds of light receptor—rods and cones—are distributed unevenly over the retina. The rods are densely packed in a ring located at about 16° of visual angle from the fovea and outside this region their density falls gradually as the distance from the fovea increases. Within the ring the density falls rapidly as the fovea is approached. The cones are packed tightly at the fovea and the density falls off rapidly on either side, so that at 10° from the fovea the density is only about 5 per cent of that at the centre (Pirenne, 1967).

The receptors are connected to a network of neurons known as bipolar cells and these, in turn, are connected to the ganglion cells, which are the neurons which convey the impulses from the eye out through the optic nerve. Within the fovea each receptor is usually connected to one bipolar cell and this, in turn, usually feeds into a single ganglion cell. Outside the fovea, on the other hand, many receptors may be connected to a single bipolar cell and many bipolars to a single ganglion cell (Haber and Hershenson, 1973).

As a result of this neural organization, it is much easier to discriminate details near the fovea than in other parts of the retina. Thus Riggs (1965) has shown that pattern acuity falls to about 50 per cent of its optimal value if the stimulus is presented 1° off-centre and to only 15 per cent at 8° off-centre.

One consequence of these variations in retinal sensitivity is that the useful field of vision is restricted to an area around the fixation point. As mentioned above, the precise dimensions of this region depend on the purpose to which the visual information is put, and there is no way of deriving any fixed estimate of its extent. However, it *is* possible to get an idea of the extent of the field in certain representative situations by referring to studies in which subjects are required to perform a variety of different tasks.

In one such study Edwards and Goolaksian (1974) investigated the accuracy with which subjects were able to detect or recognize stimuli which appeared either 10°, 15°, 25° or 58° from a fixation point. The subjects' tasks included detecting the onset of a light, identifying letters and classifying three-letter words into one of four semantic categories. At the smallest angle all of the tasks were performed at well above the chance level and this remained true at 15° in all tasks except word classification. However, at the largest visual angle subjects were only able to detect whether or not a light had been presented.

Presumably reading is more similar to the word classification task than the other two conditions of this experiment. If so, the results of this study suggest that the useful field of vision may extend no more than 10–15° from the fixation point (see also Mackworth, 1965, and Bouma, 1970, for similar conclusions).

Can we conclude on the basis of this evidence that the effective field of vision in reading extends 10° on either side of the fixation point? This seems most unlikely because a circular field of 10° radius could easily take in 80 letters from a normal line of print and as many as 5000 letters if we include all of the material in range from the lines above and below the fixation point. It seems implausible that the visual information required to identify any one of 5000 letters is available in a single fixation.

This suggests that the technique for estimating the extent of the effective field of vision has to be refined. The most obvious problem with the approach just considered is that it is based on the presentation of a single target form whereas in normal reading the subject is faced with a densely packed array consisting of several hundred letters. This could be extremely important because there is strong evidence that recognition performance falls as the number of letters increases. For example, Bouma (1970) found that the probability of identifying a briefly presented target letter is much lower when it is flanked by two other letters than when it is presented alone. This means that in order to obtain a realistic estimate of the extent of the visual field in reading it is important to use stimuli consisting of several letters arranged in exactly the same way as they are in normal print.

One straightforward and time-honoured approach to the problem is to present a subject briefly with a string of letters or a line of text and instruct him to report as much of the display as he can. Early experiments of this kind showed that subjects are able to report no more than four or five letters from a random string and perhaps 19 or 20 letters from a line of text (see Huey, 1908). These measures correspond to approximately 1° and 5° respectively. However, it is unlikely that either of them provides a satisfactory estimate of the width of the useful field of vision. The first result probably *underestimates* the size of the useful field since it has been demonstrated by Sperling (1960) that when subjects perform in this task they can see more letters than they can store or report. The second measure, on the other hand, might *overestimate* the size of the field since in the text condition an unknown proportion of the letters could have been guessed rather than identified from the visual input. Thus the only conclusion that can be drawn from these studies is that the useful field of vision is at least 1° wide.

An ideal technique for the present purposes would be one in which it was possible to examine recognition accuracy at different locations in a page-like display without overloading memory. An experiment reported by Mackworth (1965) goes some way towards achieving this, but even in this study there are problems that make it difficult to estimate the useful field of vision. The subjects were presented briefly with three critical letters, one at the fixation point and one on each side of it. The task was to say whether the three letters were the same. In one condition the critical letters were embedded in a line consisting of 14 irrelevant letters and in another there were 21 additional lines of letters. The results showed that performance was reasonable if the outside letters were no further than 2° apart, but was very poor for larger visual angles. This result points to a useful field of vision in order of 2°. However, the field could be considerably bigger than this because it is by no means certain that performance outside this region was limited by *spatial* variations in the quality of the visual input. On the contrary, the poorer recognition scores might have occurred because subjects generally took longer to locate the target letters when the separation was increased, and consequently they had to rely increasingly on impoverished information in a decaying visual trace. In other words, Mackworth' results could have occurred with a visual field of *any* size in excess of one or two degrees, and so the experiment does not provide any answer to the question under consideration.

There do not appear to be any more satisfactory attempts to determine the area over which subjects are capable of identifying letters in a page-like display, and so the question about the useful field of vision must remain unanswered for the moment. However, McConkie and Rayner (1975) and Rayner (1975a) have recently tackled a similar, but slightly more practical question, and their studies have been much more conclusive than the earlier investigations. Instead of trying to specify the area over which information is *potentially* used during a fixation, these authors have designed experiments to determine the range over which various kinds of information are *actually* used while a person is reading. This question is clearly not identical to the earlier one, since a person may ignore some of the information available to him. Nevertheless, it is useful to know the answer since it provides a lower bound for the area over which information could potentially be used and, in any case, the question is interesting in its own right.

It the first study, McConkie and Rayner (1975) used computer controlled apparatus both to display the reading material on a screen and to measure and record the subject's eye movements. A novel feature of the experiment was that the contents of the visual display could be changed as the subject scanned it. The computer was programmed so that at any particular time a segment of English text was displayed in the immediate vicinity of the subject's fixation point. However, outside this 'window' of text (i.e. on the current line and on all other lines of the page) the display was filled with meaningless strings of letters. When the subject moved his eyes to another position, a new 'window' of text was created around the new fixation point and the previous window was replaced once more by meaningless background. In each condition of the study the text consisted of a 500-word passage of prose and the end result of the programming was that the subjects saw the appropriate part of this passage wherever they looked as they scanned the display.

In order to determine the span of effective vision the investigators monitored their subjects' performances in several different conditions as the window size was varied to contain between 13 and 100 character positions. On one condition the letters in every position outside the window were similar in shape to the letters which they replaced in the text. In another, the shapes of the extraneous letters were always different, while in a third all of the new letters were *X*s. In each case, the spaces between the words in the original passage were either left as spaces (outside the window) or they were filled.

The authors argued that if the window is sufficiently large the subjects should be able to extract as much information as they can use from each fixation, and consequently their performance should not be affected in any way by the characteristics of the material outside the window. On the other hand, with smaller windows some of the crucial information might be destroyed, in which case it would be expected that at least some aspect of reading performance (e.g. fixation duration or saccade length or number of regressions) would be affected.

The main experiment was conducted using six high-school students and it was found that there were no reliable differences between the conditions for the windows containing 31 or more characters. This suggests that no useful information is picked up outside this area. Within this area (i.e. for window sizes up to and including 25 character positions) at least one dependent variable (saccade length) was reliably affected by the presence or absence of spaces and punctuation in the surrounding material. This result suggests that the information which is used to guide saccades can be picked up at least as far as twelve character positions (3°) from the fixation point. A second dependent variable (fixation duration) was more affected by the shape of the extraneous letters. This shape effect was significant for window sizes of 17 and 21 character positions, but not for any larger windows. This result indicates that letter-shape information is picked up at distances of up to ten character positions ($2\frac{1}{2}°$) from the fixation point. In a later study using the same technique McConkie and Rayner (1976) found that the region over which this information is picked up extends further to the right than to the left. In fact, there was no evidence that the subjects in this experiment used visual information that was located more than 1° to the left of the fixation point (see also Rayner, Well and Pollastek, 1980).

A similar study by Ikeda and Saida (1978) examined the effect of window size on reading rate. In this experiment five subjects were tested and it was found that their performances were unaffected until the width of the window was reduced to an average of 12.8 Japanese characters. This corresponds to a display which extends as far as 4.9° from the fixation point, and while this is larger than the highest estimate given by McConkie and Rayner (1975) it is likely that the discrepancy can be accounted for in terms of the differences in the size and type of characters used in the two studies.

The results reported by McConkie and Rayner (1975) suggest that spaces can be picked up over a slightly wider area than letter-shape information. However, Rayner (1975a) argued that because of the artificial nature of the displays, the subjects might have been forced to read in an abnormal way.

Hence the generality of the findings may be questioned. In an attempt to avoid the problems associated with the 'window' technique, Rayner (1975a) conducted a slightly different kind of experiment using the same apparatus. The basic material in this study consisted of 225 short paragraphs. On each trial, one of these paragraphs was displayed in a slightly mutilated form and the subject was instructed to read it. The mutilation always took the form of replacing one of the words in the paragraph (the *critical word*) by an extraneous string of letters of the same length. The computer was programmed in such a way that the critical word was reinstated as soon as the subject's eyes crossed an invisible boundary that was located between nine letters before and four letters after the beginning of the critical word.

In the five main conditions of the experiment the critical word (e.g. traitor) was initially replaced (1) by itself (a control condition) or (2) by another word that made equally good sense in the paragraph and which also had the same outline shape and the same outer letters (e.g. teacher) or (3) by a meaningless string

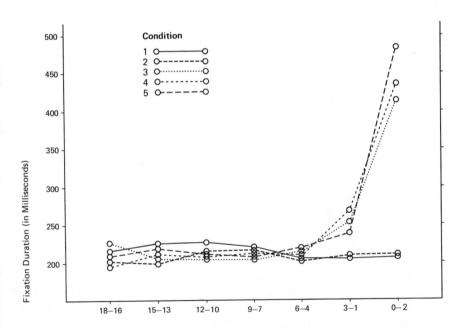

Figure 2.2 Data from Rayner's (1975a) experiment. The graphs represent the mean duration of the last fixation prior to crossing the boundary as a function of its location and of the nature of the stimulus pattern in the critical word location. Conditions: target location initially filled (1) by the target word itself (e.g. traitor); (2) by another word with the same shape and the same outer letters (e.g. teacher); (3) by a nonword with the same shape and same outer letters (e.g. tcoaber); (4) by a nonword of the same shape only (e.g. fcaobcn); and (5) by a nonword with the same outer letters only (e.g. tifjrir)

of letters with the same shape and outer letters (e.g. tcoaber) or (4) by a string of letters with the same shape but different outer letters (e.g. fcaobcn) or (5) by a string of letters with the same outer letters as the critical word but with a different shape (e.g. tifjrir).

Rayner examined two main aspects of the eye movement data to see how the subjects' performances were affected by these manipulations. First, he looked at the durations of some of the fixations that occurred before the critical word was reinstated, and he found that when subjects fixated on a position up to three character spaces to the left of the replacement stimulus the duration of the fixation was longer for the meaningless strings than for either of the words.

When the fixation was further to the left than this there was no difference between the five conditions (see Figure 2.2). This suggests that subjects were able to recognize that a string of letters was not an English word at a range of three letters. It follows that, on some of the fixations at least, they must have identified at least five letters to the right of the fixation point. (The reason for this is that at least two letters would have to be identified before the subject could tell that the stimulus was not a word.) It is tempting to assume that subjects were not able to identify any letters beyond this, but it is not really safe to draw this conclusion because it is possible that such letters *were* identified, but that the processes were not completed quickly enough for the outcome to influence the time at which the next saccade was launched.

The other feature of the data which Rayner (1975a) examined concerned the durations of fixations in the region of the critical word and immediately after its reinstatement. He found that the duration varied systematically from condition to condition, which means that subjects must have picked up misleading word- and letter-shape information before the critical word was reinstated. The results showed that these differences were evident whenever the preceding fixation occurred within about twelve character spaces (or 3°) of the target word (see Figure 2.3). This tends to confirm that visual information can be picked up at a range of at least 3° from the fixation point.

At this point it may be useful to summarize the results of the experiments on the useful field of vision in reading. The results make it clear that there is no *fixed* range over which people can pick up information. The limits of the field are only partly determined by the physical and physiological constraints of the visual system; other important factors being the subject's task or orientation and the contents of the stimulus display. In particular, the data show that although subjects can identify letters at distances of up to 10° from the fixation point under ideal conditions, they do not appear to do this while they are reading. Instead, they identify about five letters (1.25°) to the right of the fixations and between none and four letters to the left. They also detect spaces up to 3° to the right, and pick up information about the shapes of words and letters over the same range. However, this information is apparently not used to identify the material. The reason for this is uncertain. It may be that there is not enough visual detail in these positions for the letters to be identified, but a more likely explanation is that subjects make a strategic choice not to

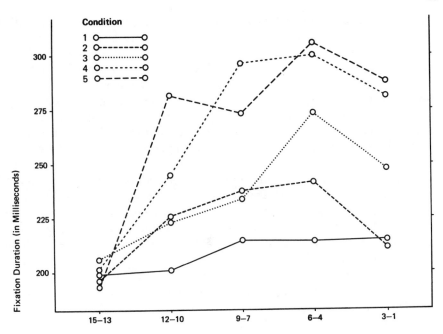

Condition

1 o———o
2 o– – – –o
3 o·········o
4 o– · – · –o
5 o— — —o

Area of Prior Fixation (Number of Character Positions to the Left of the Target Word)

Figure 2.3 Data from Rayner's (1975a) experiment. Here the graphs represent the mean durations of fixations falling on the target word immediately after crossing the boundary as a function of the location of the prior fixation and of the initially displayed stimulus pattern in the critical word location. Conditions (1) to (5) are the same as those given in the legend for Figure 2.2

try to identify words that extend more than a few letters away from the fixation point, but to leave them instead to be processed during the next fixation.

2.4 EXTRACTION OF INFORMATION FROM A SINGLE FIXATION

The evidence which we have considered so far tells us something about the area from which visual information might be extracted during reading, but it does not throw much light on the process by which this is achieved. In the next few pages we shall describe and evaluate a number of studies which have tried to determine the sequence of operations that occur when visual information is extracted from a fixation. To anticipate a bit, we shall argue that the stimulus information is registered in two different kinds of visual store before the letters and words in the display are eventually recognized, and later we shall present evidence that one of these stores is used to integrate the visual information that is extracted from successive fixations.

Much of the evidence on the process of extraction is derived from experiments which attempt to simulate the events that occur in a single fixation. In these studies a stimulus is presented for a fraction of a second and the subject typically has to report some or all of the contents of the display. If the stimulus duration is reasonably short (less than 200 ms, say) the viewer will be unable to fixate on the display more than once and, in this sense, the task simulates a single fixation in reading. However, the conditions of the task differ in several respects from those that occur in reading. For example, the 'fixation' in the experimental task is not preceded and followed immediately by a saccade, and consequently it is not likely to be affected by saccadic suppression in the way a normal fixation is. Also, artificial fixations are not preceded and followed by *other fixations* containing further information to be extracted and processed. Thus there are likely to be fewer competing processing demands than there are in normal reading. In view of these, and other, differences it is clear that experiments of this kind cannot provide us with conclusive evidence about the processes that occur during reading. Even so, they are worthy of close examination, because they provide a valuable source of hypotheses about these processes. The most important suggestion is that the information within a fixation is immediately placed in a visual store where it is held until it is destroyed shortly after the next saccadic movement. Evidence for this will be considered in the next section.

2.5 VISUAL MEMORY

There is a considerable amount of experimental evidence that the spatial pattern in a brief display is retained in visual memory for a short period after the stimulus itself has been terminated. This kind of storage is usually referred to as *iconic memory* or the *icon* (Neisser, 1967). Much of the evidence is derived from an experimental paradigm known as the Partial Report technique, which was developed by Sperling (1960). In this technique, the subject is typically presented with a brief display consisting of three or four rows of letters and he is instructed either to read a single row (Partial Report) or to report as many letters as he can from anywhere in the display (Whole Report). In the former condition the row to be reported is usually identified by an auditory signal presented shortly after the end of the stimulus. Sperling found that the proportion of items correctly reported in the Partial Report condition was higher than that in the Whole Report condition, and he concluded that for a fraction of a second the subjects are able to store more items than they can eventually report. Various aspects of the data led him to believe that this additional information is held in a visual trace which decays within less than a second.

Since this work was originally carried out it has become clear that the Partial Report advantage may not be wholly attributable to the fact that stimulus information is held in a visual trace. Under certain conditions subjects may be able to inflate their Partial Report scores by occasionally anticipating which of the rows will be sampled (Holding, 1970). Furthermore, the size of the difference may be influenced by the fact that there are fewer items to report in the Partial Report condition (Dick, 1971); and finally, von Wright (1972) has demonstrated that the magnitude of the Partial Report advantage depends on the subject's uncertainty about the type of report required on each trial and on whether the response is to be made verbally or in writing. These findings have provoked a certain amount of disagreement about the validity of Sperling's interpretations of the Partial Report data (Holding, 1975a, 1975b; Coltheart, 1975a, 1975b; Coltheart, Lea and Thompson, 1974; Dick, 1974; Sakitt and Appelman, 1978). On balance, the evidence suggests that Sperling's theoretical conclusions were substantially correct. However, the interpretation of individual Partial Report experiments is complicated by methodological difficulties such as those outlined above. For this reason the following discussion, which outlines the properties of iconic memory, will be based primarily on the results of other, less controversial experimental paradigms.

The first property we shall consider is the storage capacity of the icon. The evidence suggests that the trace is capable of retaining a large amount of detailed spatial information.* This is perhaps demonstrated most convincingly in a series of experiments conducted by Eriksen and Collins (1967, 1968). In these studies the subjects were presented in quick succession with two stimuli consisting of dot patterns. The displays were constructed in such a way that the arrangement of dots appeared to be random if either of them was viewed alone. However, when the two patterns were superimposed, they formed a composite image containing a nonsense syllable. The subjects were instructed to attempt to identify this target and the results showed that they were able to do this without difficulty when the interval between the patterns was very short, but not when it was increased to 200 ms or so. This indicates that the subjects were able to register the precise locations of several hundred dots in the first stimulus and retain this information until after the second stimulus had arrived.

The quality and detail of the information stored strongly suggests that the trace was *visual*, and the fact that subjects were unable to discern the target after 200 ms indicates that its persistence must have been very brief. Both of these conclusions have been supported by the results of numerous other studies. The visual quality of the store is confirmed by the finding that the persistence increases when the intensity of the background field is decreased (Haber and Standing, 1969, 1970), and by the fact that it is apparently terminated abruptly when the stimulus is followed by a new pattern (Sperling, 1967; Haber and Standing, 1970). The suggestion that the trace only survives for a very short period is supported by the results of several studies in which subjects were

* Recently there has been a lively discussion about the locus of storage and the mechanisms that underlie iconic memory. Sakitt (1976a) has argued that the information is retained either in the rod photoreceptors or at the membrane of the receptors, and others have strongly disputed this view (e.g. Banks and Barber, 1977; Adelson, 1978; Meyer and Maguire, 1977; McCloskey and Watkins, 1978). In another development Sakitt (1976b) and Coltheart (1980) have distinguished between several different kinds of visual persistence that might occur under different experimental conditions. While these theoretical issues are interesting in their own right it seems unlikely that they have direct implications for the process of reading and so they will not be pursued any further here.

required to make direct estimates of the duration of the visual persistence. In a typical study of this kind, Haber and Standing (1970) instructed subjects to adjust the timing of periodic clicks until they coincided with the apparent onset or offset of visual stimuli. The click settings indicated that the trace disappeared approximately 200 ms after a brief (60 ms) stimulus, and almost instantaneously after a longer (500 ms) stimulus. These findings have been corroborated by the results of a number of other experiments using related experimental techniques (e.g. Briggs and Kinsbourne, 1972; Efron, 1970; Haber and Standing, 1969). For the purposes of studying reading, perhaps the most important property of the icon is the fact that it is influenced by stimuli that follow (or precede) it. The interference effect that occurs when an unwanted stimulus follows a display is referred to as *backward masking* and the impairment caused by an earlier stimulus is known as *forward masking*.

Masking effects have generally been interpreted in one of two ways (e.g. Kahneman, 1968). According to one view, the Integration Hypothesis, the two stimuli combine to form a composite image and, as a result of this, neither the first nor the second can be perceived clearly. According to the second interpretation, the Interruption Hypothesis, performance is impaired because the processing of the first stimulus is interrupted by the arrival of the second. This interruption might occur either because the raw data in the visual trace are replaced by the data for the new stimulus, or because processing of the first stimulus is cut short by the need to deal with the second (Turvey, 1973).

It is doubtful whether all masking phenomena can be accounted for on the basis of either hypothesis alone. In fact, Turvey (1973) has argued that the data cannot be explained even if both theories are combined. In support of this conclusion, he presented evidence that the nature of the masking mechanism depends among other things on the temporal separation between the two stimuli, their relative intensities and durations, on the nature of the masking stimulus and on whether the two stimuli are presented to the same eye or to different eyes. These distinctions have important implications for general theories of perceptual mechanisms. However, our present concerns are much more limited, since we are mainly interested in the kinds of masking that occur under the conditions of reading (i.e. when the target (or fixation) duration is about 200 ms, when the masks (i.e. the preceding and following fixations) also last about 200 ms, when the intensities of the target and mask are roughly the same and when they both contain pattern information and, finally, when both eyes receive the same stimuli). In these particular circumstances it is likely that the trace of the test stimulus is slightly impaired by forward masking over the first 20–30 ms (Turvey, 1973, Expt XV) and that at the end it is replaced within a few milliseconds by the features of the masking stimulus (Turvey, 1973; Scheerer, 1973). In other words, it is likely that any perceptual process using the icon as raw data is interrupted shortly after the arrival of a masking stimulus.

For the present purposes the most important conclusion is that visual information is initially registered in a high-capacity visual store which lasts no more than 300 ms when the stimulus is followed by an empty field of approximately the same intensity, and that the information is replaced almost immediately if it is followed by another stimulus.

The discussion so far has been concerned exclusively with the first of the two kinds of visual memory mentioned earlier. It is clear that there must be other ways of retaining visual information since if all visual information disappeared within 300 ms we would probably be unable to recognize faces or perform numerous other everyday tasks. In fact, there are several studies which demonstrate that visual information can be retained in a form of storage which lasts for periods of several seconds.

A number of these studies have used familiar verbal materials, such as letters and digits, as stimuli. For example, Posner, Boies, Eichelman and Taylor (1969) showed that subjects are quicker at deciding whether two successively presented visual letters have the same name when they are, in fact, physically identical (e.g. a, a) than when they are presented in different cases (e.g. a, A). They concluded that the visual representation of the first must have been available when the second arrived. In another study employing verbal stimuli, Kroll, Parks, Parkinson, Bieber and Johnson (1970) found that subjects who are continuously engaged in an auditory distraction task are more successful at retaining a visual target letter than an auditory one. This suggests that the two kinds of stimuli are retained in different forms. In a third study, Scarborough (1972) showed that subjects are able to store up to five visually presented items without showing any appreciable deficit in a concurrent auditory memory task. These investigations establish clearly that visual stimuli can be retained in a form that differs from that used for storing auditory stimuli.

More direct evidence that the form of storage is *visual* rather than (say) abstract (Pylyshyn, 1973) comes from studies that use non-verbal stimuli that are difficult to name. In one study of this kind Mitchell (1972b) presented subjects with a letter-like nonsense shape followed immediately by a pattern mask. After delays varying from 0.5 to 6 seconds a second nonsense shape was displayed and the subject was instructed to indicate whether the two shapes were the same or different. Each subject was interrogated to see whether he had invented a name or description for any of the shapes, and the data for those that were labelled in this way were analysed separately. The results showed that matching performance for the remaining unnamed forms was significantly above the chance level in all conditions and that performance fell as the delay increased. Since the stimuli had no names or descriptions it seems likely that the information was retained in a visual form. Similar conclusions have been reached by Cermak (1971), using a different class of nonsense forms; by Phillips and Baddeley (1971) and Phillips (1974), using 5×5 matrices of black and white squares; and by Dale (1973), using a task in which subjects were required to mark the position of a dot presented very briefly in a two-dimensional display. Taken together these studies provide strong evidence visual information can be retained in some form of visual storage long after the stimulus and the icon disappear.

In order to assess the role of Short Term Visual Memory (STVM) in reading it is necessary to consider a number of its properties in some detail. These properties differ in several respects from those that characterize the icon. First, the stimulus information is retained over a much longer interval. This is particularly true when the stimulus duration is 500 ms or more since in these conditions STVM is fairly durable (see Phillips, 1974) whereas iconic persistence is virtually non-existent (Haber and Standing, 1970). Secondly, the contents of STVM are not destroyed by backward masking. In the studies conducted by Phillips and Baddeley (1971) and by Mitchell (1972b), a masking stimulus was displayed immediately after the first shape in each pair and the level of matching performance was high in spite of this. This indicates that the contents of the trace are not influenced by other stimuli in the same way as the information in iconic memory. (However, it should be pointed out in passing that there are some investigators who argue that they may be subject to interference of some kind (e.g. Posner *et al.*, 1969; Bongartz and Scheerer, 1976; Merikle, 1976)). Thirdly, the capacity of STVM is much more limited than that of the icon. Mitchell (1972a) conducted an experiment in which subjects were shown a 200 ms display consisting of a row of four Gibson forms followed after either 0.1, 1 or 3 seconds by one further form presented alone. The task was to indicate whether the single probe form had appeared anywhere in the original array. The level of accuracy in this task was relatively low (75 per cent) even at the shortest delay, indicating that the subjects were unable to retain enough visual detail in each of the four locations to perform the task as accurately as they would have been able to do with a single form. The results of a series of experiments conducted by Scarborough (1972) also suggest that the capacity of STVM is relatively low. In these experiments it was found that subjects were capable of storing no more than four or five visually presented items while retaining a concurrent auditory load. Even if it assumed that none of this information is retained in 'abstract' storage of the kind considered earlier, the results still indicate that only a small amount of material can be retained in STVM.

These differences and a few others discussed by Mitchell (1972a) and Phillips (1974) suggest that iconic memory and STVM are distinct forms of storage. However, there is some evidence that they are related and, in particular, that the information which enters STVM is extracted from the icon. Mitchell (1972b) found that visual matching performance varied as a function of the interval between the onset of the first stimulus and the following mask. Since this relationship was evident even when the stimulus duration itself was kept constant, the result suggests that the icon provides the raw data for some perceptual process that converts a portion of the information into a more durable form to be held in STVM. The nature of this 'perceptual process' is not at all clear, however. Mitchell (1972a) suggested that the process may simply be one of making memorial copies of a selection of visual features of the kind described by Hubel and Wiesel (1959). Phillips (1974) argued, in contrast, that it might entail computing the relation between separate elements of the stimulus to form what he terms a 'figural articulation' of the shape. However, neither of these proposals is supported by empirical evidence and so further research is obviously needed before the issue can be resolved.

In summary, the evidence suggests that the information present in a brief display can be registered in two different kinds of visual store. The first one, iconic memory, retains a large amount of detailed information for a short period—usually less than half a second. This trace is quickly replaced with new information when a further stimulus arrives. The second store, STVM, lasts for several seconds, but the storage capacity is much more limited. In this case there is only sufficient visual detail to enable a few letters to be identified or for a few simple forms to be matched. In contrast with the icon, the contents of STVM are not lost when a new stimulus arrives. Visual information is copied from the icon to STVM and this process continues until the raw data are either replaced or fade away.

2.6 THE USE OF VISUAL MEMORY IN THE EXTRACTION PROCESS

What roles do these two kinds of visual memory play in the reading process? The evidence summarized above suggests that the iconic trace following a fixation should not extend appreciably beyond the duration of the fixation itself. A stimulus lasting for 200–250 ms has a very short persistence and, in any case, the iconic trace should be destroyed by the visual input during the following saccade or during the first few milliseconds of the next fixation. This suggests that the icon merely functions as a register which holds the visual data momentarily while they are operated upon by some kind of read-out process.

The role of STVM depends on whether the material taken in by the fixation is identified directly from the icon or whether some (or all) of the information is transferred to STVM before being identified. If the icon itself holds the raw material used by the recognition processes, this would imply that STVM is bypassed completely and therefore plays no role at all in the reading process. On the other hand, if information is transferred to STVM so that this more durable form of storage can be used to hold the raw data for further processing, then the role of STVM could be quite important since on this assumption all stimulus information must pass through the store at some time.

In the earlier work on the extraction process it was assumed that all recognition occurred directly from the icon. For example, Sperling (1963, 1967) proposed that the items in the display are identified rapidly and then stored, first, in the form 'programs of motor instruction' (i.e. abstract codes or instructions that can subsequently be used to pronounce the items) and, subsequently, in the form of an auditory or acoustic trace. More recently most investigators have assumed that some or all of the information is transferred to STVM before being recognized (Allport, 1977; Bongartz and Scheerer, 1976; Coltheart, 1972; Henderson, 1972; Mitchell, 1972a, 1972b; Phillips, 1971).

One of the reasons for moving away from Sperling's earlier type of model is that it has great difficulty in accounting for certain serial position effects and for the retention of order information in tasks where subjects have to report the contents of a briefly presented display. The problem is that order information is retained so accurately that it is difficult to imagine a mechanism that would perform the function adequately. Broadly speaking, there are two ways in which order information could be retained according to the direct recognition model. One possibility is that the position of each item is described in some abstract, non-visual manner at the time of recognition and that this code is subsequently used to reconstruct the order information. The second possibility is that the order information is coded temporally. For example, if the string of letters were read strictly from left to right (say) then the position of each letter could be represented by the time at which it was read. Neither of these mechanisms is capable of explaining the fact that the retention of order information is essentially perfect when a string of digits (say) is displayed for 100 ms (as shown, for example, in one of the experiments reported by Mitchell, 1976). A mechanism of the first kind would be extremely complex and would not be capable of accounting for a variety of experimental effects concerning the familiarity and orientation of the stimuli (see Mitchell, 1976). A mechanism based on temporal coding would also face difficulties since data reported by Sperling (1967) and Merikle, Coltheart and Lowe (1971) suggest that several stimulus items are processed in parallel, in which case it is unlikely that the items are read from the icon in a strict and systematic order. If this is correct, temporal codes are unlikely to provide a reliable basis for retaining order information. Whether or not this is true, subjects generally have problems in judging the order of events that are separated by small intervals. In an experiment specifically designed to examine this capability in a recognition task Mitchell (1976) presented subjects with sequences of three digits separated from one another by pattern masks. The intervals between successive digits ranged from 100 ms to 1 second and it was found that at the fastest rate of presentation more than 15 per cent of the items were reported in the wrong ordinal position. The temporal separation of the stimuli in this condition obviously exceeds the maximum time intervals that could occur if the whole display were only available for 80 ms (say), and so it is clear that temporal cues would not be precise enough to explain the accuracy with which order information can be retained in the Sperling task.

In short, there is no obvious explanation of the almost perfect retention of order information unless it is assumed that the information is retained in STVM. If this assumption is made, the phenomenon is easily explained, since if a visual trace is available the order of the items can easily be checked by consulting this trace whenever it is necessary to do so.

These results suggest that STVM plays a central part in the extraction of information during a single fixation, and if follows that it must play an important role in normal reading by holding a visual description of the stimulus until recognition completed. It is also possible that STVM is used as a medium for combining the information extracted from different fixations. This is considered in the next section.

2.7   INTEGRATION OF INFORMATION EXTRACTED
FROM SUCCESSIVE FIXATIONS

Since the mean size of a saccadic movement is only about eight letter spaces it follows that several fixations must occur while a person reads a single sentence. The information extracted from each of these fixations obviously has to be pooled before the sentence can be understood. Broadly speaking, this integration could occur in two ways. The contents of the individual fixations could either be identified as far as possible before any attempt is made to combine the different sources of information or, alternatively, the contributions of the successive fixations could be integrated prior to recognition. On the second hypothesis, the visual inputs might be combined in such a way that the raw material of the identification process includes information from more than one fixation.

It is difficult to see how an integration process of the first kind could cope with inputs of the kind that occur during normal reading. Given the evidence summarized in the preceding sections it seems clear that there must be occasions on which the material at the edge of the effective field of vision is so indistinct that it is impossible for the reader to identify the word(s) it stands for. On such occasions the best the reader should be able to do (on the first hypothesis) is to identify and retain the information in the form of a set of unrelated letters. But if he did this, it would almost certainly cause problems at a later stage, particularly if the saccade immediately following this fixation is one that covers several letter spaces. In this situation the partially identified word might fall at the opposite edge of the field of vision and it might even fall completely outside this area. If this happened the reader would end up with, at best, two uncoordinated samples of the word in question. He would then be faced with the problem of combining them to identify the word and, without the benefit of spatial information to specify the relative positions of the two sets of letters, this would seem to be a virtually impossible task. Similar problems would occur if the saccade following the first fixation were very short (say, two letter spaces). Here the new fixation would presumably contain much of the information already extracted from the previous fixation and the resulting duplication of information would have to be edited out of the representation in the subsequent 'integration' process. Again, this would not be a straightforward task in the absence spatial information from the two fixations. There would even be some difficulty if the saccade were 'perfectly' spaced so that the second fixation fell precisely in the correct position for it to provide the letters that were missing from the end of the word. If this happened the two halves of the word would still have to be brought together in the appropriate way before the word could be identified.

The difficulty in explaining how this kind of integration process would achieve its goals has led many writers (e.g. Neisser, 1967; Hochberg, 1970; Mackworth, 1972; McConkie and Rayner, 1976; Rayner, 1975a, 1978) to prefer the second proposal; namely that it is unrecognized visual information that is integrated.

According to this hypothesis, the visual information in a new fixation is added to information previously stored in STVM. In one version of the hypothesis, it is assumed that information about the size and direction of the eye movement is used to locate the information from the new fixation in precisely the correct position within the existing visual structure. Given this assumption it is easy to account for the fact that text can be read even when different parts of some of the words apparently arrive in different fixations and when there are wide variations in the lengths of saccades. According to the hypothesis, the information from two or more fixations is entered into a common visual trace which is then used as the raw material for the word identification process. If information is combined in this way it should make little or no difference whether all of the information needed to recognize a word comes from a single fixation or whether portions of it are extracted from several different fixations. Similarly, it should make little difference if two fixations cover the same ground. (In this situation the amount of visual detail in the corresponding part of the trace might be increased a little, but otherwise the contents of STVM should be unaffected.) Finally, given this account, it is possible to explain how a person might be able to read a word in the middle of a portion of the text apparently missed out during a long saccade. The word may be too far from the fixation points on either side for it to be recognized on the basis of the visual information from either fixation alone. However, when the contributions from both sides are combined, there might be sufficient detail for the word to be identified.

Intuitively, the visual integration hypothesis seems quite compelling, and it is certainly more appealing than the alternative hypothesis outlined above. However, we obviously need to consider empirical evidence before we can decide which of the hypotheses is more likely to be correct. As it turns out, the small amount of evidence currently available appears to be *against* the visual integration hypothesis. However, it will be argued that the case against this suggestion is not as damaging as it first seems and that there is no reason to abandon the hypothesis.

The first line of evidence to be considered is something of a red herring. Rayner (1978) reported a finding which he initially took to be evidence in *favour* of the visual integration hypothesis. After further investigation, however, it became clear that it was inappropriate to interpret the finding in this way, and so Rayner's original arguments have not contributed to the case for visual integration. The experimental finding was as follows. The subject started each trial by looking at a fixation stimulus. After a short delay a word, or a string of letters, was presented in a position 1°, 3° or 5° from the fixation point and the subject was instructed to fixate on the new stimulus. While the eye movement was taking place the stimulus was sometimes replaced by another one—a word with a different shape or with different letters. The subject's task was simply to name the newly presented stimulus.

Rayner argued that, according to the visual integration hypothesis, the time taken to name the new stimulus should reflect the quality of the integrated visual trace derived from the two fixations. Thus he predicted that the test word would be named very rapidly on trials when the first stimulus provided information that was compatible with that in the second (i.e. when the two stimuli had similar shapes and when the first one was presented close enough — 1° or 3° — for its features to make a significant contribution to the integrated trace). In contrast with this, he expected that the response latencies would be relatively slow when the two sources of visual information were incompatible with one another (i.e. when the stimuli differed in the outline shape or outer letters).

These predictions were borne out by the data and to this extent it could be argued that the results were consistent with the visual integration hypothesis. However, it is clear that the results of this experiment could equally well have been produced by priming mechanisms other than the one outlined by Rayner. In particular, they could have been caused by some form of facilitation that takes place irrespective of the spatial locations of the preliminary and target stimuli. In order to test this possibility Rayner, McConkie and Ehrlich (1978) repeated and extended the experiment. The main conditions of the first study were retained as one of the conditions in the new experiment. In this condition, the target word was presented in the same location as the preliminary parafoveal stimulus and the subject had to make an eye movement before fixating the word and naming it. In a new condition (the *simulation* condition), the target word was presented not in the parafovea but at the initial fixation point. In this case the stimulus was the same as it would have been following the eye movement in the first condition, but the subject did not actually have to make a saccade to locate it. If the original results had occurred because visual information from the two fixations had actually been *combined* in the (initially) parafoveal location, then the priming effect would have been reduced or eliminated in the simulated condition because in this condition the two stimuli were in different positions and consequently they should not have been integrated. In fact, the results showed that the priming effects in the two different conditions were almost indistinguishable, and this suggests that the mechanism responsible for the effect is not a form of visual integration. Thus, the results of this modified experiment show that Rayner's earlier findings cannot be taken as avidence in *favour* of the visual integration hypothesis. However, they do not, by themselves, provide any strong evidence *against* the theory.

A more direct attack against the theory itself has been made by McConkie and Zola (1979). In this investigation subjects were required to read passages displayed on a computer screen in alternating letter cases (e.g. *In ThE eStUaRiEs*...). During certain of the subject's saccades the text was changed completely so that each of the upper-case letters became a lower-case letter and vice versa. On the remainder of the saccades the display was left unchanged. If visual information from successive fixations had been integrated then some difficulty might have been expected on the 'change' fixations (i.e. those on which the word and letter shapes were incompatible with those extracted during the previous fixation). The results showed no evidence of this. Fixation durations and saccade lengths on these occasions were almost identical with those recorded when the material remained unchanged.

McConkie and Zola (1979) interpreted these findings as evidence against visual integration and argued that information is carried over from one fixation to the next in the form of letters, phonemic codes or some other non-visual representation. On the surface this argument is quite persuasive but on closer examination certain difficulties emerge. One problem is that the information derived from different fixations can only be compared or combined meaningfully if each fixation carries information which specifies which of the letters (or other non-visual units) from the two fixations correspond with one another. If each fixation merely delivers uncoordinated fragments of words to some higher centre then it is difficult to see how this information could be combined in any effective way. Obviously, this problem could be overcome if the fragments were labelled according to the position from which they originated on the page, but this option is presumably not open to McConkie and Zola (1979) since it involves carrying *spatial* information from one fixation to the next. Without a facility of this kind the explanation of the facilitation (or interference) effects may not be viable. A second, and perhaps more serious, problem with McConkie and Zola's interpretation of their data is that while their own study showed no effect of changing letter- or word-shape from one fixation to the next, previous studies *have* reported differences of this kind. For example, it will be recalled that in Rayner's (1975a) reading task the period for which a subject fixated a critical word was shown to vary as a function of the information displayed in its place prior to the fixation. (See Figure 2.3 for a detailed graph of the results.) More specifically, the average fixation time was longer when the previewed stimulus differed in shape from the target word (e.g. *chfbt* when the target word was *chest*) than when it was similar in shape (e.g. *chovt*). It is difficult to see how this result could have occurred if no visual information is carried forward from one fixation to the next.

These observations suggest that it may be premature to dismiss the notion of visual integration in reading. Although McConkie and Zola (1979) failed to find the differences expected on this hypothesis, this may simply have been because their experiment was not sensitive enough to pick up the important effects. There are several features of the experiment that could have reduced its sensitivity. One possible problem is that the subjects in both conditions may have extended the durations of their fixations to allow for potential problems in processing alternating texts, in which case the preset durations may have been sufficiently long to obscure any additional processing produced by the discrepancies between the displays in different fixations. It is also conceivable that a composite image consisting of letters printed in both cases in every position (e.g. **ESTUARIES**) is just as easy to read as the alternating case stimuli in the 'unchanged conditions'. If this is true, then no difference would have been expected on the visual integration hypothesis.

It should be evident from the foregoing discussion that the issue of integration of information from successive fixations cannot be resolved on empirical grounds at the moment. However, as argued above, the visual integration hypothesis offers a much fuller and more persuasive account of the relevant phenomena than the alternatives, and for this reason we shall accept it as a working hypothesis.

To recapitulate, the proposal is that visual information from the fixated area of the text is copied via the icon into STVM during most of the period of fixation. The new information is combined with the visual material retained from previous fixations in a manner which may be likened to the construction of a scene by superimposing a series of overlapping transparencies of small parts of the scene. Featural information from later fixations is subsequently added to the developing internal representation in the same way. At any point in the process the current contents of STVM may be used as the raw data for the process or processes that are used to identify the words in the text. These procedures will be considered in detail in the next chapter, but before moving on it is necessary to deal with one other process which has an important effect on the extraction of visual information from the page—the control of eye movements.

2.8   THE CONTROL OF EYE MOVEMENTS

The information that is extracted from a page is partly determined by the processes discussed above (i.e. those that occur during individual fixations), but it is also influenced by the distribution of fixations in different parts of the page. This means that the efficiency of the reading process depends, to some extent, on the control of eye movements. Recently, a good deal of attention has been paid to the nature of the mechanisms by which this control is exercised (Shebilske, 1975; O'Regan, 1975; Haber, 1976; Rayner and McConkie, 1976). Broadly speaking, three kinds of model can be distinguished in the literature. The simplest possibility is that eye movements are not influenced in any way by moment-to-moment variations in the materials under consideration, but vary unsystematically—perhaps as a result of motor or physiological factors. This may be referred to as a Random Control model. The second possibility is that eye movements are controlled by variations in the momentary difficulties encountered in processing the text (Workload Control model). On this hypothesis, it is suggested that the control mechanism responds to increases in local workload either by programming shorter saccades (to reduce the amount of new information that it added to the processing 'queue') or by prolonging the fixations (to allow more time for processing the current material). In different versions of the model it is assumed either that the movements are guided by the *anticipated* workload over the next few fixations (O'Regan, 1979), or by the actual workload associated with the fixations preceding the movement (Rayner and McConkie, 1976), or, finally, that they are controlled by an accumulation of material that builds up over several fixations (Bouma and de Voogd, 1974). The third type of model proposes that eye movements are directed towards particular kinds of stimuli on the page so that these words or parts of words can be submitted to special analysis (Stimulus Control model). These target stimuli may be determined by the general characteristics of the reading task. For example, it is presumably useful to look at words rather than the spaces between them, and it may be particularly worthwhile to fixate on the beginnings of words (Hochberg, 1970, p. 86). It may also be useful to *avoid* certain kinds of stimuli such as short function words that can easily be guessed from the context (Hochberg, 1970, p. 86). Other classes of target stimuli may be specified not so much by the general requirements of reading, but by moment-to-moment expectancies based on the reader's knowledge of the structure of language. Thus, Hochberg (1970) has suggested that people can direct their eyes towards specific words that are needed to confirm their hypotheses about the content of the passage. In most versions of the Stimulus Control model it is proposed that eye movements are guided by the physical properties of the stimulus alone. However, it has also been suggested (e.g. by O'Regan, 1975) that saccades might be guided by more abstract properties of the material such as the grammatical class of the words, and Kennedy (1978) has even suggested that semantic analysis of material in the periphery might identify potentially informative regions of the text, and that this more abstract information might be used to direct the eyes to the more important areas of the page.

There are two aspects of scanning behaviour that need to be accounted for by any model of eye movement control. The first is the length of successive saccades and the second is the duration of the fixations. Rayner and McConkie (1976) have shown that these two measures are uncorrelated and consequently they have argued that they must be controlled by different mechanisms. We shall therefore consider the measures separately in most of the following discussion.

Let us start with the control of eye movements. Here a very cursory examination of the data immediately shows that we can dismiss the Random Control model. Contrary to the model there is a good deal of evidence that saccade lengths are influenced by the characteristics of the reading material. To start with, subjects tend to vary saccade size in such a way that they avoid the spaces between words (Abrams and Zuber, 1972) and between sentences (Rayner, 1975b; Rayner and McConkie, 1976). They also seem to adjust their saccades to take account of word length. O'Regan (1975, 1979) and Rayner (1979) found that readers make larger eye movements when leaving long words than when leaving short words, and also that eye movements which *land* in long words are longer than others. Furthermore, Rayner and McConkie (1976) demonstrated that the probability of fixating on individual letters of a medium length (six-letter) word was greater than the corresponding figure for words that were either longer or shorter than this. There is also a tendency for the position of a fixation *within* a word to vary systematically with the length of the word as a whole (Rayner, 1979). There is even evidence that systematic effects occur when word length is kept constant. For example, O'Regan (1975,

1979) found that the eyes tend to skip past the word *the* more often than they do for any other three-letter words. Moreover, Rayner (1977) showed that the probability of fixating the definite article varies as a function of its position within the sentence.

All of these results indicate that eye movements are influenced in one way or another by the reading matter. With this evidence we can confidently rule out the Random Control model. However, it is not quite so easy to choose between the remaining models since many aspects of the data can be explained equally well by both of the alternatives.

Stimulus Control models can account for the results if it is assumed that the eyes are directed (1) towards *words* rather than towards the spaces or punctuation marks between them; (2) towards material *beyond* the word currently being fixated (to explain O'Regan's finding that saccades leaving long words are longer than others); (3) towards locations well within each new word (to account for the finding that movements *into* long words are longer than average); and (4) *away* from short words in general (and from the definite article in particular).

Workload Control models can provide an explanation of several of the findings by proposing that the control mechanism responds to local changes in processing requirements by programming saccades of varying lengths. Two assumptions have to be made before this account becomes viable. The first is that 'local processing' includes the analysis of materials lying to the right of the fixation point. More specifically we have to assume that the control mechanism produces long saccades whenever the processing immediately to the right of the fixation point can be completed without difficulty (i.e. whenever it seems likely that the next bit of analysis will be carried out quickly and easily). The second assumption is that it is easy to process textual features such as punctuation marks, spaces and short words like 'the', and that these features will therefore be among the materials associated with large eye movements. With these assumptions it is possible to account for the main features of the data since the form of control just outlined would clearly produce a tendency for subjects to skip over spaces, punctuation marks, short familiar words and the endings of words.

While each of the models provides a reasonable account of most of the data, neither is without its difficulties. In the case of the Stimulus Control models the problems can almost certainly be overcome, but with Workload Control the difficulties are damaging enough to question the viability of the model.

The main finding which challenges the Stimulus Control model is one that was reported in a study by O'Regan (1979). In this study the landing position of saccades in the region of the word *the* was compared with that for both high-frequency and low-frequency three-letter verbs appearing in equivalent positions in control sentences. The results confirmed O'Regan's (1975) earlier finding that fixations tend to overshoot the word *the* by a greater distance than they do for three-letter control verbs. However, this effect was significantly greater when the word *the* was compared with low-frequency verbs (e.g. *met*, *ran*) than when it was compared with high-frequency verbs (e.g. *was, are*). This suggests that the saccade length may be determined not only by the *size* of the parafoveal word but also by its *frequency*. Since frequency is obviously not a physical property of the stimulus the result appears to be more compatible with the Workload Control model than with the Stimulus Control model. However, it would be premature to reject the second model on the basis of this finding alone since there were one or two peculiarities in the data. Of particular importance was the fact that the tendency to skip *the* was greater in the control for the low-frequency condition than it was in the high-frequency control condition, and this difference occurred despite the fact that the two conditions were ostensibly equivalent. This means that differences in the relative tendencies to overshoot high- and low-frequency words was partly due to unexplained differences in the control condition. In other words, it is not clear whether or not there is a significant difference in saccade sizes in the vicinity of the high- and low-frequency words themselves. In the absence of this information it is impossible to tell whether saccades are influenced by anything other than the physical properties of the words and so O'Regan's reservations about the Stimulus Control model may be unfounded.

In the case of the Workload Control model the problems are more severe. Data that present difficulties include some from an experiment conducted by O'Regan (1975). Here it was found that subjects tend to make larger eye movements when entering long words than when entering short words. This is the opposite of the result expected on the Workload Control model, since long words tend to have relatively low frequencies and should therefore require more processing than short words do. If more work is anticipated, the size of the saccade should be set so that it is shorter rather than longer than average. The fact that it was not shows that the Workload Control model cannot account for all aspects of the data. At best, the processing load can only be a *partial* determinant of saccade size.

Overall, the evidence indicates that the strongest influence in the control and guidance of eye movements is likely to be the properties of the stimulus in the vicinity of the current fixation rather than the amount of processing entailed in the analysis of this stimulus. One outstanding question concerns the exact nature of the stimulus properties that are used by the control mechanism. As mentioned above, the most common suggestion is that it is merely the spatial and physical properties of the stimulus that determine the distribution of fixations. However, Kennedy (1978) has argued that eye movements may be guided by certain semantic properties of the material. More specifically, he has suggested that the eyes may be directed towards areas that contain information that is potentially interesting and important to the reader.

The main support for this hypothesis comes from an experiment in which subjects's eye movements were monitored as they read short, three-sentence passages. In the experimental group the third sentence always contained a word which was closely associated with one of the words in Sentence 1. In the control group this word was replaced with a low associate of the earlier word in Sentence

1. The results showed that the subjects in the first group tended to fixate on the critical word in Sentence 3 earlier than those in the control condition did, and Kennedy (1978) interpreted this as evidence that the subjects had specifically directed their eyes towards an area of the text that had been shown to be important by preliminary semantic analysis. Unfortunately, there are difficulties with this interpretation. One problem is that the data collected by Rayner (1975a) suggest that it is not possible to carry out semantic analysis of words that are more than four or five letters to the right of the fixation point (see Section 2.3). If this is true, the subjects' fixations would have to approach very close to the critical word before the results of this analysis became available for guiding subsequent saccades. At these short distances the critical word would tend to be fixated next whether or not it had been subjected to preliminary analysis, and so it is difficult to see how this information could have been used to help the subject to fixate the critical word at an earlier point in the experimental condition. Another problem derives from the fact that subjects in the experimental condition read a series of passages containing highly associated words in Sentence 3. This might have prompted them to develop a strategy of searching out the related word. If this happened the difference in the patterns of eye movements in the two conditions may be attributable to a strategy built up in the early trials of the experimental condition rather than to the use of peripheral semantic information to guide the saccades on any particular trial. Considering the difficulties facing the 'semantic control' hypothesis and the availability of alternative explanations for Kennedy's data, it seems safest at present to assume that this kind of stimulus control does not occur in normal reading.

We can now turn to the mechanisms that control the *durations* of fixations. As before, there is no difficulty in ruling out the Random Control model since there is compelling evidence that fixation time varies systematically as a function of the properties of the materials taken in by the fixation. Thus fixations that land in the spaces between sentences or on punctuation marks are shorter than those falling elsewhere in the text (Rayner, 1975b; Rayner and McConkie, 1976) while fixations that occur in the region of a nonword are longer than those falling on normal text (Rayner, 1975a; see Figure 2.3.). Similarly, Rayner (1977) and Just and Carpenter (1980) have reported that subjects tend to pause longer on rare words than on frequent words, while Rayner (1977) has presented evidence which suggests that subjects may dwell for a relatively long time on the main verb of each sentence.

Given that these results argue against Random Control, what conclusions can be drawn about the mechanisms that control fixation durations? Stimulus Control models are primarily concerned with the *placement* of fixations rather than their durations and, while it is possible that the duration is somehow affected by the physical shapes of the stimuli within the field of vision (as opposed to the processing associated with these stimuli), there is no particular support for this kind of explanation. The finding that fixations were longer for difficult materials such as rare words and nonwords suggests that the durations are partly determined by the current processing load. In other words, they are consistent with models based on the notion of Workload Control. It is not clear from these data whether each duration is controlled individually, or whether it is determined by the backlog of material to be assimilated from several preceding fixations (cf. Bouma and de Voogd, 1974). However, Rayner and McConkie (1976) have argued that adjustments are made on a fixation-to-fixation basis. They reasoned that if processing load is determined by the contents of more than one fixation, then local processing difficulties should carry over from one fixation to the next and so, on the 'backlog control' hypothesis, successive durations should be positively correlated. They tested this on the data for six of their ten subjects and found that the correlations were small. They apparently considered that this evidence was sufficient to rule out the 'backlog' hypothesis. However, they reported that the six correlations 'ranged from 0.10 to 0.16, with an average of 0.13' (p. 833) and, by using a one-sample t-test on the correlation measures, it is easy to show that this mean differs significantly from zero even if it is assumed that the variance between the correlation values is the maximum value compatible with the data reported ($t(5) = 9.69$, $p < 0.001$). This suggests that fixation durations are *not* controlled individually. Other data point to the same conclusion. For example, in an experiment discussed in detail earlier. Rayner (1975a) found that the fixation which occurred *after* one containing a nonword was typically longer than one following ordinary material (see Figure 2.3). This may be largely due to the fact that there are discrepancies between the visual features extracted from the two fixations (the interpretation discussed in the previous section). However, this is probably not the whole story, since the duration of a fixation following a short saccade (< 6 letters) was 30 ms shorter if it followed a fixation containing a word (Condition 2) than if it followed a fixation containing a nonword that was visually equivalent (Condition 3). This suggests that processing difficulties encountered with nonwords in the first fixation were carried over into the second.

If this conclusion is correct it suggests that fixation duration may be partly determined by processing difficulties encountered over several previous fixations.

To summarize, then, there is evidence that both saccade lengths and fixation durations are influenced by material on the page. However, they appear to be controlled by different mechanisms. The empirical evidence that is presently available does not permit any confident conclusions to be drawn about the nature of these mechanisms. Nevertheless, it seems that fixation durations are influenced by the processing demands associated with (at least) the last two fixations and that saccades are influenced by the presence of certain physical shapes (particularly spaces) within the range of vision. The lengths of the saccades may be influenced by processing demands as well, but there is no clear evidence that this occurs on a moment-to-moment basis.

2.9 SUMMARY OF CHAPTER 2

When a person reads he makes a series of brief eye movements to enable him to fixate on several different areas of the page. Investigations of saccadic suppression indicate that little or no useful information is made available for further processing during these movements. During the fixations, however, information is registered in a high-capacity visual store (the icon) and some of it is subsequently processed in depth. The icon remains available for most of the duration of the fixation, but its contents are then replaced by new material. During this interval some of the visual features are copied into a second store (STVM) where they are probably integrated with the visual information extracted from earlier fixations. This pooled source of visual data together with the icon provides the raw material for the processes that identify the visual patterns on the page as letters and words. These processes are considered in detail in the next chapter.

In certain circumstances details can be picked up at distances of 10° or more from the fixation point. However, this may not be possible when the material is arranged conventionally in lines of print. In any case, when people are actually reading, the evidence suggests that they only tend to use information from a small region ranging from approximately 1° to the left to 3° to the right of the fixation point. What is more, apparently only the information in the centre of this region is used immediately for the purposes of recognition.

Part of the reason for this may be that only a small amount of information can be retained in STVM and it is possible that the average distance between fixations is determined primarily by this fact. Whether or not this is the case, it is clear that STVM plays a central role in the extraction of visual information from the page. It follows that if there are people who have difficulty in retaining information in this store then these individuals should suffer from reading deficits of one kind or another. Evidence for this will be considered in Chapter 7.

Evidence on the control of eye movements suggests that the physical placement of fixations is largely determined by the distribution of the material on the page. Readers tend to direct their eyes towards points that are slightly to the left of the middle of long words and they tend to avoid parts of the text containing short words, punctuation marks and spaces. The *durations* of fixations are partly determined by the progress achieved in the analysis of the last two or three fixations. Fixation durations are short whenever the analysis is straightforward, but they are prolonged slightly if problems are encountered in the visual, lexical or linguistic analysis of the material.

CHAPTER 3

Word recognition

The previous chapter dealt with the way in which visual information is extracted from the page. In the next phase of reading this visual input is used to recover the semantic and syntactic information which the reader needs to understand the text. Perhaps the most important question at this stage concerns the nature of the retrieval process. How is appropriate information about the words on the page recovered from memory?

As a start in tackling this question it is useful to consider a simple analogy—that of an ordinary dictionary. A dictionary allows one to discover the meaning, pronunciation and syntactic class of words once the appropriate entry has been located, and for this reason investigators such as Conrad (1974), Coltheart, Davelaar, Jonasson and Besner (1977), Forster (1976) and many others have found it fruitful to assume that people possess an *internal dictionary* or *subjective lexicon* which operates in a broadly similar fashion. According to this view, the reader's task is to use the visual representation of the word to locate the appropriate lexical entry in his mental dictionary. Having done this, he can then proceed to recover at least part of the information needed to understand the text. In this approach, the problem of retrieving word information is divided into two parts—the problem of locating the lexical entry and the problem of recovering the relevant information once the entry has been identified.

The vast majority of the research in this field has concentrated on the first of these two phases and within this body of work it is possible to identify two broad themes. The first is a general consideration of the sources of information that are typically drawn upon in the course of locating the lexical entry, and the second is a more specific debate on the way this information is actually used to achieve this goal. These two general questions will be considered in turn.

3.1 SOURCES OF INFORMATION THAT COULD *POTENTIALLY* BE USED IN WORD RECOGNITION

There are several sources of stored information which a reader could potentially use in locating the lexical entry for a word. First, he could use his knowledge of the shapes of letters to identify the individual letters of the word. The resulting string of letters could then be used to locate the lexical entry. There is a little doubt that the target entry could be reached by such a route.

Almost all readers can identify individual letters without difficulty and most can probably identify a word given its constituent letters. The second potential source of information is a set of rules or procedures for pronouncing letter strings. Information of this kind would enable the reader to convert the printed material into an articulatory form or into a series of sounds which could then be used to recognize the word by its sound. It is obvious that at least a few pronunciation rules of this kind are retained in memory since it is possible to pronounce strings of letters that we have never seen before (e.g. *liggertike*).

A third source of information that could pay a part in word recognition is a body of knowledge concerning spelling regularities. (These are known as *orthographic rules*). Information of this kind could be used to guide processing and may be particularly useful when parts of the stimulus are missing or indistinct. A fourth source of information that might be used in word recognition is knowledge about the visual characteristics of individual words or parts of words. This might include information about the length of the word, its outline pattern, regions within the word that are densely packed with straight or curved lines and so on. Finally, it is conceivable that contextual information could be used to facilitate the process of identifying a word. Such information might help by biasing the reader's choice in favour of highly predictable words.

Although any of these sources of information could *potentially* be used in word recognition this obviously does not establish that they *are* used, and it certainly does not imply that they make any contribution during normal reading. Some of the potential sources may never have any influence at all on the recognition process. Others may be accessed so slowly that the information is recovered too late to have any influence under normal reading conditions.

In the next few sections we shall consider in turn whether each of the sources of information is used in word recognition.* In this discussion we shall draw a distinction between the kinds of information used to process impoverished stimuli (i.e. words that are presented very briefly or followed by a masking stimulus) and the information used to process clear and legible words. The reason for treating these two issues separately is that readers probably use different processing strategies in different situations (see, for example, Coltheart, 1978; Terry, 1976–1977; Terry, Samuels and LaBerge, 1976; Spoehr, 1978) and it is generally not safe to generalize from one situation to another.

3.2 SOURCES OF INFORMATION USED TO ACCESS DEGRADED WORDS

Most of the work using impoverished words as stimuli has been concerned with issues other than the attempt to determine the sources of information that are used to gain access to the lexicon and, as a result, it is not always easy to draw inferences about the access process itself. However, the results of these

---

* Much of the discussion of contextual effects will be deferred until Chapter 5 because it depends on ideas that will not be considered in detail until the next chapter.

experiments are worth considering because they often suggest hypotheses that can be tested in more suitable circumstances. In the following discussion we first consider the implications of indirect evidence of this kind and later we proceed to studies that are more directly concerned with the access process itself.

Two major techniques have been used to investigate the processing of impoverished stimuli and both of them concentrate on the subject's ability to identify individual letters. In the first task the subject is required to report as many letters as he can from a briefly presented display. This task has already been considered in passing in Section 2.6. In the second task—a forced-choice task introduced by Reicher (1969) and refined by Wheeler (1970)—a display consisting of one to eight letters is flashed briefly on the screen and followed immediately by a pattern mask together with two further letters. The subject is instructed to indicate which of these two letters originally appeared in a particular part of the initial display.

The results obtained in both kinds of experiment typically show that letter recognition performance varies according to the nature of the stimulus. For example, in the forced-choice task Reicher demonstrated that performance is more accurate when the initial display consists of a four-letter word than when it contains a single letter or a string of four unrelated letters. This effect, which is referred to as the *word superiority effect*, is reasonably reliable and has been replicated many times (e.g. by Wheeler, 1970; Smith and Haviland, 1972; Thompson and Massaro, 1973; Johnston and McClelland, 1973; Baron and Thurston, 1973), and over the past few years research employing degraded stimuli has been dominated by attempts to explain it. A number of relatively trivial explanations of the phenomenon were eliminated at an early stage by Wheeler (1970) and since then almost all accounts have been based on the notion that performance with words benefits because subjects are able to draw upon sources of information that would not otherwise be available. Thus, it has been suggested that the effect may result from the use of higher-order perceptual units such as phonological rules, spelling patterns and word-shapes (see Smith and Spoehr, 1974, for a detailed review of this work).

Which of these units can actually be shown to play a role in the forced-choice and the whole report recognition task? Starting with the 'larger' units, there is some evidence to suggest that units associated with *whole words* play a part in the recognition of letters presented in brief or degraded displays. Manelis (1974) found that the level of performance in the forced-choice task is higher when the stimulus is a real word than when it merely consists of a string of letters that conforms to English spelling rules.* This suggests that words must have some unique property (or properties) which can be used to improve performance in the recognition task.

* One or two investigations have failed to replicate this effect (e.g. Baron and Thurston, 1973, and Spoehr and Smith, 1975, Expt 2). However, there seems to be little doubt that it is a genuine phenomenon because significant differences between words and regular nonwords have been obtained in several studies other than that reported by Manelis (e.g. Juola, Leavitt and Choe, 1974; Spoehr and Smith, 1975, Experiment 1; McClelland, 1976; McClelland and Johnston, 1977).

The most obvious property possessed by words and not by letter strings is that they have a familiar shape. Subjects may be capable of using this information to facilitate the processing of words. Direct evidence for this comes from a forced-choice experiment conducted by McClelland (1976). Subjects were presented with stimuli consisting of monosyllabic words or nonwords printed either in lower-case letters, in upper-case letters or in alternating cases (e.g. *RaGe*). The results showed that the percentage of letters correctly identified was significantly lower in the alternating case condition. Since neither the identity of the letters nor the order in which they appeared was altered when the letter cases were changed, the result must be attributed to the availability of visual features that extend over more than one letter (i.e. the shape of the word or, perhaps, of some part of it).

Next we turn to units that are smaller than words. Part of the evidence comes from studies which show that recognition performance is better with letter strings that are regular and word-like than with strings that do not resemble words (Gibson, Pick, Osser and Hammond, 1962; Aderman and Smith, 1971). This result suggests that some additional source of information is available in the first case. Since the stimuli differ only in the sequential structure of the letter strings this information must be based on the subject's knowledge of the letter combinations that are likely to occur in English. As mentioned earlier, this knowledge may be derived from either one of two main sources: knowledge of spelling rules and knowledge of pronunciation rules. Unfortunately, it is not always easy to differentiate between these two possibilities because words that are orthographically regular tend to be pronounceable and vice versa. However, there is some evidence to suggest that pronunciation rules (at least) play a distinct role in the forced-choice recognition task. This comes from an experiment conducted by Spoehr and Smith (1973). Subjects were presented with one- or two-syllable words and on each trial they were required to decide which of two letters had been present in the display. The results showed that a higher proportion of letters were correctly reported for one-syllable words. On the basis of this, and other evidence, Spoehr and Smith argued that syllable-like perceptual units known as 'vocalic centre groups' play an important part in word recognition. In particular, they suggested that these units are used as a basis for constructing a phonological representation of the word and that this information is used in the subsequent analysis of the stimulus.

Other investigators have argued that spelling patterns may also play a role in recognition, but there is much less consensus on this than there is on the use of pronunciation rules. Gibson, Pick, Osser and Hammond (1962) conducted an experiment in which subjects were required to report as much as they could remember from briefly presented displays that either conformed to normal English spelling rules (e.g. *glurck*) or did not conform to these rules (e.g. *ckurgl*). The results showed that their performance was better when the strings were orthographically regular. Since the strings with regular spelling were also more pronounceable than the others this result could be explained in terms of either pronunciation rules or spelling rules. However, in a later experiment Gibson,

Shurcliff and Yonas (1970) replicated the result using congenitally deaf children, and since it is unlikely that these subjects could have made effective use of pronunciation rules it seems clear that at least part of the effect must have been based on the use of spelling rules.

Another study which points to the use of orthographic structure was carried out by Baron and Thurston (1973). Subjects were presented with either words or nonwords and were required to make a forced-choice decision about one of the letters. On the 'word' trials the alternative letters were selected in such a way that both of them would be pronounced in the same way in the complete word (e.g. *warn, worn*). The results showed that the normal word superiority effect occurred under these conditions. If the effect obtained in previous studies had resulted exclusively from the use of phonological information then it would have been eliminated in the present study since the use of homophones would make it impossible to discriminate between the alternative words on the basis of their sounds. The fact that this did not happen suggests that subjects may make use of non-phonological perceptual units such as spelling patterns.

Finally, Spoehr and Smith (1975) presented some evidence that spelling patterns (as well as vocalic centre groups) play a part in the processing of letter strings. They found that forced-choice performance was better for stimuli in which the letter combinations were similar to those that occur in corresponding positions in English words (e.g. *blst*) than for stimuli in which the combinations are not permissible in these positions (e.g. *lstb*). Since the letter strings were relatively unpronounceable in both conditions they took this as evidence that orthographic rules are consulted at some point in the process.

While these studies tend to suggest that spelling rules are used in the perceptual analysis of letter strings, the evidence is by no means conclusive. The deaf subjects in the experiment reported by Gibson *et al.* (1970) could have performed better with the 'regular' letter strings because they were able to make effective use of lip movements during the task (see Coltheart, 1977, p.162). The word superiority effect obtained by Baron and Thurston (1973) could plausibly be explained on the basis of other perceptual units such as pronunciation rules. The use of such rules during perceptual processing might, for example, have allowed processing resources to be freed in the word condition enabling more attention to be paid to the visual analysis of the letters. Finally, the results obtained by Spoehr and Smith (1975) could be explained without recourse to spelling patterns if it is assumed that the subjects adopted special strategies to deal with the unpronounceable letter strings. For example, they might have inserted a vowel in the middle of the sequence, making strings like *blst* pronounceable but leaving others like *lstb* relatively unpronounceable. If something like this occurred, the main experimental findings could be explained in terms of perceptual units other than spelling patterns.

In addition to these general reservations about the evidence in *favour* of the 'spelling pattern' hypothesis there are one or two studies which provide reasonably direct evidence *against* the hypothesis. Manelis (1974) compared the letter recognition performance for strings made up of common letter combinations with those consisting of rarer patterns and found that there was no evidence of a correlation between either bigram or trigram frequency and the accuracy of performance. In a similar, but more detailed, study McClelland and Johnston (1977) found no difference between the level of performance for high- and low-bigram-frequency words and letter strings. If spelling units had played a part in the recognition process some kind of relationship would have been expected, and so these studies throw some doubt on the hypothesis. All in all, there is slightly more evidence *against* the use of spelling units than there is *for* it.

To summarize, research based on the recognition of individual letters appearing in briefly presented displays suggests that several different processing units might contribute to performance. There is some evidence that word-shape and units underlying pronunciation may play a role in the process and, although the weight of evidence is rather against it at the time of writing, it remains possible that spelling patterns play a role as well.

Do these units also make a contribution to the process of accessing the lexical entry for a word? It may be that many of the foregoing effects occur because strings of letters can be processed more efficiently if they are treated as familiar words. If this is true, it is conceivable that the units which influence performance do so by facilitating the process of identifying the stimulus word. On this hypothesis word-shape and pronunciation units would be considered to play an important role in accessing the lexical entry for a word. However, this conclusion only follows if one accepts one particular account of the word superiority effect, and there are several reasons for having reservations about the validity of this interpretation of the phenomenon.

One problem is that in recognition tasks of the kind reviewed above familiar units may play a role not only in the extraction of information from the stimulus, but also in retaining the information until the response alternatives become available and in comparing the information with the alternatives (see Krueger, 1975). In many of the studies cited above, these alternatives cannot be eliminated, and so there is no guarantee that any of the sources of information in question are used to locate the lexical entry for the target word. Conceivably, further experiments could be carried out to uncover the role of units in the extraction process; but even if this were done, it is not at all clear that we would be in a position to answer the original question because there is a second important difficulty with tasks of the kind reviewed in this section, and this is that the pattern of results obtained in these studies is often extremely sensitive to minor changes in the experimental procedure. Thus, even if it could be demonstrated that one or other of the units played a role under a particular set of conditions one could not be sure that the same unit (or units) would be used in any other circumstances. The sensitivity to procedural details in these tasks is perhaps best illustrated by the way in which the word superiority effect changes and even disappears under various conditions. Manelis (1974) found that the magnitude of the word superiority effect depends upon the proportion of trials in which the stimulus is a word rather than an unrelated string of letters (see Aderman and Smith, 1971, for a demonstration that similar variations occur with the spelling pattern effect). Johnston and McClelland (1973) and Juola,

Leavitt and Choe (1974) found that the superiority effect is eliminated if the letter string or word is not followed by a masking stimulus, while Spoehr (1978) has observed that the effect of number of syllables on forced-choice performance disappears if there is no masking. Purcell, Stanovich and Spector (1978) have shown that the word superiority effect disappears if the angle of the display is increased, and Krueger (1975) has presented evidence that it only occurs in the left hemisphere of the brain. Finally, Mezrich (1973) has shown that the effect is actually reversed if subjects are instructed to report the whole array before making a decision, and Massaro (1973) and Thompson and Massaro (1973) have reported that similar kinds of reversal occur under other conditions.

Taken together, these findings demonstrate that relatively small changes of procedure in the recognition task can cause subjects to vary their processing strategies and that this sometimes has a dramatic effect on their performances. This means that it is impossible to be confident in generalizing from the results of forced-choice letter recognition experiments to other kinds of experimental task. In particular, it does not appear to be safe to draw any conclusions about the perceptual units that might be used when the primary task is to locate the lexical entry for a word rather than to make a forced-choice decision about one of its letters.

The best that can be concluded from the forced-choice and whole report studies is that they give us an idea of the kinds of information that can be used when subjects have to make decisions about component parts of impoverished words. Obviously, it may be fruitful to see whether the same sources of information are used to identify the words themselves. In particular, it would be profitable to try to determine whether word-shape and pronunciation rules play a part in the identification of degraded words. Unfortunately, there is much less work on normal word recognition than there is on the forced-choice task, but there is at least a suggestion that word-shape may contribute to the process. This comes from an experiment carried out by Coltheart and Freeman (1974). On each trial of this experiment, an eight-letter, disyllabic word was presented for 50 ms and the subject was required to say the word. Each word was presented three times during the experiment: once in lower-case letters, once in upper-case letters and once with the case alternating from letter to letter. The results showed that performance in the alternating case condition was worse than that in the other two conditions. This suggests that units associated with the shape of the word play a role in the identification process under these conditions. There does not appear to be any direct evidence that pronunciation rules and orthographic rules contribute to the process so all we can do is retain these possibilities as working hypotheses.

3.3 SOURCES OF INFORMATION USED IN PROCESSING CLEARLY PRINTED WORDS

Experiments employing undegraded stimuli have examined the contribution of most of the sources of information that we have considered up to now. They have considered the role of the individual letters in the word, of information about spelling rules and pronunciation rules, and of information associated more directly with the lexical unit itself. Each of these potential sources of information in word recognition will be examined in turn.

3.3.1 The identity of individual letters

Most of the evidence suggests that the letters of a word are *not* recognized as part of the process of identifying the word itself. On occasion this conclusion has been reached on rather dubious grounds, but recent studies have provided reasonably convincing evidence against the use of letter units.

Perhaps the most contentious case against letter units was one that was put forward by Johnson (1975). Johnson based his conclusions on a series of studies in which the time required for subjects to match complete words was compared with the matching time for single letters. The results of one experiment showed that subjects took longer to indicate whether the first letter of a word was the same as a previously presented letter than to say whether the whole word was the same as a previously presented word. A second study revealed that the time taken to match two individual letters was about the same as that required to match two words consisting of several letters. Thirdly, the data showed that the matching time for words was unaffected by their lengths. Johnson interpreted each of these findings as evidence that word recognition is not mediated by letter recognition. Basically, his argument was that if letters had been identified first they would have been matched more quickly than words. Also, on this assumption longer words would require more letters to be identified and should therefore take longer to match than words with fewer letters.

Subsequent investigators have pointed out several difficulties concerning Johnson's interpretation of the data. The first problem is that letters that appear as parts of words almost certainly suffer from lateral masking (cf. the work of Bouma, 1970, discussed in Chapter 2) whereas letters presented alone do not. This would tend to slow down performance in all conditions involving words or other multiletter displays, and so it is virtually impossible to draw any conclusions about the relative matching latencies for single letters and letters in words (Sloboda, 1976; Massaro and Klitzke, 1977). The second difficulty is more specific to Johnson's second finding. The problem here is that the matching time for words is not a stable measure. It depends critically on the sample of words employed in the experiment, and it has been shown that Johnson's finding can be reversed simply by altering the materials. In particular, the average response time is slower if the word pairs presented on the 'different' trials are always very similar (e.g. life—line) than when they are dissimilar (e.g. life—last) (Sloboda, 1976). Indeed, Massaro and Klitzke (1977) have found that letter matching is significantly faster than word matching when similar words are included on some of the 'different' trials. This suggests that Johnson's findings are not at all robust with respect to relatively minor changes in experimental procedure.

Other experiments point to the same conclusion. Using a matching task in which the stimuli were presented simultaneously rather than successively, Marmurek (1977) found that Johnson's first finding was reversed (i.e. letters in words were matched faster than words) and that single letters were matched more quickly than words. Other research with the simultaneous matching task shows that, in contrast with the results obtained in Johnson's experiment, response latency increases with word length (Eichelman, 1970).

Taken together these results throw considerable doubt on Johnson's (1975) reasons for concluding that individual letters are not used as perceptual units. They also suggest that the processes and strategies which are used are so task-specific that the results of this kind of experiment are unlikely to tell us anything useful about ordinary word recognition.

More recently Cosky (1976) has carried out a study that offers a more direct test of the suggestion that letter units are used to identify clearly printed words. Cosky approached the problem by comparing the recognition times for words made up of letters that are easy to identify with those for words made up of less 'discriminable' letters. Clearly, words of the first kind should be processed more rapidly if the letters are identified *en route* to the lexical entry. The relative discriminability of the letters was determined in a number of different ways. In certain of the tests the subjects were shown a series of letters and non-alphabetic characters (e.g. #, +, etc.) or inverted letters and in each case they were required to say as quickly as possible whether the stimulus was a (normally oriented) letter or not. In other tests the subjects were instructed to name a letter which was either presented alone or flanked by two non-alphabetic characters. In each case the latency data were used to rank the letters in order of discriminability. The results showed that the different measures correlated reasonably well with one another, which suggests that the individual tests were measuring similar characteristics of the letters. The data from one of the classification tests were used to designate 13 of the letters as 'easy' to identify and the rest as 'difficult' to identify.

In the main part of the experiment subjects were instructed to pronounce words that differed in the discriminability of their constituent letters and also in their lengths and their frequency of usage. The results showed that the last two variables had a highly reliable effect on reaction time, but there was no evidence at all that recognition time is influenced by variations in the discriminability of the constituent letters. This suggests that the recognition of a clearly printed word does not entail the identification of the individual letters within it. However, as Cosky himself pointed out, models involving prior letter recognition cannot be ruled out completely on the basis of these data. The measures of letter difficulty employed in the study may not reflect the differences in letter recognition time that occur in normal word recognition. Alternatively, letter recognition may proceed in parallel with other processes that take longer to complete, in which case differences in letter processing would presumably not be reflected in the overall time to recognize the word. Even if we accept these reservations, however, there does not appear to be any strong evidence that the identities of individual letters are used to access the lexical entry in fluent reading.

3.3.2 The use of spelling patterns

There does not appear to be any direct evidence that information about spelling patterns is used to gain access to the lexical entry for a clearly printed word. However, they do appear to be used in a variety of other tasks and this suggests that the hypothesis can be considered a plausible one. Krueger (1970) found that subjects are able to locate a target letter more rapidly when it appears in a list of nonwords that conform to English spelling rules. Chambers and Forster (1975) showed that the time subjects took to say whether two strings of letters were the same or different depended on whether the sequences were orthographically legal (e.g. crawn) or not (e.g. crhot) (see also Barron and Pittenger, 1974). Unfortunately, these tasks do not resemble ordinary word recognition very closely and so it is impossible to generalize from the findings in order to draw any reasonable conclusions about normal reading tasks. It therefore remains a matter of speculation whether spelling patterns are used in fluent word recognition.

3.3.3 The use of pronunciation rules

It is frequently suggested that readers use pronunciation rules to gain access to lexical information. However, as with spelling rules, there seems to be little direct evidence that this occurs with clearly printed reading materials.

There are a number of ways in which the hypothesis could be tested. Perhaps the simplest is to compare performance for words that are easy to pronounce with that for words that are more difficult to pronounce. Following this approach, Baron and Strawson (1976) instructed subjects to read lists of words (aloud) as rapidly as possible. In one condition the pronunciation of the words always conformed to normal pronunciation rules (e.g. *sweet*). In another, the pronunciation of every word was irregular (e.g. *sword*). The results of this experiment showed that the regular lists were read more rapidly than the others which suggests that phonological coding plays a part in performance. A similar conclusion is suggested by an earlier study which showed that performance is influenced by the number of syllables in the word when other factors are held constant (Klapp, Anderson and Berrian, 1973). However, these studies do not establish that pronunciation rules are used to *access* words in the lexicon. It may be that the effects of pronounceability are confined to the process of vocalizing the word after it has been identified. Indeed, certain other aspects of the data reported by Klapp *et al.* (1973) strongly suggest that this may be what happens. The results showed that the syllable length effect disappears when overt vocalization is not required. This suggests that the effect is associated with response preparation, in which case it does not tell us anything about the way in which lexical units are accessed. To investigate this issue it is essential to use silent reading tasks.

In one silent reading experiment Meyer, Schvaneveldt and Ruddy (1974) displayed pairs of letter strings and instructed subjects to indicate as rapidly as possible whether both strings were English words. On trials when they were, the two words were either pronounced in the same way (e.g. *bribe, tribe*) or else they were pronounced differently although the spelling was similar (e.g. *couch, touch*). The results showed that the subjects responded more rapidly when the pronunciation of the two words was similar, suggesting that phonemic recoding plays a role in this task. In another study Taylor, Miller and Juola (1977) recorded the time taken for subjects to match pairs of words and found that they responded more rapidly to one-syllable words than to two-syllable words of the same length. Again, this points to the conclusion that performance is influenced by the use of phonological codes. However, neither the double lexical decision task used by Meyer *et al.* (1974) nor the matching task employed by Taylor *et al.* (1977) closely resemble normal reading, and consequently it is not safe to draw any conclusion from these studies about the strategies used to access words in conventional reading.

There is some evidence that the meaning of a word or phrase may sometimes be accessed by a phonological route. Meyer and Gutschera (1975) conducted an experiment in which subjects were presented with a question (e.g. 'Is a kind of fruit?') followed shortly by a test word (e.g. *pear*). The task was to indicate as rapidly as possible whether the word was a member of the category in question. Some of the non-members were homophones of a word that was an instance of the category (e.g. *pair*) while others were not. The results showed that subjects took longer to say 'no' to homophones than to other words, indicating that the pronunciation of the words was used at some stage in the process.

A similar conclusion is suggested by the results of an experiment reported earlier by Baron (1973). In this study subjects were shown short phrases and they had to indicate whether these phrases made sense in the form in which they were printed. Some of the phrases were completely sensible (e.g. *tie the knot*). Others sounded right but contained words that were spelt inappropriately (e.g. *tie the not*), and the rest neither sounded correct nor looked correct. The results showed that subjects made more errors on trials of the second kind than on trials when the phrase sounded wrong. The response times on such trials also tended to be slightly longer although this effect did not reach significance.

While these data suggest that phonological recoding occurs at some point before the response is made in these tasks, the results do not establish that this occurs prior to lexical access. It is quite possible that the words are initially located without any reference to pronunciation rules, and that the interference produced by the sound of the phrase occurs because the words are subvocalized *after* they have been identified.

It is probably impossible to devise tasks which completely eliminate post-lexical effects of this kind. However, there are tasks that minimize the effects by requiring subjects to do little more than identify the target word. One task of this kind is the lexical decision task.

Using the lexical decision task, Rubenstein and his colleagues have provided reasonably clear evidence that people use phonological recoding at some point in making word/nonword decisions. In one study Rubenstein, Lewis and Rubenstein (1971) showed that nonwords that sound like words (e.g. *burd*) are slower to classify than other equally regular nonwords (e.g. *losp*). (This difference has been dubbed the *pseudohomophone* effect.) The experiment has been criticized by Clark (1973) on the grounds that the finding may not generalize to new materials and, indeed, a few failures to replicate the finding have been reported (e.g. Frederiksen and Kroll, 1976). However, in a detailed review of the field, Coltheart (1978) has pointed out that several successful replications have been reported as well, and so it seems likely that the phenomenon is a reliable one. In a later study Rubenstein, Richter and Kay (1975) found that highly pronounceable nonwords such as *losp* can be identified as nonwords more rapidly than less pronounceable strings (e.g. *likj*). Both of these findings suggest that phonological encoding plays a role in the lexical decision task. However, as Coltheart (1978) has stressed, the effects demonstrated in these experiments are restricted to *nonwords* and so, strictly speaking, the conclusion should also be confined to nonwords. Thus the experiments do not necessarily tell us anything about the way in which ordinary words are identified. In particular, it is possible that the lexical entry is always located more rapidly by a direct route based on the visual representation alone than by a route based on phonological encoding (Coltheart, Davelaar, Jonasson and Besner, 1977).

In order to examine the role of phonological encoding in the identification of *words*, as opposed to *nonwords*, Coltheart, Besner, Jonasson and Davelaar (1979) examined the YES latencies for words that are pronounced according to standard pronunciation rules (regular words) and those that are not (exception words) (see Coltheart, 1978, for a detailed discussion of these rules). The prediction was that if access to the lexicon is based on phonological codes, regular words should be identified more rapidly than exception words. However, there was no evidence of any difference at all and so the authors concluded that subjects do not use grapheme-to-phoneme correspondence rules to access the lexical entries for ordinary words in this task.

To recapitulate, there have been several demonstrations that phonological encoding occurs with at least certain kinds of material. However, there is no evidence that this occurs prior to lexical access when the stimuli are words. In fact, the lack of difference between performance with regular and exception words strongly suggests that fluent readers do not use pronunciation rules to gain access to the lexical entry.

3.3.4 The use of word-shape

The final possibility is that the overall shape of the word or perhaps some part of it can be used to gain access to the lexical entry. The results obtained using a variety of experimental techniques suggest that this can occur under appropriate circumstances. However, as will be seen, only one or two of these tasks are sufficiently similar to the processes that occur in reading to warrant the conclusion that such units are used in ordinary word recognition.

The first task that will be considered is the speeded matching task. In this technique two words or strings of letters are presented in a display and the subject is required to say as quickly as possible whether they are the same or different. Using this technique Eichelman (1970) has found that words are matched more rapidly than random strings of letters of the same length. Barron and Pittenger (1974) showed that the word advantage for 'same' judgements is still evident when words are compared with orthographically regular nonwords and the difference remains even when the two types of material are matched for bigram and trigram frequency.

One interpretation of these results (although it is not the one favoured by either set of investigators) is that words are processed more rapidly because they have a familiar shape (i.e. familiar outlines and internal combinations of features). Some support for this suggestion comes from the finding that the word advantage is reduced when the materials are presented in a mixture of upper- and lower-case letters (Pollatsek, Well and Schindler, 1975; Taylor, Miller and Juola, 1977, Expt 3; Bruder, 1978). The main effect of mixing the cases is probably to reduce the familiarity of the word (or possibly of other perceptual units), and so it seems likely that familiar visual units play a significant role in the matching task. In two of the experiments (Taylor *et al.*, 1977, Expt 3, and Bruder, 1978, Expt 3) it was the advantage of words over regular nonwords that was reduced. In these studies the units must have been based on whole words since an advantage over regular strings cannot be explained satisfactorily on the basis of smaller units.

A second line of evidence which suggests that familiar word units may play a role in recognition is provided by a task in which subjects are required to search for a target letter in various kinds of text. In one study of this kind, Healy (1976) instructed subjects to mark the letter *t* whenever it appeared in a 100-word passage of prose. In another part of the study the passage of prose was replaced by a random list of letters. She found that the percentage of *t*s missed in the various occurrences of the word *the* in the prose condition was much higher than that for targets appearing in the same ordinal position in the control condition. A second experiment showed that the difference remained when the word order in the experimental condition was randomized, suggesting that the difference cannot be attributed to the fact that linguistic redundancy is used to skip the word *the* in the prose condition. Further experiments showed that the difficulties in detecting the letter *t* cannot be accounted for by the fact that it is not pronounced in the word *the* and that there tend to be more errors in high- than in low-frequency words.

In her interpretation of these results, Healy suggested that individual letters may sometimes be relatively difficult to detect because they fall within reading units which are treated as wholes. The fact that performance is influenced by word frequency tends to confirm that whole word units may be implicated in the process.

While the matching task and the search task both provide evidence that familiar shape units can paly a role in processing words, both of them differ substantially from normal reading, and so as usual there is no way of telling whether the units are normally used to gain access to the mental lexicon. In the case of the matching task the difficulty is compounded by the fact that the advantage of words over nonwords disappears when the stimuli are presented in succession rather than simultaneously, or when word and nonword trials are randomized rather than being blocked together in the same experimental session (Taylor *et al.*, 1977). These observations suggest that relatively small procedural changes cause subjects to change their processing strategies. If the word advantages are as sensitive as this to experimental changes it is obviously impossible to generalize the findings to different conditions such as those that are likely to occur in fluent reading.

The problem of generalizing from one task to another also makes it difficult to accept the conclusions of certain studies that have argued that word-shape does *not* play a role in recognition. Smith, Lott and Cronnell (1969) conducted an experiment in which subjects searched through a passage of prose looking for 20 target words. In the three main conditions the materials were printed in upper-case letters, in lower-case letters or in alternating cases, and the result showed that the number of targets located was not influenced in any way by the way in which the text was printed. If this result is taken at face value it suggests that word-shape does not influence the speed and efficiency of recognition. However, as Coltheart and Freeman (1974) have pointed out, any variations in word recognition that occurred in this task might easily have been obscured by the heavy demands of checking and remembering the 20 target words. It is clear that more sensitive and more ecologically valid tasks are needed to evaluate the hypothesis.

Perhaps the most direct way of examining the role of word-shape in recognition is to compare subjects' reading times for materials with familiar word-shapes with those in which the shapes are unfamiliar. This has been done by Pickering (1975) using single words, by Baron (1977) using lists of unrelated words, and by Fisher (1975) and Cohen and Freeman (1978) using coherent passages of prose.

In Pickering's experiment the subjects were required to make lexical decisions about words that were either printed conventionally or in a mixture of upper- and lower-case letters. The results showed that their responses were slower when the familiar word-shape was disrupted. In Baron's study the subjects were required to read aloud a list of 30 proper names in which the first letter was either typed in the upper case (e.g. *Ann, Dan,* etc.) or—in the unfamiliar condition—in the lower case (e.g. *ann, dan,* etc.). In other conditions the lists consisted of words that do not often occur at the beginnings of sentences and so are only rarely seen with a capital letter at the beginning (familiar condition: *ate, ant*, etc.; unfamiliar condition: *Ate, Ant*, etc.). The results showed that the total time required to read the lists presented in the unfamiliar manner was significantly longer than that for the familiar lists.

A similar result was obtained by Fisher (1975) using a silent reading task. The subjects were required to read 200-word passages printed in either upper-case or lower-case letters (familiar conditions) or in alternating cases (unfamiliar condition) and were later tested for comprehension. The results showed that both the comprehension score and the reading rate were lower in the alternating case condition. Unfortunately, it is not clear whether either effect was statistically significant. The experimental conditions that are relevant to the present discussion comprised only a small part of the study and the bulk of the statistical analysis concentrated on other unrelated phenomena such as the effect of removing the spaces between words.

In the remaining study Cohen and Freeman (1978) instructed subjects to read short passages aloud. One of the passages was printed in alternating cases and another was printed in the conventional way (i.e. in lower-case letters except for capitals at the beginning of sentences). The results showed that the reading rate was reduced in the alternating case condition, but this effect was only marked for the slower readers (11 per cent reduction in speed). The difference for the fastest readers was only 2 per cent. This discrepancy between the two group might indicate that they use different strategies to recognize words, but a more likely interpretation of the virtual absence of an effect in the fast readers is that their performance was distorted by a ceiling effect. For example, it may be that they were unable to pronounce the words any faster than they could identify them in the alternating case condition, in which case there would be no way they could improve their performance when the text was presented in a more familiar manner.

Taken together the results considered in this section suggest that word-shapes may play a role in a variety of tasks which bear some resemblance to normal reading. More direct tests with tasks that are actually based on reading tend to confirm that units of this kind may be used to access lexical information in these conditions.

3.4 SOURCES OF INFORMATION USED IN WORD RECOGNITION: A SUMMARY

The experiments that have been conducted with degraded materials provide positive evidence that the overall shape of the word (or part of the word) can be used to access its lexical entry. There is also some evidence that other units, particularly those associated with pronunciation and orthographic rules, may play a role in tasks that are considered to be related to word recognition (e.g. tasks involving the identification of individual letters in a briefly presented array). Whether or not these units are also used to access the lexicon is a matter for further detailed research, but a reasonable working hypothesis for the time being is that they may be used for this purpose under suitable conditions.*

The research on clearly printed words provides no clear evidence that any perceptual units other than the featural description of the word itself play any role in accessing the lexical entry. In particular, there is some evidence *against* the prior identification of individual letters and *against* the use of pronunciation rules for accessing the lexicon, while the evidence relating to the use of orthographic units is too indirect to be of any use in evaluating their role in the process of identifying words.

Taken at face value these data seem to suggest that in fluent reading the identification of words is not preceded by the classification of any of the sub-units that comprise it (i.e. word recognition is *direct* or *non-mediated*; Smith, 1971). However, it should be stressed that this conclusion is not universally accepted. Some investigators such as Massaro (1975) and Rozin and Gleitman (1977) have argued against direct recognition on the grounds that a system operating in this way would be inefficient. The problem, as these writers see it, is that a direct recognition system makes no use of the fact that a reader is typically able to recognize a word by its sound before he comes to read it. Instead of utilizing the existing phonological representation of the word the reader has to create a separate *visual* description for each new word he learns and this requirement, it is argued, may place excessive demands on memory. Researchers of this persuasion find it much easier to accept a model in which the letters of a word are identified and pronounced so that the existing *phonological* description can be used to access the lexicon.

Mediated models of this kind would certainly place fewer demands on memory and this might be seen as an argument in their favour. However, it is not a very persuasive one since no one has ever shown that the memory system would be unduly taxed by doubling the memory requirements. In fact, there is positive evidence that this kind of duplication can and does occur. This comes from case studies of patients who lose the ability to pronounce letter strings as a result of an accident, but nevertheless retain the capacity to read almost as well as other adults (Beauvois and Dérouesné, 1978; Shallice and Warrington, 1980: see Section 7.2.3 for further details). If these patients had not previously memorized visual as well as phonological descriptions of most of the words in their vocabularies, it is difficult to see how they could have retained the ability to read. If one or two individuals like this are able to (or strictly were once able to) retain dual codes for an extensive vocabulary of words then there is no reason why this should not be within the capabilities of the majority of fluent readers. Thus there does not seem to be any reason to qualify our conclusion that the identification of clearly printed words is not preceded by the identification of letters, spelling patterns or any other subword units.

Throughout this discussion of the sources of information used to identify words we have retained the distinction between the perceptual processing that

---

*In addition to the sources considered here there is evidence that contextual constraints may contribute to the recognition process. This issue is taken up in Chapter 5.

readers engage in when they are confronted with degraded materials and when they are required to read clearly printed text. The initial reason for making this distinction was that readers might use different strategies for the two types of material. In the event, the best that can be said from the current evidence is that there is some suggestion that different strategies might be used. For example, while there is reason to believe that pronunciation rules could be used to recognize impoverished stimuli, the evidence suggests that this is not one of the strategies used to identify undegraded words. More direct evidence that variations in stimulus quality can lead subjects to use different strategies comes from investigations of the effect of context on word recognition. This work is considered in detail in Chapter 5 (see Sections 5.5 and 5.6), but for the purposes of the present discussion it is worth noting that the influence of context depends strongly on the quality of the stimuli. (Strong contextual constraints are obtained with impoverished stimuli, but with clearly presented stimuli these effects are either very weak or non-existent.)

These data suggest that reading undegraded material is not the same as reading impoverished text. If this is true, questions are raised about why there should be differences in the way these two types of stimuli are processed. One possible explanation for these differences (based on the Coltheart *et al.* (1977) account of the differences between processing *words* and *nonwords*) is that there are two or more parallel routes to the lexicon and that these alternative routes tend to be used in different circumstances. Thus subjects may *rely* on the preliminary recognition of sublexical units or *bypass* this information depending on whether the stimuli are presented in an impoverished or in an undegraded form. The route that is eventually employed could conceivably be determined by the subject's choice, but a more plausible suggestion is that all routes are followed simultaneously and that the pattern of data depends upon which of the alternatives reaches the goal first. Thus the direct route might operate efficiently with clearly printed materials, in which case most words would be recognized in this way under normal reading conditions. With degraded materials the processes associated with the direct route might be slowed down so that they rarely reach a decision before the word has been recognized by indirect procedures. In this case the data would reflect the characteristics of the alternative route.

According to this hypothesis, word recognition may be viewed as a race between alternative processes. The outcome of the race is determined by the relative efficiency of the different processes under varying conditions. If this notion is accepted there are factors other than the stimulus quality that might influence the outcome. One obvious consideration is the subject's familiarity with the word to be read. If it is new or unfamiliar the processes that are specific to the individual words (i.e. the direct processes) are unlikely to be very efficient and so operations that build up the sound of the word using pronunciation rules are liable to predominate in these conditions. In the case of a fluent reader, only a small proportion of the words would be unfamiliar and this strategy would not have to be used very often. However, it is worth considering carefully because it may be a particularly important strategy for inexperienced readers and, as will be argued later (see Section 8.2), it may play a crucial role in improving the efficiency of the direct route.

Another factor which might influence the outcome of the lexical race concerns the point in processing at which extraneous information becomes available. For example, the context in which a word appears might guide the analysis of the word if the contextual information is available for long enough in advance for the reader to take it into account, but if it is presented immediately before the target word appears there may not be enough time for it to influence the course of processing. This point is developed more fully in Chapter 5.

The discussion so far has concentrated on the sources of information that might be drawn upon to recognize words under different conditions. Very little has been said about *how* this information is used or about how decisions are made about the identity of the word. The evidence summarized above suggests that different procedures may be used in different circumstances. It therefore seems sensible to examine the process employed under three broad kinds of condition—those that entail the identification of impoverished stimuli, those that occur when the stimulus is unfamiliar or novel and those associated with familiar undegraded materials.

3.5   MODELS OF WORD RECOGNITION:

IMPOVERISHED STIMULI

There has been a great deal of work directed towards elucidating the processes by which impoverished words are identified. Much of it uses stimuli that are either presented very briefly or followed by a masking stimulus of some kind. Unfortunately, very few of the studies have used materials similar to those that are encountered in 'natural' reading tasks (e.g. handwriting), and there is little reason to believe that the procedures that *have* been investigated in the psychological literature play an important part in normal fluent reading. For this reason the topic will be dealt with rather briefly and no attempt will be made to do justice to the time and energy that has been devoted to this kind of recognition task in the literature.

Broadbent (1967) outlined a variety of models that have been used to account for the perception of impoverished stimuli. Perhaps the most obvious suggestion is that subjects' performances are influenced by the fact that they try to guess words whenever they fail to identify them directly. The simplest model of this kind is the Pure Guessing model. According to this suggestion the subject's guesses are based exclusively on the properties of the words in his vocabulary. That is, the choice of a word might be influenced by its frequency (say) but would not be affected, for example, by the fragments of the word that might have been successfully processed.

A more likely account of guessing is one in which the subject's choice is influenced both by the characteristics of the incomplete information extracted from the stimulus and by biases in favour of certain words or classes of words. Broadbent called this the Sophisticated Guessing model. One particular version of the model states that the range of potential words is first narrowed down by reference to available featural information, and that a specific word is chosen from these alternatives on the basis of word frequency.

Not at all models of word recognition emphasize deliberate guessing in this way. Broadbent (1967) considered several models in which there is no separate provision for guessing. The most important class of models in this category treats word recognition as a form of statistical decision making. In models of this kind it is assumed that each word in the subject's vocabulary is represented by a device which registers the amount of evidence there is in favour of the item in question in the stimulus information. In the absence of stimulation this value averages around some predetermined resting point. However, on the arrival of any stimulus resembling the target word the value is incremented and the critical word is judged to be present if this measure increases beyond some prespecified criterion. Models of this kind can account for many of the findings previously attributed to guessing by positing that the decision criterion varies with the type of word in question. (For example, it may be lower for common than for rate words.) Broadbent (1967) referred to models of this type as Criterion Bias models.

Which of these types of model provides the best account of the recognition of degraded words? The evidence suggests that the Pure Guessing model is unable to account for the magnitude of the word frequency effect or for certain other phenomena associated with the perception of rare and common words (Broadbent, 1967) and is therefore unsatisfactory as a model of word recognition. However, recent versions of both the Sophisticated Guessing model and the Criterion Bias model seem to be able to account for most aspects of the data. A viable version of each of these models will be described briefly before any attempt is made to distinguish between them.

One of the more successful versions of the Sophisticated Guessing model is the account of word recognition put forward by Rumelhart and Siple (1974). According to this model, visual features are extracted from the stimulus while it remains available and this information is used to exclude all words that are incompatible with the feature list and to select a sample of words that remain consistent with it. More specifically, candidate words are eliminated if they do not possess one or more features that are present in the stimulus sample or, alternatively, if the number of features in the description of the word exceeds the number in the sample by some critical value. A choice between the remaining items is then made on two grounds: the likelihood that a given word would yield the feature list under consideration and the subject's prior expectation that a particular word will occur. Thus, if there are two words, both of which would be equally likely to give rise to the partial visual description generated by the first stage of the analysis, then the choice between them will be made on the basis of factors such as the frequency of the words and the context in which the stimulus appears. The model is expressed in a detailed mathematical form and is capable of accounting for most of the major experimental findings obtained with impoverished stimuli (e.g. the word frequency effect, the word superiority effect and various contextual effects to be discussed in more detail in Chapter 5 (see Section 5.5)).

The version of the Criterion Bias model which we shall consider is the Activation model presented by Adams (1979). According to this model words are recognized indirectly (i.e. following the activation of individual letters). The letter units themselves are activated both directly and indirectly. The visual features extracted from a particular part of the stimulus excite various letter units directly, and these units in turn activate others that frequently appear in adjacent positions in English words. Thus, in addition to the direct activation an individual letter unit is energized indirectly by the letter units excited in the positions on either side of it.

In the next stage of the model, combinations of letter units feed into various lexical units and these units are activated to varying extents depending on the precise collection of letters initially stimulated and on the frequency of the word represented by the lexical unit. As soon as a word unit is excited, this in turn leads to reciprocal activation of each and every unit representing its constituent letters, and the effects continue to reverberate in the system until the level of activation in one of the lexical units reaches its criterion and the word is recognized.

This model is capable of accounting for the word superiority effect. (Letters that are parts of words benefit from reciprocal activation by lexical units whereas others do not.) It can also explain the word frequency effect. (High-frequency words are more strongly activated by their component letters.) Indeed, Adams (1979) has argued that it can handle all of the important experimental findings in word recognition just as well as the Sophisticated Guessing model can, and she has described at least one situation in which her Criterion Bias model fares better than the alternative (see Adams, 1979, Expt IV). Strings of letters were displayed briefly and followed by a mask. Subjects were required to indicate whether or not the letters spelt an English word. Guessing was discouraged by allowing subjects to say 'I don't know' and by penalizing wrong answers. If the standard word advantage is attributable to the effects of guessing then it should be minimized by discouraging guessing in this way. In fact, on the guessing hypothesis there is reason to assume that there should be a *nonword* advantage in this task because there is a case for assuming that fewer letters need to be identified in order to categorize the string as a nonword. For example, if only two adjacent letters are identified and these violate orthographic rules it follows that the string must be a nonword, whereas all of the letters need to be identified before the subject can be confident that the stimulus is a word. In fact, in contrast with this suggestion, the results showed that words were classified more accurately than nonwords. This suggests that the letters making up words are actually more perceptible than those in nonwords and not merely guessed more accurately. Thus Adams argued that these data are more consistent with the Criterion Bias model which attributes the word advantage to the build-up of reciprocal activation between letter and word units. However, as she stressed, this does not rule out the possibility that word recognition performance is influenced by sophisticated guessing. In fact, in the introduction to her study she argued that 'something like sophisticated guessing must be a normal component of the perception process' (*op. cit.*, p. 140). Thus, the identification of degraded words may be influenced both by criterion biases of the kind discussed above and by sophisticated guessing procedures.

One way in which the processes might be combined is this. The appearance of the word might directly activate a series of letter units, spelling units and word units and these in turn might produce further activation in one another. During this process the criterion value of one or more words might be exceeded in which case the *first* unit could be selected for the purposes of labelling the stimulus. If the reciprocal excitation between the lexical and sublexical units reached some kind of equilibrium without any of the word criteria being reached, then, after a prespecified delay, a sophisticated guessing procedure could be used to make a choice between the most likely alternatives.

3.6 MODELS OF WORD RECOGNITION: UNFAMILIAR OR NOVEL STIMULI

A central assumption of the models considered above is that the reader has access either to the spelling or to the visual description of all potential target words. (If this were not the case the word unit could not be activated directly by the constituent features or letters.) This presupposes that the subject has had a certain amount of prior contact with the word. If the word is only known to the reader in its spoken form (or if its visual description is poorly defined) then it is obviously necessary to use recognition procedures that differ from those described above. Presumably at some point this involves working out the *pronunciation* of the word and using the resulting phonemic description to gain access to the lexicon. If so, we need to ask how the visual representation of the word in Short Term Visual Memory (STVM) can be converted into a usable phonemic description.

There are two main suggestions as to how this might occur. Both presuppose that the first stage of analysis entails identifying the individual letters of the word, but after this different procedures are used to derive the pronunciation of the word. According to one view, words are recoded by consulting a repository of rules for converting individual letters or short strings of letters into appropriate strings of phonemes. (These are the grapheme-to-phoneme corres-pondence (GPC) rules referred to earlier in Section 3.3.3 and discussed in greater detail in Section 8.5.) According to the second suggestion, a new string of letters is pronounced not by referring to general *rules*, but by comparing the current word with words of known pronunciation. Thus, a string of letters like *zite* might be pronounced by comparing it with a word like *kite*. Baron (1977) has referred to these two positions as the *correspondence* strategy and the *analogy* strategy respectively.

The evidence suggests that one of these strategies (the analogy strategy) is definitely used by adults, but it is very difficult to establish empirically whether GPC rules are used as well.

The most convincing support for the use of analogy strategies comes from a series of experiments conducted by Glushko (1979). Subjects were simply required to pronounce words or strings of letters as rapidly as possible. In one of the studies the main contrast of interest was that between the pronunciation time for pseudowords like *heaf* (which resembles words that are pronounced in at least two different ways—the regular way as in *leaf* and irregularly—e.g. *deaf*) and the reading latency for strings like *hean* (for which all of the most similar words are only pronounced in one way—cf. *clean*). If GPC rules had been used to perform the task, the regular correspondence rules would presumably have been applied in both circumstances, in which case there would be no reason to expect any difference in pronunciation time. On the other hand, if subjects had used the analogy strategy their considerations of similar words would have yielded conflicting evidence on pronunciation in the first condition but not in the case where all similar words are pronounced in a single way. Response times would therefore be expected to be longer in the first condition. The results of the experiment showed that letter strings like *heaf* did take longer to pronounce than words like *hean*, and so it seems clear that the subjects were using some kind of analogy strategy.

If people are capable of using this kind of strategy it is almost impossible to tell whether they can make use of GPC rules. As Glushko (1979) has pointed out, the problem is that virtually any pattern of results that might be obtained with GPC rules could equally well occur as a result of using the analogy strategy. As discussed above, letter strings could be pronounced by breaking them down into segments that appear in familiar words, and if this happened exception words (i.e. those yielding conflicting analogy information) would be more difficult to pronounce than regular words. Individual differences between readers might be explained if some people use long strings of letters to look for analogies and others use single letters or pairs of letters.

If it is impossible to make any behavioural distinction between the two strategies it may seem sensible to abandon the notion that GPC rules are used in any way at all and explain all pronunciation in terms of the analogy strategy. However, this framework would differ from that used by the overwhelming majority of investigators to date, and this would cause inconvenience in considering their work. Given that there is no positive evidence *against* the use of GPC rules, the simplest approach to the issue seems to be to assume that *both* strategies may be used in parallel and this is what we shall do in the remaining chapters.

3.7 RECOGNITION OF CLEARLY PRINTED AND FAMILIAR STIMULI

We can now turn to the recognition procedures that are arguably the most important in fluent reading. These are the procedures that people use to identify clearly printed and familiar stimuli. It will be recalled from the earlier discussion in Section 3.3 that with materials of this kind access to the mental lexicon does not appear to be mediated by the use of extraneous sources of information. A suitable model of recognition must, therefore, explain how the lexical entry could be accessed by procedures that rely exclusively on the visual description of the words.

There have been three general types of answer to this question. The first suggestion is that the entry is located by means of a systematic search through the entire lexicon. According to this hypothesis, the graphemic information from the stimulus word is compared with the visual information associated with successive lexical units. The process continues until a satisfactory match is found (cf. Forster and Bednall, 1976; Glanzer and Ehrenreich, 1979). The second proposal is that the lexical entry is activated *directly* (i.e. without any intervening search). This could be achieved if each word in the mental lexicon were represented by an evidence-collecting device of the kind postulated earlier in the discussion of Criterion Bias models (see Section 3.5). Evidence would begin to accumulate in these devices as soon as the stimulus was presented and eventually one of the units would reach its criterion. The word associated with this unit would be selected as the target word. The most influential proponent of this kind of model has been Morton (1969). The third kind of model of word recognition can be viewed as a hybrid of the first two. Essentially it is assumed that the process is carried out in two phases. In the first phase a particular subset of the lexicon is isolated for special consideration. This might occur in the same way as it does in the direct activation models, except that the level of activation in *several* of the units would exceed the criterion and all of these entries would be included in the subset or *shortlist*. In the second phase the items in the shortlist are examined individually in roughly the same way as they are in the search models. As before, the stimulus is considered to have been identified when a satisfactory match is found with one of the items in the shortlist. The main adherents of this kind of model have been Becker (1976) and Forster (1976).

The first of these three models has major shortcomings and has, therefore, been given very little serious attention in the literature. Some of the main difficulties will be outlined in the next few paragraphs and the remainder of the present section will be devoted to a detailed examination of the direct access and shortlist models.

One of the more obvious problems facing the simple search model is that the search and matching processes in such a model would have to be extraordinarily rapid. To get some idea of how rapid these basic steps would have to be it is only necessary to consider the following facts. First, a fluent reader typically requires less than three-quarters of a second to indicate whether a string of letters is a word or a nonword. Secondly, such a reader may be familiar with 20 000 to 100 000 words (Smith, 1971). If we make the plausible assumption that it is necessary to examine *all* of the lexical entries before announcing that a regular nonword is *not* an English word, then it follows that a single comparison cannot take longer than 750/20 000 ms (i.e. less than 0.04 ms). (In fact, it would have to be considerably less than this figure because this rough calculation takes no account of the time occupied by response execution and other non-search processes.)

While these timing considerations certainly make serial search models seem implausible, they are not really decisive because we cannot entirely rule out the possibility that simple, highly-overlearned operations can be completed very rapidly. More concrete evidence against simple search models comes from an experiment conducted by Glanzer and Ehrenreich (1979). In this study subjects were presented with a number of word/nonword lists in which the words either came from a narrow or a wide range of frequencies. In each case the subject was required to indicate whether or not the stimuli were English words. There were several findings that are difficult to account for on a simple serial search model. Perhaps the most clear-cut of these was a demonstration that subjects responded to high-frequency words more rapidly when they appeared in *pure* lists than when they were presented together with words of other frequencies. According to the serial search model, the time taken to locate a word should be determined primarily by the time taken to rule out all of the entries that occur before it in the lexical listing. This in turn should be determined by the position of the target word in the list and the degree of similarity between the stimulus display and each of the lexical entries that occur before this target item. Since neither of these entries should vary for a particular stimulus, it is difficult to see why response time should vary as a function of the stimuli that appear elsewhere in the experimental list. On the basis of these and other data, Glanzer and Ehrenreich ruled out the general search model and went on to purpose a variant of the shortlist model for word recognition.

Another line of evidence against simple search models has been suggested by Coltheart, Davelaar, Jonasson and Besner (1977). Their argument was based on the assumption that the search time for a word reflects the time taken to rule out the lexical entries that are processed before the target word is reached. They reasoned that the search process should be retarded if several of these entries resemble the stimulus display. To test this prediction they compared the lexical decision times for letter strings that are similar to varying numbers of different words in English. (For the purposes of this study a string was considered to be similar to a word if it differed from it in only one letter position, i.e. *task* and *bank* would be treated as being similar to *tank*.) The results for *words* showed that the number of similar words had no effect on performance: the response time was no faster when only one or two words resembled the target word than when there were several such words in the lexicon. On this evidence alone it could be argued that the task was simply insensitive to the differences under examination. However, this argument is difficult to sustain because there *was* an effect when the stimuli were nonwords and this effect is stable enough to have been reported by other investigators (e.g. Stanners, Forbach and Headley, 1971; Stanners and Forbach, 1973). If

58

the effect occurs with nonwords then it is difficult to explain why it does not occur with words. Consequently, Coltheart *et al.* (1977) took their results as evidence against search models in general.

Unfortunately, this conclusion is not as decisive as it seems. One problem is that the search model predicts that the similarity effect should be smaller for words than it is for nonwords,* and so the fact that the paradigm was capable of picking up the nonword effect does not necessarily establish that it was sensitive enough to detect an equivalent word effect. A more important problem is that recent work has shown that the lexical decision time for words *can* be affected by the similarity between the target and other words. In particular, Chambers (1979) has shown that there are delays in processing words that differ from others only in the order of a pair of letters (e.g. *bale, able*—see Section 3.9 for further details). This suggests that Coltheart's earlier failure to find the effect may have been due to the fact that the 'similar' words were not similar enough to cause appreciable delays. These developments weaken this second line of evidence against search models. However, the general doubts about the plausibility of the model remain and, together with the experimental problems raised by Glanzer and Ehrenreich (1979), they seem to constitute sufficient grounds for rejecting the model and so it will not be given any serious consideration in the remainder of the discussion of the word recognition process.

Before attempting to evaluate the direct access and shortlist models it is necessary to describe these models in greater detail. We shall start with the direct access model.

As mentioned above, the most fully worked out version of the model is that put forward by Morton (1969). The central feature of this model is the evidence collector—a device that is selectively tuned to respond to stimuli that resemble the shape of the word it represents. Morton has called this basic unit the *logogen*. The recognition system consists of several thousand logogens—one for each morpheme. Each unit is connected to a device for pronouncing the word (termed an *output logogen*) and it is also linked indirectly with other information about the word (e.g. its semantic specification). When a string of letters is presented, the collection of visual features causes a variety of logogen units to be activated and this process continues until one of them reaches a preset threshold. At this point the logogen 'fires' and the word is considered to have been recognized.

According to the model, recognition time can be influenced in two distinct ways. First, it can be affected by variations in the *rate* at which the level of activation of a given logogen increases. This will depend primarily on the degree to which the logogen is tuned to the stimulus under analysis and more generally it can be regarded as a measure of the *sensitivity* of the evidence-collecting device. The second way in which recognition time can be influenced is by

---

*This follows because a nonword would have to be checked against the entire list of lexical entries including the complete set of similar words. A word, on the other hand, would only have to be compared with the 'shape mates' that precede the target word in the search list.

shifting the criterion for triggering the logogen. This could be achieved either by changing the threshold value or by altering the resting level of activation (i.e. the degree of activation which is present before the stimulus is displayed).

In the simplest version of the model both parameters are fixed in advance. The target logogen count simply increases at a stinulus-determined rate until the criterion is reached and the word is recognized. In some of the more complex versions the 'criterion' is assumed to change after the stimulus has been presented. For example, in a version of the model used for developing a mathematical treatment of word recognition, Morton (1969, 1970) assumed that the probability of choosing a logogen is determined not only by the level of activation (or 'response strength') of that particular logogen but also by the response strength of all the other logogens in the system. More specifically, he assumed that the probability is given by the ratio of the response strength of the logogen under consideration to the total response strength of the units elsewhere in the system. These refinements were introduced to account for data obtained in experiments employing impoverished stimuli but, as Schuberth and Eimas (1977) have pointed out, the treatment can easily be extended to handle intact stimuli by assuming that response time is inversely related to the probability of selecting a particular logogen (see Assumption 2, p. 34). In practice this could be achieved in several ways, but perhaps the simplest way of incorporating the refinement is to assume that thresholds are variable and that the thresholds for all logogens are raised in line with the general activity in the system (see Coltheart, Davelaar, Jonasson and Besner, 1977, for a closely related proposal).

We can now turn to the 'shortlist' or 'verification' models of Forster (1976) and Becker (1976; Schvaneveldt, Meyer and Becker, 1976; Becker and Killion, 1977). Although there are several differences in the details the broad features of the two models are similar. In both cases it is assumed that certain physical characteristics of the stimulus are used to isolate a set of entries that resemble the stimulus word. As Becker has pointed out, this could be achieved by a mechanism similar to that proposed by Morton: the subset could consist of the entries for all of the logogens that exceed some (relatively lenient) criterion. As soon as the shortlist has been assembled (or located) it is assumed that the individual entries are subjected to a more detailed examination. The stimulus trace is compared in turn with the stored physical description of each shortlisted candidate. On Becker's model the word is considered to be recognized as soon as a satisfactory match has been found. On Forster's model, however, this decision is postponed briefly until one further comparison, the *post-access check*, has been completed. In either case, the final selection is based on a matching or verification process that is more detailed than the procedure that generates the initial shortlist. According to the shortlist models, recognition time can be influenced by various factors including the time taken to prepare the shortlist, the size and structure of the list, and the time taken to carry out individual comparisons in the verification process.

How do these two classes of model compare in accounting for word recognition data? To prepare the ground for this discussion it may be useful to summarize some of the main findings that have to be accounted for. The most important of these findings is almost certainly the *word frequency effect*—the tendency for frequent words to be identified more rapidly than those that are only used rarely in written English. This effect has been demonstrated repeatedly in studies using the lexical decision task (e.g. Rubenstein, Garfield and Millikan, 1970; Frederiksen and Kroll, 1976, Expt II; Schuberth and Eimas, 1977). It has also been shown in naming studies (e.g. Forster, 1976; Frederiksen and Kroll, 1976, Expt I; Perfetti, Goldman and Hogaboam, 1979) and in studies that record the reading times (Mitchell and Green, 1978) or fixation times (Just and Carpenter, 1980) that occur when subjects are reading long passages of prose.

Another highly stable finding is the *degradation effect*. This is simply the finding that a word takes longer to identify if the quality of the stimulus is reduced.* This effect has been demonstrated using a variety of forms of degradation including the reduction of stimulus intensity (Becker and Killion, 1977), the removal of a random collection of dots from the stimulus form (Perfetti and Roth, 1981), the superimposition of a dot pattern on the display of a word (Meyer, Schvaneveldt and Ruddy, 1975) and the presentation of slightly misleading previews of the word in parafoveal vision (McClelland and O'Regan, 1981).

A third finding that has to be accounted for by models of word recognition is the *word similarity effect* mentioned earlier in the present section. This is Chambers's (1979) finding that in suitable circumstances it takes a shorter time to recognize words with distinctive shapes than to identify words that are similar to other English words. It is also necessary to provide an explanation for the Coltheart *et al.* (1977) demonstration that it takes longer to *rule out* a nonsense word that is similar to several genuine English words.

The fourth result that has to be explained is one that might be termed the *case alternation effect*. This is simply that it takes longer to respond to words printed in alternating cases (e.g. *wOrD*) than to words presented in a more conventional lower-case form. This has been shown using both the lexical decision task (Pickering, 1975) and a word-naming task (Besner, 1980).

The final result to be considered here is the *stimulus ensemble effect* reported by Glanzer and Ehrenreich (1979)—the demonstration that the time taken to identify a word is influenced by factors such as the range of words that might have been presented in a given session.

In addition to these five basic findings, word recognition is affected in a variety of ways by context. However, these effects will not be considered immediately since they depend on a more extensive analysis of the ways in which context operates. These issues will be taken up in Chapter 5 (see Section 5.6.2).

We are now in a position to start evaluating the viability of the two models.

---

*It should be noted that with minor stimulus degradation it is possible to increase response latency without significantly changing the error rate. It therefore seems appropriate to consider this kind of degradation effect separately from the effect discussed in Section 3.5.

First, we consider how the data are handled by the logogen model (and a few of its variants) and then we proceed to assess the case for the verification model.

3.7.1 The logogen model

In most versions of the logogen model, word frequency is assumed to have an effect on the *criterion* for detecting a word rather than on the sensitivity of the detector. Thus, Morton (1969, 1970) assumed that the logogen units for high-frequency words have a lower threshold than those for low-frequency words.* The implication of this is that the logogen counts for high-frequency words will only have to be increased by a small amount before the threshold is reached (i.e. a small amount of sensory evidence will be sufficient for the word to be identified). With low-frequency words, on the other hand, the amount of visual information required will be greater and the response time will be longer. While this account of word frequency has been adopted by most subsequent workers (e.g. Schuberth and Eimas, 1977; Becker and Killion, 1977), Morton himself has recently changed his mind about the explanation of the effect. He now believes that word frequency effects are introduced *after* the logogens have fired and that they have little or no effect on logogen activation itself (Morton, 1980). More specifically, he has suggested that the word frequency effect is attributable to variations in the time taken to check the meaning(s) of a word after it has been identified.

Turning to the degradation effect, the fact that degraded words take longer to identify than others can be explained in two different ways. The first possibility is that the sensitivity of the logogen falls in line with any reduction in stimulus quality. This would mean that the logogen count is increased at a slower rate with degraded stimuli than it is with intact stimuli. For any given threshold value the end result would be that recognition time should increase with the degree of impoverishment of the stimulus. The second possibility is that degraded stimuli are subjected to preprocessing before they are brought into contact with the logogen system. For example, the stimulus may be 'cleaned up' (Sternberg, 1967) before it starts to activate the logogen. On this account the recognition time for degraded stimuli would be increased not because the logogen activation rate is changed but because there is a delay before the activation process can be initiated.

On the first explanation the effect of stimulus degradation should interact with any variable that produces a criterion shift within the target logogen. In particular, if the threshold is reduced the advantage of the fast over the slow activation rate (i.e. the advantage of intact over degraded stimuli) should be less than it is when the threshold is set much higher. It follows that any model that combines this explanation of degradation with a criterion-shifting account of the word frequency effect must predict that there should be an interaction between these variables. In fact, experimental studies have consistently failed to find any

---

* Alternatively, they might have a higher initial resting count, but the distinction is not very important because both kinds of adjustment produce equivalent effects.

evidence of such an interaction (Stanners, Jastrzembski and Westbrook, 1975; Becker and Killion, 1977; Schuberth, Spoehr and Lane, 1981), and so this particular combination of explanations must be ruled out. However, the present account of the degradation effect is quite compatible with Morton's more recent interpretation of the word frequency effect, since there is no reason why a variable causing a change in sensitivity should interact with one that has its effect *after* the logogen has fired (cf. Sternberg, 1969).

The second explanation of the degradation effect appears to have no difficulty in accounting for the data. The absence of any interaction between degradation and word frequency can be accounted for if we assume that the stimulus representation is completely 'cleaned up' before the logogen is activated. On this assumption the time required to increment the logogen count from its resting level to the threshold should be completely independent of the initial quality of the stimulus and so the effects of context on degradation should be additive.

As with the previous effect, the logogen model could account for the word similarity effect in two different ways. The first possibility is that the logogen threshold is raised when the word it represents is difficult to distinguish from other words. It is easy to imagine a machanism which raises the thresholds of words like *silt* and *clam* whenever the reader misidentifies them as *slit* or *calm*. If this occurred over a few years of the reader's experience the thresholds of such words would settle down to a value that is higher than that for other words of the same frequency. The end result would be that the words would take longer to identify than other comparable words (i.e. there would be a word similarity effect). The second proposal is based on the 'variable criterion' version of the logogen model (see p. 59). It will be recalled that this variant of the model assumes in effect that all logogen thresholds are raised in line with the general activity in the system. The word similarity effect could then be explained by assuming that there is increased activity in the system when the physical stimulus resembles more than one word.

The first suggestion can easily account for the similarity effect in words. However, as has been mentioned above, there is also a similarity effect for *nonsense words*. Using a lexical decision task, Chambers (1979) found that it takes longer than average to rule out a string that closely resembles an English word (e.g. *gadren*). Similarly Coltheart et al. (1977) demonstrated that lexical decision time is greater for strings that are similar to several English words than for strings that only resemble one or two words. While it is plausible to suppose that the logogen thresholds for certain classes of words are permanently raised, it is very difficult to maintain that this kind of mechanism is responsible for the effect in nonwords. In fact, as Coltheart et al. (1977) have pointed out, there is no obvious way in which Morton's original version of the model could have handled nonword decisions. With a nonsense stimulus the logogen system should either carry on collecting evidence until one of the units eventually reaches its threshold (in which case the subject would mistakenly declare that the stimulus was a word) or else the process should carry on indefinitely without anything happening at all. In order to overcome this problem Coltheart and his colleagues proposed that in certain circumstances the process of collecting evidence is terminated after the passage of a certain amount of time and that a 'no' response is initiated when this 'deadline' is reached. To account for the similarity effect they assumed that the deadline is not fixed in advance but varies according to the amount of activity within the logogen system as a whole. As in the 'variable criterion' version of the logogen model, it is assumed that the deadline is set at a relatively short interval is the display only stimulates a small amount of activity in the system (i.e. if the string is not similar to many English words) and at a longer interval when the general activity in the system is higher. Given these refinements the variable deadline/variable criterion version of the logogen model is capable of accounting for all of the data on similarity effects.

The next finding to be considered is the case alternation effect. This can be accounted for on the logogen model if it is assumed that a proportion of the visual features that contribute to logogen activation are features that extend over more than one letter (sometimes called 'transgraphemic' features, but more generally features that characterize the word-*shape*). If these features are distorted or changed by presenting the word in an unconventional format, then the result should be that the sensitivity of the detector unit is reduced and the response latency is increased.

Like other variables that are assumed to affect sensitivity, the case alternation effect should interact with any manipulation that causes a shift in the logogen criterion. More specifically the effect should be reduced when the threshold is lowered. Considering the criterion-shifting account of the word frequency effect, then, the prediction should be that the effect of alternation is greater for low- than for high-frequency words. Unfortunately, Pickering (1975) has found that there is a significant interaction in the *opposite* direction, while Besner (1980) has reported two experiments in which the two manipulations had additive effects. It is not clear which of these findings is closer to the truth, but it is obvious that neither of them provides any support for the explanation of case alternation just offered. There are two possible ways out of this dilemma. The first is to abandon the criterion-shifting account of the word frequency effect and turn to Morton's more recent explanation in terms of post-access effects. This would predict that the effects of word frequency and case alternation should be additive and it is therefore only tenable if Pickering's results are in some way artefactual. The second solution to the problem would be to assume that the detector units for high-frequency words give greater weight to trans-graphemic (or word-shape) features than those for low-frequency words do. If this were the case, distorting or removing these features would reduce the sensitivity of high-frequency logogens more than those for rarer words. In suitable circumstances this could produce either the additive effect shown by Besner or the interactive effects shown by Pickering. This modification is rather *ad hoc*, but it is not entirely implausible, since it would seem reasonable for readers to familiarize themselves with the overall shapes of the more common words in the language.

The last finding to be considered in the present evaluation of the logogen model is the stimulus ensemble effect reported by Glanzer and Ehrenreich (1979). It will be recalled that one instance of the effect is the finding that high-frequency words are responded to more slowly when they appear in mixed lists than when they appear in lists consisting entirely of high-frequency words. This result can be explained on the logogen model if it is assumed that the thresholds for all high-frequency words are lowered when the subject is confident that all of the words will come from this class. Similar changes would explain comparable effects obtained with pure and mixed lists of low- and medium-frequency words. If this explanation is correct, the change should interact with any variable that influences logogen sensitivity. This prediction could easily be tested, but no one seems to have done this at the time of writing.

The evaluation of the logogen model will be resumed when further evidence (on contextual effects) has been described in Chapter 5. Summarizing the position so far, it seems that the logogen model can account for most of the relevant data in one way or another. However, in order to retain the model it has been necessary to make a number of additional local assumptions (e.g. preprocessing of degraded stimuli; variations in the salience of transgraphemic features; variable deadlines for nonwords, etc.). These changes are undesirable in that they detract from one of the major strengths of the logogen model—its simplicity. However, as we shall see, the shortlist model fares little better in this respect.

3.7.2 Shortlist models of word recognition

According to the shortlist or verification model, the word frequency effect is handled in a fairly straightforward manner. Both Forster and Becker simply assume that the items in the shortlist are ordered according to word frequency and that the verification process works through the candidates one by one. Given these assumptions, a high-frequency word at the 'top' of the list will be processed sooner than a word near the 'bottom' of the list and the result would be that the overall response latency would show a word frequency effect.

The degradation effect presents a few more problems since there are at least three potential explanations of the phenomenon. The first is that a word that is degraded and has stimulus features missing may be compatible with more candidates than it would have been if the stimulus had been intact. In this case the shortlists for degraded stimuli would tend to be longer than those for intact words and the result of this would be that more candidates would have to be checked in the former condition and so the average response latency would be greater in this condition. The second possibility is that comparison or verification time (or post-access checking in Forster's version of the model) is greater when the stimulus is degraded. This would increase the time required to rule out each of the candidates preceding the target word and the overall result would be that response times would be greater than those associated with undegraded words. The third possibility is that the process of preparing the shortlist is postponed until after the stimulus has been 'cleaned up' by preprocessing operations. On this account, first put forward by Schuberth, Spoehr and Lane (1981), the degradation effect would simply be attributed to the fact that processing would be held up longer by the process of preparing the more impoverished stimuli for subsequent analysis.

While all three suggestions can account for the degradation effect itself, the first two are unable to account for the evidence that the effects of word frequency and degradation do not interact (see p. 62). If more candidates are included in the shortlist as in the first suggestion, then the difference in the time required to process those near the top (i.e. the high-frequency words) and those near the bottom (low-frequency words) should be greater than it is with undegraded stimuli. Similarly, if it takes longer to process each candidate, then the low-frequency words at the end of the list should be more affected than the words at the beginning. In contrast, the preprocessing account has no difficulty in explaining the additive relationship between word frequency and degradation. According to this explanation the processing required to deal with stimulus degradation should have no detrimental effect on the subsequent search processes and so there should be no interaction between the two.

The first two explanations considered above could both provide plausible accounts of the word similarity effect. Words (or nonwords) that are similar to several other English words could produce relatively long candidate lists and these would take longer to search than the shorter lists produced by more distinctive words. Also, it may take longer for the verification process to reject candidates that are very similar (but not identical) to the target word. The first account would be more appropriate for explaining the Coltheart et al. (1979) finding that lexical decision time is affected by the *number* of similar words, while the second hypothesis would provide a more suitable explanation of why the response is delayed when there is a single highly similar alternative (as in Chambers's, 1979, experiment). It is worth noting that on the second account the similarity effect should only occur when the alternative is a word that has a higher frequency than the target word (as it was in Chambers's study).* If the frequency of the other word were *lower* it would appear somewhere *below* the target word in the shortlist and should therefore never be reached in the search process.

Turning to the case alternation effect, this could potentially be explained by assuming again that unconventionally printed words generate larger shortlists or that they slow down the verification process. Neither of these explanations is particularly satisfactory, however, since both predict that the

---

* Since this was written Fox (1981) has checked this prediction. The results showed that there was a similarity effect when the target word was the shape-mate with the *higher* frequency as well as when it was the one with the *lower* frequency. This result is not easily explained on the shortlist model.

case alternation effect should decrease with increasing word frequency and, as has already been mentioned, this is not what happens (see p. 63). One possible explanation of the effect is that with alternations the target word fails to make the shortlist on some proportion of the trials. On these trials, we can assume that the shortlist is searched exhaustively, and that a new shortlist is prepared as soon as the subject discovers that the target word is missing. The overall effect of this additional processing would be to increase the mean response latencies by some quantity that is not dependent on word frequency.

Finally, the stimulus ensemble effect can be explained if it is assumed that the shortlists are selected not from the whole lexicon but from a shorter list of (say) high-frequency words (Glanzer and Ehrenreich, 1979). This would reduce the number of candidates in the shortlist and should therefore reduce the time taken to locate all targets except those that are very near to the 'top' of the list.

To recapitulate, the shortlist model seems to be capable of accounting for most of the data on word recognition, but it requires just as many modifications as the logogen model did. On the evidence considered so far there is no reason to favour one model over the other. A final decision about the models will be postponed until after contextual effects have been considered in Section 5.6.2.

3.8 HOW ARE LOGOGENS ACTIVATED (OR HOW ARE CANDIDATES SHORTLISTED)?

In both the shortlist model and the logogen model it is assumed that there is some procedure for selecting candidates for special attention. In the logogen model there is only a single candidate—the target word—and the word is considered to have been recognized when the logogen fires. In the shortlist model several candidates reach some kind of threshold and these are then used to compile a shortlist that is subsequently searched in an attempt to locate the target word itself. In both cases it is assumed that the selection is based on the activity of some kind of word detector unit. However, until now we have had relatively little to say about the nature of this activation process. Morton (1969, 1970) suggested that the logogen count for a particular lexical entry is increased whenever the sensory mechanism detects an 'attribute' which is a member of one of the logogen's defining sets. Most subsequent versions of the word detector model have incorporated this suggestion, but there is some disagreement about what kinds of 'attribute' are used in word recognition. Morton himself proposed that visual, acoustic and semantic properties of words all play some part in activating logogens. However, the logogen model was designed to explain aspects of behaviour other than visual word recognition, and so it does not necessarily follow that all of these properties play a role in fluent reading. It is obvious that the recognition of printed materials must make use of visual attributes. Also Morton assigned an important role to semantic properties.* However, in view of the evidence summarized in Section 3.3.3, it does not seem likely that acoustic attributes are used to activate logogens in fluent reading.

---

*This concerns contextual effects and is dealt with in some detail in Chapter 5.

Morton (1970) suggested that the 'visual' attributes for a word like *cat* might include properties such as three letters, initial *c*, final *t* and so on. However, the suggestion that visual attributes are based in part on letter categories seems to be questionable given the evidence that information derived from identifying individual letters is not used in fluent word recognition (see Section 3.3.1). An alternative possibility is that the visual attributes used in word recognition are 'distinctive features' such as the presence of vertical or horizontal lines, curves, ascenders and descenders, closed and open shapes and so on (Smith, 1971).* Thus the presence of a curved line at some point within the stimulus shape might be treated as a unit of evidence in favour of identifying the display as the word *cat*.

It seems likely that a model in which logogens are activated by visual features could provide a reasonable account of fluent word recognition. Of course, there would have to be a great deal of flexibility concerning the specific features which a logogen could accept as evidence. If this were not the case it would be impossible to recognize words in different type-faces, in different cases or in alternating cases. At the same time, there must obviously be a limit to the range of features that are capable of exciting each logogen. Otherwise there would be no way of excluding items from the search list in the shortlist model and there would be no way of distinguishing between pairs of words that are physically similar on the logogen model. Some idea of the specificity of tuning can be gained by considering the data reported by Chambers (1979). As we have already mentioned, she used an interference paradigm in a lexical decision task to investigate the kind of stimulus information that is used to access the lexical entry. Subjects were presented with words or nonsense words that either differed from another word in one letter position (e.g. *lotor* from *motor* or *collar* from *dollar*) or in the reversal of the order of two adjacent letters (e.g. *gadren* from *garden* and *bale* from *able*). Previous work (e.g. by Taft and Forster, 1976) had shown that it takes longer for subjects to say that a nonsense string is *not* an English word when it is very similar to such a word than when it bears little resemblance to any word in the English language. Similarly, it takes longer to respond positively to a real word when it is very similar to other words. Chambers (1979) interpreted these interference effects as evidence that inappropriate lexical entries were activated during the course of the lexical decision process. Given this assumption, the paradigm can be used to determine the kinds of departure from the 'ideal' string that can still lead to activation.

The results of the experiments showed that there was no interference effect when the test string differed by one letter from an English word (i.e. strings like *lotor* and *moton* did not seem to activate the lexical entry for *motor*). However, as indicated above, there *was* an interference effect when pairs of letters were interchanged (e.g. subjects took longer to classify words like *bale* than control words like *buff*). Chambers (1979) interpreted these results as

---

*In fact, Smith (1971, p. 120) argues that we do not yet know enough about the visual system to specify the features that might be used in word recognition and so he deliberately avoids trying to do so.

evidence that *all* of the letters in a word have to be present before the lexical entry is activated, but that it is not essential for all of the adjacent letters to be presented in the correct order.

These results certainly tell us something about the kinds of information that detector units will accept as evidence. However, the conclusion that activation depends on the presence of *all* the letters of a word does not seem to be completely justified by the failure to find interference effects when a single letter of a word is changed. It could be that the modified stimulus is capable of activating the related word to some extent, but that this excitation is not sufficient to hold up the decision about the current stimulus. In fact, the evidence reported by Coltheart *et al.* (1977) suggests that a single letter change is *not* sufficient to prevent all activation of the lexical unit. They found that subjects take longer to reject nonsense words that differ by a single letter from several different words than they take to rule out strings that resemble no more than one or two words. This shows that a stimulus must have at least *some* effect on words that differ from it in only one letter position.

A detailed account of the visual activation of logogens would have to deal with a number of other points which have not been considered fully up to now. For example, it would be useful to know whether the presence of some features can increase the logogen count more than that for other less critical features. Can the logogen count be *decreased* when inappropriate features are encountered in some part of the word? Are there separate tallies for upper- and lower-case words and for words printed in different type-faces, or is there a single count that is incremented by any feature that is compatible with any conceivable form in which the word might be printed?

At the moment is only possible to suggest an answer to the first of these questions. It seems to be necessary to assume that different weights are attached to different kinds of feature and to features appearing in different positions in the word. The reason for this is that there is convincing evidence that the beginnings and ends of words play a more important role in word recognition than the letters (or features) in the middle (Bruner and O'Dowd, 1958; Forster and Gartlan, 1975, cited in Forster, 1976). This phenomenon can only be accounted for easily if it is assumed that the features positioned at the beginnings and ends of words increase the count of the relevant logogens more than features appearing elsewhere.

As a general way of handling these phenomena it could be assumed that word detectors are activated following reference to a stored set of 'rules for visual access' for each word. These rules, or *productions* (Newell and Simon, 1972; Newell, 1973), might take the form: if feature f_i appears in character position n then increment the logogen count for word w_j by k_j units.* Under a system of this kind the salience of end letters could be handled in a simple way

---

* There would have to be supplementary rules to handle Chambers's evidence that the position of the letter does not have to be exactly correct for the logogen to be activated. These additional rules may take the form: if f_i appears in positions $n-1$ or $n+1$ increment the count by m_j units (where $m_j \leq k_j$).

by assuming that the value of k_j is high for all features that occur in the outer letters of the word and lower (or possibly even zero) for the internal letters.

A general scheme of this kind would be capable of handling most of the data obtained in word recognition studies and it is therefore a useful working hypothesis about the way in which logogens operate. However, there is one line of work in the field that is difficult to reconcile with the proposal that logogens are only activated directly by visual features. This is work which suggests that compound words (i.e. those with a suffix or prefix or those made up of simpler words like *handstand*) are recognized by first analysing the words into their components and then using these derived components (rather than the visual features themselves) to finalize the process of specifying the word. Indirect recognition of this kind would go against the spirit of the model outlined above. However, it may not be necessary to abandon our working hypothesis because, as we shall see in the next section, there is no conclusive evidence that word analysis or *morphological decomposition* of this kind plays any significant role in word recognition.

3.9 MORPHOLOGICAL DECOMPOSITION

The main proponents of morphological decomposition in recent years have been Taft and Forster (1975, 1976). These authors have argued that compound words like *unlucky* are analysed into simpler components before they are accessed. (In this particular example 'morphological' analysis would yield components corresponding to the base word (*luck*), the adjectival suffix (*-y*) and the negative prefix (*un-*).) According to this hypothesis, word recognition consists of two distinct phases. In the first phase the word is broken down into its morphological units and in the second phase the base word is looked up in the internal lexicon. The advantage of such a system is that it reduces the number of lexical entries that have to be maintained in storage. However, there are some drawbacks as well, one of which is the fact that relatively complex processing has to be carried out before the lexical entry can be accessed.

Taft and Forster (1975) presented two different kinds of indirect evidence for the decomposition hypothesis. In both cases this evidence centred on the status of base words. It was argued that if lexical access were based on morphological analysis in the manner outlined above, then all of the base words that the reader might encounter would have to be represented in the lexicon. This would apply even to bases that are not themselves English words (e.g. *juvenate* from the word *rejuvenate*). Given these assumptions Taft and Forster predicted that subjects would have some difficulty in deciding whether or not letter strings like *junenate* were English words. With materials like this the lexical entry for the base word would presumably be activated by the stimulus producing a tendency for the subject to decide that it *is* an English word. Other information would indicate that the base alone is not a legitimate word, and the resulting conflict would presumably increase the decision latency for materials of this kind. Taft and Forster conducted an experiment in which the decision times for strings like *juvenate* were compared with those for nonwords that are not bases (e.g. *pertoire* from *repertoire*). The results confirmed the prediction that the response latencies to stems would be longer. However, this is not convincing support for the decomposition hypothesis since the data can be explained reasonably well without assuming that the base words are represented in the lexicon. For example, it may take longer to say 'no' to stem words because they are physically similar to more real words than other letter strings are. (This suggestion follows the 'variable deadline' explanation of similarity effects given in Section 3.7.1.) Manelis and Tharp (1977) have shown that the base words used by Taft and Forster (1975) occur more often in English words than the corresponding non-base controls do, and this obviously lends plausibility to an interpretation of the data based on similarity effects.

The second line of evidence in favour of the decomposition hypothesis was the finding that words which are stems of common English words, as well as being words in their own right (e.g. *vent*), take longer to classify than other words of approximately the same frequency (Taft and Forster, 1975). Unless the authors unwittingly allowed differences other than base word status to creep into the two classes of material, this result strongly suggests that stems as well as words are represented in the lexicon. However, it should be pointed out that even if such entries do exist this does not necessarily imply that readers make any use of them in the fluent identification of compound words. Thus this particular line of evidence does not provide any direct support for the decomposition hypothesis.

A more direct test of the hypothesis has been reported by Manelis and Tharp (1977). In this study the lexical decision times for pairs of affixed and non-affixed words (e.g. *faster* and *sister* respectively) were compared and the results showed no significant difference. This result argues against the suggestion that morphological decomposition occurs prior to lexical access since any morphological analysis of the words would presumably have produced a lexical entry in one case and a meaningless letter string in the other. The additional processing that would obviously be required in the second case would presumably have produced longer response latencies in this condition.

The Manelis and Tharp investigation was restricted to words with suffixes and so it could still be argued that morphological decomposition occurs when the stimulus word has a prefix. However, there does not seem to by any evidence for this either. Clayton (1980) carried out the test with prefixed words and, as in the earlier study, there was no difference between the lexical decision times for affixed and control words.

In a follow-up to their earlier article, Taft and Forster (1976) presented evidence for another kind of decomposition—the decomposition of words with two or more underlying morphemes (e.g. *football*). They argued that words of this type are analysed into their constituents and accessed on the basis of the one that appears first. Much of the empirical support for this proposal has been based on the latency data for various nonword decisions. In one experiment it was found that subjects took longer to classify nonwords when the first constituent was a word (e.g. *footmilge*) than when it was a nonword (e.g.

mowdflisk). However, the presence of a word in the second position (e.g. *trowbreak*) apparently had no effect on performance. The authors interpreted these (and other) nonword results as evidence that subjects recognize polymorphic words by attempting to access the first constituent and using the outcome of this operation to access the complete word. However, like the nonword effects in the earlier study, it seems likely that the data could be explained equally well in terms of differences in the degree of similarity between the test string and the entries in the lexicon (i.e. in terms of a variable deadline model—see Section 3.7.1). Of course, it is necessary to assume that test strings with English words at the beginning activate more logogens than those with words at the end. However, this does not seem implausible: it would occur if more weight were given to the visual features at the left of the stimulus array than those in other positions.

A final experiment reported by Taft and Forster (1976) was based on words rather than nonwords and is therefore not open to alternative explanations of the kind outlined above. The lexical decision time for polymorphic words with common words as first constituent (e.g. *headstand*) was compared with that for frequency-matched words with a rare first constituent (e.g. *loincloth*). The results were consistent with the view that the words were accessed via the first constituent; the decision latencies were shorter when the first constituent was a high-frequency word. However, the materials employed in this experiment may have encouraged subjects to use an unusual strategy. Almost all of the letter strings employed in the experiment consisted of two words run together and, while it may be appropriate to access the word via the first constituent in these circumstances, it certainly does not follow that people use the same technique to identify polymorphic words in more conventional reading tasks.

To recapitulate, the present evidence suggests that base words may be represented in the internal lexicon and that, in some circumstances, letter strings may be decomposed into their constituents prior to lexical access. However, the data available at the time of writing do not indicate that we need to revise our earlier conclusion that in fluent reading the logogens are activated directly by visual features without any intermediate processing.

3.10 SUMMARY OF CHAPTER 3

Most of the work on word recognition has centred on two main issues: (1) What sources of information are called upon in the process of accessing the lexical entry? (2) How are these sources of information actually used to locate the internal representation of the word?

The answers to both of these questions depend on the form in which the stimulus word is presented and particularly on the degree to which it is impoverished. They also depend on whether the reader is familiar with the word in its typed or printed form. For these reasons the processes used for recognizing degraded words, (visually) unfamiliar words and normal familiar words were considered separately in the body of the chapter.

For degraded stimuli there was reasonably clear evidence that information about word-shapes (or the shapes of parts of words) may be used in the process of accessing the internal representation of the word. There was also reason to believe that readers might make use of spelling patterns and pronunciation rules, but here the evidence was relatively indirect since it was based on demonstrations that these sources of information can be used in *letter recognition* rather than in *word identification* tasks. Evidence on the potential contribution of other units was not available.

In the case of unfamiliar words it is almost certain that subjects use a pronunciation strategy to convert the stimulus into a phonemic form so that it can be recognized in terms of its sound. However, opinion is divided as to whether this is achieved by using words that resemble the target word as analogies or by referring to abstract pronunciation rules (e.g. GPC rules). The later suggestion was adopted for the sake of convenience.

Finally, the evidence concerning the sources of information used in the recognition of stimuli that are both undegraded and familiar suggests that neither letter units nor orthographic rules nor pronunciation rules play an important part in the process. The only information that seems to be important in normal reading conditions is the visual description of the word (but see Chapter 5 for a minor qualification of this statement).

Turning to the question of *how* a word is identified, the major debate in the literature on impoverished stimuli has been between the supporters of Criterion Bias and of Sophisticated Guessing models of word recognition. At the time of writing a reasonable conclusion seems to be that *both* kinds of process may play a role in word recognition. The initial stages of processing might operate in the manner specified by the Criterion Bias models (i.e. with evidence-collecting devices (logogens) being activated directly by the stimulus information). If the level of activation reaches a prespecified threshold determined by the subject's expectations, word frequency, etc., then the word will be identified according to these principles. However, if the quality of the stimulus is poor and the critical value is not reached, than a Sophisticated Guessing procedure might be used to reach a decision. For example, subjects may make a weighted choice between the items that are compatible with the stimulus information as in Rumelhart and Siple's version of the model.

In the case of *clearly printed* words the major discussion has been between proponents of direct access models (i.e. logogen or Criterion Bias models) and the supporters of a particular class of search models referred to as shortlist or verification models. In the first kind of model it is assumed that words are identified by a process in which all word units are activated simultaneously until the point at which one of them reaches its threshold and is thereby identified. In the second kind of model it is assumed that the visual description of the word is first used to select a small set of candidates for detailed consideration. Detailed records of the normal visual descriptions of these words are then compared one by one with the stimulus trace until a satisfactory match is found and the word is identified. In order to account for the data in both cases it is necessary to make a number of additional, situation-specific assumptions and there is little reason to favour one model rather than the other. However, this issue is taken up again in Chapter 5 and at that point there is some evidence on contextual effects which seems to tilt the balance in favour of the logogen model.

Irrespective of the precise mechanisms by which words are identified, it is clear that one of the outcomes of the process is that additional stored information about the identified words can now be recovered from the reader's internal lexicon. This information may include the meaning (or alternative meanings) of the word, its correct pronunciation, its grammatical class and so on. Such information provides the raw material for the comprehension processes that derive the overall meaning of the text. These processes are considered in the next chapter.

CHAPTER 4

Comprehension of sentences and texts

In the previous chapter we considered the processes by which the visual input is used to locate the appropriate entry in the internal lexicon. We shall assume that with little extra processing it is possible to recover information from memory about the syntactic category of the word and about its meaning—or meanings, if there is more than one*. The next phase of the reading process is to combine the meanings of the successive words to produce the meaning of the sentence and eventually the text as a whole. It will be assumed that this is carried out by a set of procedures which draw upon raw material in the form of semantic and syntactic descriptions of the individual words and use this information to produce an end-product corresponding to the meaning of the text.

In order to appreciate what is entailed in this process it is essential to be aware of the kinds of information that are typically extracted from a passage of prose. Some of these types of information can be illustrated by considering the following pair of sentences:

The popular young teacher was given a pet by a couple of her children. They decided to take the turtle back to the shop when they found that she liked soup.

Although this 'passage' is quite short it succeeds in conveying a great deal of information. For example, we know (from the first sentence) that an action took place at some time in the past, and that this action involved transferring an object from one group of people to another person. We also have some idea of the obligations incurred in this transaction and other circumstances surrounding it. We are told the occupation of the recipient (*teacher*) and the identity of the object (*pet*). We are also given some information about the other people: they are *her children*. The word *her* used in this phrase refers to the teacher and so we can deduce that she is a woman. We also know that the attributes *popular* and *young* apply to her.

From the second sentence we learn that two or more people (*They*) decided to do something after another event occurred. The people referred to by the

---

* However, something extra may be required before the reader is able to *name* the word. Marcel (in press) has demonstrated that there are circumstances in which a person can show that he knows the *meaning* of a briefly presented word without being able to say exactly *which* word it is. This could be handled on the logogen model by assuming that each logogen has two threshold values: one for making the meaning of the word available, and a second, higher threshold for making the word available as a response (Marcel and Patterson, 1978). However, we shall not concern ourselves any further with this issue here, since it is unlikely that post-access pronunciation of words plays an important part in silent fluent reading, which is our major current concern.

word *they* are the same as the *children* mentioned in the first sentence. Skipping a few words we come to the word *turtle* which presumably must refer to the same creature as the word *pet* did previously. The *shop* (four words later) has not been mentioned before, but we can easily work out that it is likely to be the place where they bought the turtle (or did they just find it there, or even steal it?). The word *she* very probably refers to the teacher, but it could refer to the turtle (at a pinch). The sentence suggests that the decision to take the pet back was a consequence of the discovery that *she liked soup*. One way of making sense of this is to assume that it was *turtle* soup that the teacher was partial to and that the children took the pet back because they feared for its life.

As this example shows, a reader has to make a number of different kinds of decisions about a text before he can understand it. At least five broad types of decision can be distinguished. First, the reader has to identify the basic 'units of meaning' in each sentence. The meaning of this phrase will be considered in more detail later, but the idea can be illustrated by considering the first sentence in the example. Here the central idea can be expressed as follows: Group (X) gave Object (Y) to Person (Z). It is doubtful whether a person could understand the sentence without identifying a 'unit of meaning' which corresponds in some way to this abstract statement. Similarly, the sentence conveys a number of subsidiary 'units of meaning' (e.g. Z is popular, Z is young, X belong in some sense to Z, etc.). All of these elementary units have to be isolated before the sentence can be completely understood.

The second kind of decision which a reader has to make concerns the relationship between the people, objects, places and properties that play a role in each 'unit of meaning'. For example, in the first sentence it is essential to determine that it is the *children* who are the subject and the *teacher* who is the recipient of the action of giving and there are similar, though more complicated, relationships in the second sentence.

The third kind of decision concerns the selection of the appropriate sense of words that are potentially ambiguous. Thus, in the example it is necessary to deduce that *pet*, *couple* and *shop* are nouns not verbs, that *back* is *not* a noun and that the word *found* in this context means roughly the same as *discovered* and not *to initiate* (*a society*) or *to melt mould* (*a metal*).

The fourth prerequisite for understanding a passage properly is that the relationships between the different 'units of meaning' should be appreciated. Some links arise simply because some of the 'units make statements about the same objects or individuals. Thus, in the example the two sentences are linked to one another by the fact that words such as *teacher* and *she*, *children* and *they*, and *pet* and *turtle* are coreferential (refer to the same entity). In other cases an entire 'unit' may be linked to another one as in the example where the statement *she liked soup* is apparently to be taken as the reason that the children decided to act in the way that they did.

The fifth and final kind of operation entailed in comprehension is that concerned with drawing inferences that are implicit in the text. A chain of inferences that would offer a way of understanding the current example has already been suggested and, in general, the process of uncovering implicit meanings is probably an important aspect of comprehension because much written material deliberately leaves a great deal unstated.

These observations about the possible components of the comprehension process are based on intuitive judgements and, while this kind of linguistic analysis can be extended in a much more comprehensive and formal way (see, for example, Fillmore, 1968, and Halliday and Hasan, 1976), it is important to base our investigations of comprehension on what readers actually to rather than what intuitive or linguistic analysis suggests they *should* do. One way of investigating the kinds of information actually extracted from a text by ordinary readers is to examine the distinctions and details which they are able to notice or recall shortly after they have finished reading the passage. Assuming that this information bears some resemblance to the representation that is initially extracted from the sentence or text, it should be possible to determine whether normal readers actually carry out the five general types of operation outlined above.

4.1 THE END-PRODUCTS OF COMPREHENSION

This strategy for investigating 'normal' comprehension calls for a precise method of examining the 'end-product' of comprehension (i.e. the summary that is presumed to be retained in memory). The experimental paradigm that will be used for this purpose is one that was originally developed by Sachs (1967, 1974).

Subjects read a short paragraph which contained a target sentence like example 1a:

(1a) A wealthy manufacturer, Matthew Boulton, sought out the young inventor. (Target)

(1b) The young inventor sought out a wealthy manufacturer, Matthew Boulton. (Semantic change)

(1c) A wealthy manufacturer, Matthew Boulton, sought the young inventor out. (Formal change)

(1d) A rich manufacturer, Matthew Boulton, sought out the young inventor. (Lexical change)

(1e) The young inventor was sought out by a wealthy manufacturer, Matthew Boulton. (Active/passive change)

After various delays ranging from 1 to 16.5 seconds they turned over the page and read a test sentence which was either identical to the target sentence or which included a semantic change (e.g. example 1b), a formal change (example 1c), a lexical change (example 1d) or a change from the active to the passive voice (example 1e). They were instructed to indicate whether the test sentence was identical to one of the sentences in the paragraph. The results showed that, with delays of five seconds or more, the subjects picked up semantic changes and voice changes but tended to report that the formal and lexical sentences were identical to the target sentences. This suggests that the target sentence was stored in a form which preserves the overall meaning of the sentence, but not the details of the wording. On the basis of this finding it seems reasonable to hypothesize that the end-product of processing example 1a is different from that for example 1b, and for example 1e, but that it is identical, or at least very similar, to the end-product for sentences like examples 1c and 1d.

In the next section a number of experimental results of this kind will be used in an attempt to establish whether normal readers show signs of engaging in the five broad aspects of processing outlined above.

4.2 CHARACTERISTICS OF THE COMPREHENSION PROCESS

The first aspect of comprehension which we considered earlier was the process of breaking up the sentence or text into basic 'units of meaning'. Until now no attempt has been made to spell out exactly what is meant by this phrase. However, it is important to do this before proceeding any further.

The 'unit of meaning' that has most commonly been used in work on memorizing and comprehending text is a simple linguistic description known as a *proposition*. In essence this is an abstract statement about an entity (i.e. a person or an object) or about the relationship between two or more such entities. So, for example, a proposition may state that certain property or state of affairs is true of a person or an object (e.g. *James is thin*) or it may state that a certain action or activity takes place between two entities (e.g. *Tom punched Harry*).

A variety of different notations have been used to express the kinds of statements made by propositions. For example, *Tom punches Harry* has been represented in each of the ways shown in Figure 4.1. To a large extent the differences between these alternative forms of representation are purely notational. Thus, it is possible to rewrite the basic networks in the system used by Anderson (1976) in terms of the linear representation used by Clark and Clark (1977) and vice versa (see Anderson, 1976, Chapter 2). However, there are some real differences between some of the alternative theoretical conceptions on the nature of propositions. An important source of disagreement concerns the issue of *decomposition*. Are propositions constructed in some sense from the nouns and verbs that appeared in the original sentence, or is each of these lables analysed into simpler semantic units which then become part of the propositional representation? On this issue, theorists like Anderson, Bower and Kintsch have tended to argue that there is no need to break down the representation into primitive meanings while others like Norman, Rumelhart and Clark have taken the opposite view and have frequently adopted the practice of semantic decomposition in their attempts to construct propositional representations of sentences and texts. Another point of disagreement concerns the degree to which it seems to be important to use different propositional descriptions to represent sentences that are paraphrases of one another. In Clark's scheme, paraphrases are rarely represented in the same way, whereas this occurs quite frequently in most of the other systems and it is particularly common in the active structural network approach used by Norman and Rumelhart.

(a)   punch (Tom, Harry)   (Clark and Clark, 1977

(b)   (PUNCH, TOM, HARRY)   (Kintsch, 1974)

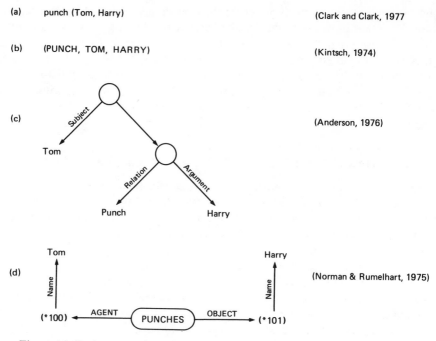

Figure 4.1 Various notations that have been used for representing propositions

While these disagreements are interesting and potentially important it is also true to say that there is considerable consensus between all of the theories on some issues. In particular, there is normally no difficulty in saying whether two words of a sentence should be incorporated into the same underlying proposition or not. This can be used to determine whether readers typically analyse texts into their underlying propositions.

4.2.1 Evidence that readers partition sentences into their underlying propositions

If sentences are broken down into propositions and stored in this form, then material that belongs to the same proposition should be integrated more closely than is the case for material that is not part of the same proposition. Thus in example 2 the verb *touched* should be more closely associated with *hippie* (which is its subject and therefore part of the same proposition) than it is with *prostitute* which belongs to a different proposition.

(2) The hippie who kissed the prostitute touched the debutante who liked the captain.

(3) The _____ who kissed the _____ the _____ who liked the _____.

In an experiment designed to test this hypothesis Anderson and Bower (1973) instructed their subjects to read a number of sentences similar to example 2.

At a later stage they were shown a partial framework of the sentence (as in example 3) and they were required to recall the missing words.

The probability of recalling words like *touched* was compared for two groups of subjects: those who recalled *hippie* but not *prostitute* and those who recalled *prostitute* but not hippie. As expected, it was found that the verb was recovered more frequently when the noun which had been remembered was part of the same proposition (as was the case in the first group) than when it belonged to a different proposition (as in the second group). Since this result is the opposite of what might be expected on the basis of the physical proximity of the word pairs in the original sentence, it provides some evidence that the sentence must have been analysed and stored in terms of its propositional structure.

Another, more recent study by Ratcliff and McKoon (1978) has come to the same conclusion using a somewhat different paradigm. In this experiment subjects were required to read lists of four sentences including examples like 4 and 5.

(4) The pauper chopped wood and lugged water.
(5) The chauffeur jammed the clutch when he parked the car.

At the end of the list they were presented with a series of 32 individual words and they had to indicate as rapidly as possible whether each word appeared in any of the sentences in the preceding group. The results indicated that the latencies of correct 'yes' responses varied as a function of the relationship between the current word and the immediately preceding test word. In particular. the response was faster when the second word came from the same proposition as the first (e.g. *pauper—wood, pauper—water, chauffeur—car*) than if the two words came from different propositions in the same sentence (e.g. *wood—water, clutch—car*). Since the average number of words separating the critical words in the original sentences was slightly greater in the first case this result cannot be explained in terms of the degree of separation in the surface structure.

As before, the data suggest that words belonging to the same proposition are more closely associated in the representation of the sentence than words from different propositions. This provides further support for the view that, in memory tasks at least, sentences are broken down into propositions at some point in the analysis.

4.2.2 Evidence that readers take note of the relationship between entities within a proposition

Once the individual propositions have been isolated it is essential for the reader to assign a role to each of the constituent elements. The clearest evidence that this does actually occur comes from recognition studies in which subjects have to discriminate between the original sentence and distractors in which the roles of some of the entities have been changed.

An early experiment of this kind by Sachs (1967) has already been described (see Section 4.1). In this study the roles of the agent and the recipient were reversed in one type of distractor (see example 1b) and the results showed that there was no tendency to confuse this with the original. This suggests that the roles of the different individuals must have been clearly labelled in the representation of the sentence and it seems safe to assume that the same happens with other cases or functions that can be specified in this way.

4.2.3 Evidence that potential meanings of ambiguous words are excluded from the representation

In the discussion so far no attempt has been made to specify how much of the potential meaning of a word in a sentences is subsequently incorporated in the propositional representation of the material. Is a complete specification of the meaning of each word copied from the lexicon into the new representation? Or are only the most salient aspects of the meaning transferred to the proposition? If the meaning is initially registered as a whole, is it subsequently retained in an all-or-none fashion, or can different parts of it be purged or forgotten independently of one another?

The evidence suggests that the lexical information is not retained in indivisible packages. For instance, Bobrow (1970) conducted and experiment in which subjects had to listen to a series of sentences, like example 6, in which the subject noun was ambiguous.*

(6) The pine board shored the river bank.

Later they were given a cue phrase consisting of the subject noun together with an adjective, and they were instructed to recall the object of the original sentence. In one condition the adjective in the cue phrase was chosen to select the same sense of the ambiguous word as that specified in the original sentence (e.g. *wooden board* in example 6). In the second condition a different meaning of the word was selected (e.g. *insurance board*). The results showed that the level of performance was better in the first case, suggesting that the two senses of the ambiguous word were not represented in an equivalent manner in the memory trace of the target sentence.

Other experiments have shown that similar effects occur even when the words are not strictly ambiguous. In one such study, Olson (1972) presented subjects with sentences like example 7.

(7) The stone tower stood alongside the old building.

Later they were shown a test sentence with four alternative words in one of the positions (e.g. *stone, round, wooden, square* in the position of the second word.) They were required to indicate which one had appeared in the original sentence. It was found that when subjects selected the wrong adjective they

---

* In this study and a number of other investigations cited in this chapter the sentences were *heard* rather than *read* by the subject. Where necessary I have assumed that similar results would be obtained in a reading task. However, the assumption may not always be valid, as was shown in an experiment by Sachs (1974).

tended to choose a word which had a similar function to the original (e.g. *wooden*) more often than words which conveyed information of a different kind (e.g. shape information in this example). This suggests that certain aspects of the meaning of a word must have been retained even when the word itself was forgotten. Other recent studies indicate that the details which are preserved are partly determined by the context in which the word appears. In one such experiment conducted by Anderson and Ortony (1975), the subjects first listened to 28 simple sentences like example 8 or 9:

(8) Television sets need expert repairmen.
(9) Television sets look nice in family rooms.

Some of the subjects heard example 8 which emphasizes the fact that a television set is an appliance. Others heard example 9 which draws attention to the fact that a television set can also be regarded as a piece of furniture. The remaining subjects heard control sentences. In each case, subjects were subsequently given a booklet of cue words, including words like *appliance*, and instructed to work through it recalling one target sentence for each prompt. The results showed that the subjects who heard a sentence emphasizing the cued sense of the target noun performed better than those who heard any of the other versions of the sentence. This suggests that the way in which the target noun is represented varies as a function of the sentence in which it appears.

It must be concluded from these studies that the arguments in a proposition do not correspond either to the words in the original sentence or to their semantic descriptions. The information that is read into the proposition apparently consists of a partial specification of the word meaning. Inappropriate shades of meaning and inappropriate senses of ambiguous words are excluded from consideration before the gist of the sentence meaning is stored in memory.

4.2.4 Evidence that readers link propositions to one another

The discussion so far has concentrated on the representation of single propositions. However, in most reading matter the text is made up of a large number of different propositions and it is therefore important to consider the way in which separate units are integrated.

Of course, it is conceivable that they are not organized or interrelated in any way at all. Textual information could in principle be retained in the form of an unstructured list of propositions. However, the experimental evidence argues against such a possibility. Lesgold (1972) carried out an experiment in which subjects read lists of sentences each of which consisted of two simpler sentences joined by a conjunction as in examples 10 and 11:

(10) The aunt ate the pie and Alice was senile.
(11) The aunt ate the pie and she was senile.

In some cases the subject of the second sentence was a proper noun (as in example 10). In others, like example 11 the proper noun was replaced by a pronoun. Later in the experiment the subjects were given a cue word (e.g. *ate*) and they were instructed to use this prompt to recall the remainder of the sentence. It was found that in the proper noun condition subjects were more likely to recall content words from the proposition containing the cue word than from the other proposition (i.e. in this example they were more likely to recall *aunt* than *senile*). In the 'pronoun' condition, however, a word from the second proposition was just as likely to be recalled as one from the first. This finding suggests that in sentences like example 11 the propositions tend to be integrated or linked to one another to a greater extent than they are in other sentences.

The tendency to relate propositions to one another in this way was also shown in a study by de Villiers (1974). Subjects heard a series of sentences including successive sentences like these two:

(12) The man bought a dog. The child wanted the animal.

Later they tried to recall the sentences, and it was found that they often reported having heard sentences which were not actually presented to them (e.g. *The child wanted the dog*). In another condition people heard a similar list of sentences except that the word *the* was replaced by the word *a* every time it appeared. In this case, people were less likely to make the mistake of 'recalling' sentences that were not in the list. These results suggest that people in the first group assumed that the animal mentioned in the second sentence referred to the dog mentioned earlier and that on this assumption they combined the two propositions.

In addition to this integration, or perhaps as a consequence of it, some propositions in a text are given a different status from others. In particular, propositions that are central to the theme of a sentence or paragraph are somehow more 'strongly' represented than those which are more peripheral. Such a difference in the salience of the propositions of a sentence was shown in an experiment by Hornby (1974). On each trial the subjects heard a sentence consisting of two clauses, one of which expressed a presupposition and the other the main focus of the sentence. For example:

(13) The one that is stroking the cat is the girl.

In this example the sentence presupposes that someone is stroking the cat but the central or focal assertion is that this someone is the girl. Shortly after hearing the sentence the subjects were shown a picture and they had to indicate whether the sentence presented an accurate description of the picture. In a few cases it *was* accurate, but on most trials the picture misrepresented either the *presupposed* constituent (by depicting someone stroking a *dog*, for instance) or the *focused* constituent of the sentence (by showing a *boy* instead of a *girl* stroking a cat). The results showed that the subjects were less likely to notice discrepancies of the first kind than those which concerned the focused component of the sentence. This suggests that the underlying propositions of a sentence are represented in a way which reflects their relative importance in the communication as a whole.

This conclusion receives further support from a number of studies conducted by Kintsch and his colleagues (Kintsch and Keenan, 1973; Kintsch, 1974; Kintsch, Kozminsky, Streby, McKoon and Keenan, 1975). The materials in these experiments consisted of sentences or short paragraphs that were generated from preselected lists of propositions. Using a scheme developed earlier by Kintsch (1974), the texts were analysed into hierarchical structures consisting of a few superordinate propositions and a much larger number of different levels of subordinate propositions. The superordinate propositions corresponded to the major themes of the text while the others expressed more peripheral information. The subjects read the sentences of passages and later recalled their contents. The data showed that the probability of recalling a particular proposition was closely related to its position in the hierarchy. In particular, superordinate propositions were remembered much more frequently than those assigned to lower levels in the hierarchical structure.

Recently, similar effects have been shown in experiments designed to investigate the retention of complete stories (Thorndyke, 1977; Mandler and Johnson, 1977). The representational framework used in these studies was based on the notion that many stories follow fairly specific conventions. For example, in Thorndyke's (1977) 'grammer' for simple stores (which is based on earlier work by Rumelhart, 1975) it is assumed that all stories are made up of a Setting, a Theme, a Plot and a Resolution. Each of these components is assumed to consist of further elements. For instance, the Plot is made up of an indefinite number of Episodes, each of which is further subdivided into a Subgoal (which is set up as a means of achieving a Goal normally expressed earlier in the Theme), an Attempt to reach this Subgoal and the Outcome of the action. By partitioning stories in accordance with ten rules of this kind, Thorndyke was able to assign the individual sentences of a story to different levels of a hierarchical plot structure. The influence of the level in the hierarchy on the recall of a sentence was tested in an experiment in which subjects read (or heard) a story and then immediately attempted to recall it as accurately as possible. This procedure was repeated for a second story, and then the subject was instructed to write a short summary of each of the stories.

The results of the recall and summary conditions alike indicated that subjects tended to retain higher-level propositions rather than low-level details in the hierarchical plot structures. These findings, together with those reported by Kintsch and Hornby, provide fairly compelling evidence that readers distinguish between propositions on the basis of the role each of them plays in the text.

4.2.5   Evidence that readers draw inferences during comprehension

In the last few pages we have considered the representation and recall of material that is expressed explicitly in the text. However, this is not the only kind of information that a person remembers after reading or listening to a passage of prose. There is a considerable amount of evidence that people tend to remember the inferences which they make from the text as well as its explicit contents.

In one experimental demonstration of this phenomenon Johnson, Bransford and Solomon (1973) presented subjects with short paragraphs like example 14:

(14) John was trying to fix the bird house. He was *pounding* the nail when his father came out to watch him and help him do the work.

Later they were shown recognition sentences some of which included information that was implicit in the earlier text as in example 15:

(15) John was using the hammer to fix the bird house when his father came out to watch him and help him do the work.

The subjects were instructed to indicate whether the new sentence was exactly the same as one of the sentences in the original paragraph. The outcome was that more than half of them agreed that it was. In a control condition the initial paragraph was altered slightly so that there was no implication that an instrument was used in the action (e.g. *pounding* was replaced by *looking for* in example 14), and in this condition the number of false recognitions was significantly lower than before. These results suggest that people remember the inferences which they draw from sentences as well as the sentences themselves.

This conclusion has been confirmed and extended by numerous other studies (e.g. Bransford, Barclay and Franks, 1972; Bransford and Johnson, 1973; Jarvella and Collas, 1974; and Frederiksen, 1975). There is even some evidence that information which is inferred and information which is expressed directly are stored in propositional representations that cannot be distinguished from one another after a few minutes. Keenan and Kintsch (see Kintsch, 1974) carried out an experiment in which subjects read paragraphs containing critical propositions that were either stated explicitly as in example 16 or were implicit in the text as in example 17:

(16) A carelessly discarded burning cigarette started a fire. The fire destroyed many acres of virgin forest.
(17) A burning cigarette was carelessly discarded. The fire destroyed many acres of virgin forest.

After a delay of 15 minutes the subjects were shown a series of test statements including the critical propositions (i.e. in this case *The cigarette started a fire*) and they were instructed to indicate as quickly as possible whether each of them was true or false. The response latency was almost identical in the two conditions suggesting that the form of the representation is comparable whether the information is expressed explicitly or implicitly.

4.2.6 Reservations concerning the use of memory techniques

The main aim of the present section has been to try to provide an empirical foundation for some of the intuitive observations made at the beginning of the chapter. This has been done largely by using data from memory experiments. Before moving on to consider the processes underlying the various different aspects of comprehension, it may be worth pausing to observe that there are several difficulties in deriving inferences from memorial data in this way.

Some of the main problems have been spelt out clearly by Fillenbaum (1974). The central difficulty is that in recalling a sentence or passage a person's performance is influenced not only by the way in which the material is represented, but also by various memorial processes such as forgetting, retrieval and reconstruction. This means that some of the information in the representation may be quickly forgotten, with the result that certain distinctions might not be reflected in the memory data. Equally, the memorial processes might *add* information which was not present in the original representation. For example, if the trace consisted of isolated words (e.g. *Harry, ball, Kicked, the*) the subject might use his linguistic knowledge during retrieval to reorder the words to construct a sentence. If retrieval effects of this kind occur, the use of memory techniques could easily lead to inappropriate conclusions about the nature of the initial representation of the material.

A second problem raised by Fillenbaum (1974) is that subjects may adopt special processing strategies when they try to remember sentences, and so the results obtained in memory tasks may not be representative of the processes that occur during more conventional reading. There is clear evidence that people process sentences differently when they are oriented towards memorizing them and when they are simply attempting to understand them (Green, 1975; Aaronson and Scarborough, 1976). Indeed, such differences are sometimes reflected in memory data. For instance, it has frequently been shown that the detailed recall of the exact wording of a sentence is improved if subjects are warned in advance that there will be a memory test at the end of the experiment (see, for example, Johnson-Laird and Stevenson, 1970; Tieman, 1972; Wanner, 1974).

These observations suggest that it may occasionally be misleading to use the results of memory experiments to draw inferences about the end-products of comprehension. Thus, it is advisable to maintain a degree of healthy scepticism about the conclusions reached in the previous section. Nevertheless, since there is not much empirical evidence to work from apart from that based on memory techniques, we shall proceed to use the present conclusions as a framework for the remainder of the discussion of comprehension.

4.3 THE END-PRODUCTS OF COMPREHENSION: A SUMMARY

The evidence derived from memory experiments suggests that when a person reads a passage of prose he constructs an internal representation which corresponds to the meaning of the text. This internal representation can be conveniently described in terms of abstract statements known as propositions and the evidence suggests that these propositions are linked to one another and structured according to their importance.

The semantic information incorporated *within* a proposition comes predominantly from the internal lexicon, but it is clear that not all of the information that can be recovered from this source finds its way into the eventual representation. In particular, inappropriate meanings of ambiguous words are not retained in the final structure. On the other hand, some of the information incorporated in the end-product comes neither from the mental lexicon nor, indeed, from the explicit structure of the text. This additional information derives from inferences that are made by the reader himself.

Theories of comprehension have to explain how a reader uses the string of words he has just recognized to build up an internal representation of this kind. How are propositions constructed? How are inappropriate word meanings eliminated and at what stage in the process does this occur? What procedures are used to link propositions? On what basis are individual propositions assessed and assigned to positions within a hierarchical structure? In what circumstances does a reader draw inferences from the material and at what points in the processing sequence to these processes occur? The remainder of the chapter will be devoted to tackling these questions. The discussion will start by examining current suggestions on the process of constructing propositions.

4.4 SENTENCE COMPREHENSION—THEORIES BASED ON THE USE OF PERCEPTUAL STRATEGIES

The most common suggestion concerning the construction of propositions is that certain superficial properties of words in the sentence are used as clues for determining the underlying structure of the sentence (Bever, 1970; Fodor, Bever and Garrett, 1974). It is proposed that people use these clues in a variety of heuristic strategies for understanding sentences. For example, Fodor *et al.* (1974) have suggested that when subjects encounter a noun–verb–noun sequence in the sentence they take the first noun to be the subject of the clause, the verb to be the action and the second noun to be its object. This provides a straightforward procedure for constructing a proposition from the surface structure of a sentence. In another strategy, referred to as the *lexical analysis strategy*, Fodor *et al.* have suggested that listeners or readers use the properties of the individual words in the sentence to help them to work out its structure. For example, if the main verb of the sentence is transitive (e.g. *kick*) they might use this fact to eliminate structural possibilities that are not compatible with transitive verbs (e.g. complement structures as in 'The warder heard that the prisoners had escaped'). In a third strategy it is assumed that subjects use specific words in the sentence as clues to the underlying structure. For instance, if the word *whom* is encountered in a text it may be taken as a signal that the sentence contains a relative clause.

Bever (1970), Kimball (1973) and Fodor *et al.* (1974) have suggested several other strategies that might be used for analysing sentences and the list has been extended by Clark and Clark (1977). Suggestions of this kind could provide a partial answer to the question of how people construct propositions. However, as Kaplan (1975) has pointed out, a complete account of this process needs to do more than specify a list of strategies that might be used to analyse sentences. It should say something about the order in which the strategies are tried and it should also indicate what happens when a strategy produces an unacceptable output. Some of these requirements can be met by incorporating 'perceptual strategies' into a more general model of syntactic processing such as the Augmented Transition Network model developed by Kaplan (1972, 1974, 1975).

4.5   SENTENCE COMPREHENSION USING AUGMENTED TRANSITION NETWORKS (ATNs)

A central feature of this model is a conceptual device known as an Augmented Transition Network (ATN) (cf. Thorne, Bratley and Dewar, 1968; Bobrow and Fraser, 1969; Woods, 1970). To illustrate the idea we shall describe a few ATNs and indicate how they might operate.

An ATN consists of a relatively small number of *states* which are connected to one another by labelled arrows or *arcs*. Figure 4.2 represents a four-state ATN which is perhaps the simplest network that can be used to process a complete sentence.

Processing a sentence consists of passing through the states in the order specified by the arrows. The *label* attached to each arc represents a condition that has to be satisfied before each transition can be made. (For example, in Figure 4.2 CAT NOUN (i.e. 'category noun') specifies that the current word must be a noun in order for control to be passed from S1 to S2 or from S3 to S4.) Associated with each arc there is also a *naming action* which is carried out when the arc has been traversed. Thus, in Figure 4.2 the word corresponding to arc (1) would be labelled as the subject of the sentence.

The way in which an ATN operates can be illustrated by considering how a simple sentence like example 18 is handled:

(18) Elephants eat sardines.

The process starts in the first state (S1). The label for arc (1) requires that the first word should be a noun. The lexical entry for 'elephants' is therefore consulted to check whether this condition is satisfied. After this has been confirmed the arc is traversed and the naming action is carried out (i.e. *elephants*

Arc	Naming Action
(1)	Assign the name SUBJECT to the current word
(2)	Assign the name ACTION to the current word
(3)	Assign the name OBJECT to the current word

Figure 4.2   An example of an extremely basic Augmented Transition Network

is named as the SUBJECT of the sentence). By a similar procedure *eat* is identified as a verb and named as the ACTION and control passes to S3. Finally, at arc (3), the word *sardines* is tested and named as the OBJECT and the processing of the sentence is completed.

It is evident that the network outlined above could not cope with the majority of sentence structures. For instance, it would fail to handle sentences with noun phrases like example 19:

(19) The old elephant ate raw sardines.

This can be dealt with quite easily be extending the network slightly as in Figure 4.3.

This network introduces three new kinds of label. The first, JUMP at arc (6), simply allows control to be passed unconditionally from one state to another. The other two, SEEK and SEND, are somewhat more complicated. SEEK NP1 asks if the current word starts a noun phrase, and the arc can only be traversed if the sentence starts with a noun phrase. To check this, control is passed to NP1 and the words are processed in terms of the noun phrase network. The first word *The* satisfies the condition for arc (5) and is therefore labelled as a DETERMINER. The word *old* meets the condition for arc (7) and so it can be designated as a MODIFIER. The word *elephant* allows arc (8) to be traversed and this completes the noun phrase. SEND NP returns the system to the point at which the noun phrase network was initially called (i.e. arc (1) in this example). The condition for traversing arc (1) is now satisfied and so control can be passed to S2. Following this, the verb is processed as in the

Sentence Network

Noun Phrase Network

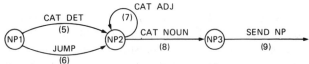

Arc	Action
(1)	Assign the name SUBJECT to the current phrase
(2)	Assign the name ACTION to the current word
(3)	Assign the name OBJECT to the current phrase
(4)	Assemble sentence representation
(5)	Assign the name DETERMINER to the current word
(6)	None
(7)	Assign the name MODIFIER to the current word
(8)	Assign the name HEAD to the current word
(9)	Assemble noun phrase

Figure 4.3 An Augmented Transition Network to handle sentences with noun phrases

simpler example considered above. Then at arc (3) the noun phrase network is called again to process the phrase *raw sardines*. When these operations have been carried out the arc is traversed and the sentence is duly completed.

This second version of the network can handle a greater variety of sentences than the previous one, but remains somewhat specific. However, it is possible to extend the network so that it can handle passives, prepositional phrases, complements, relative clauses and a variety of other syntactic structures (see Kaplan, 1975; Stevens and Rumelhart, 1975; Rumelhart, 1977). Thus, in their most general form ATNs can offer a very powerful model for the processing of sentences.

4.6 EVALUATION OF PERCEPTUAL STRATEGIES

We have already pointed out some of the weaknesses of the Perceptual Strategies approach, particularly those concerning the failure to provide a complete and systematic account of the way in which sentences are comprehended. We now turn to a more empirical evaluation of the approach. As we shall see, the experimental case for strategies is no stronger than the theoretical justification.

The two strategies that have been studied most intensively are the lexical access strategy and the strategy that uses surface-structure clues to determine the underlying structure of sentences. In the first strategy it is suggested that subjects use lexical information in their efforts to compute the structural relations within the sentence. This hypothesis has really only been tested in one way: by comparing the ease with which people process sentences containing transitive verbs (i.e. verbs that are only compatible with a single underlying structure) and those containing complement verbs (which are consistent with a variety of structural possibilities). Fodor, Garrett and Bever (1968) argued that if subjects were able to make use of lexical information as suggested by the hypothesis, they would need to entertain fewer structural hypotheses while processing sentences with transitive words than when they were analysing complement sentences. Consequently, they predicted that sentences of the first kind would be easier to handle than the others. They tested the hypothesis in an experiment in which subjects were required to paraphrase doubly self-embedded sentences like examples 20a and 20b:

(20a) The box the man the child *liked* carried was empty.
(20b) The box the man the child *slapped* carried was empty.

As expected, it was found that sentences with transitive verbs like *slapped* in example 20b were paraphrased more accurately than sentences like example 20a. However as Fodor, Bever and Garrett (1974) later pointed out themselves: 'Experiments with doubly self-embedded sentences are always suspect because of the oddity of the stimulus materials' (p. 351). In fact, there is a good deal of evidence that subjects are normally incapable of processing such sentences. Thus the results do not provide any convincing evidence that people use the lexical analysis strategy to process more conventional sentences. A more recent test of the hypothesis has been carried out by Holmes and Forster (1972) using an experimental technique known as the Rapid Serial Visual Presentation (RSVP) technique. In this task the words of a sentence are flashed on a screen in rapid succession and the subjects are instructed to recall the sentence as accurately as possible. Holmes and Forster compared the level of performance for sentences containing transitive and complement verbs and found that subjects were generally more accurate in reporting sentences of the first kind. This might be interpreted as evidence in favour of the hypothesis. However, performance in the RSVP task is almost certainly affected by non-perceptual effects (Mitchell, 1979), and so it is impossible to tell whether or not the effects are perceptual in origin (as the hypothesis requires).

In addition to the studies just outlined, there have been at least two attempts to test the hypothesis using experimental tasks designed to provide more direct measures of sentence processing difficulty. In neither case was there any support for the hypothesis. In one of these studies Hakes (1971) used an experimental technique known as the *phoneme-monitoring* technique. In this task the subjects listen to a sentence and they are instructed to press a button as soon as they hear a target phoneme. The latency of the response to this phoneme is taken as a measure of the momentary sentence-processing difficulty in the locality of the phoneme. Contrary to the hypothesis, the results of Hakes's experiment showed that there was no significant difference in the response time to target phonemes immediately following transitive and complement verbs.

In the second experiment Mitchell and Green (1978) measured the time required to read successive three-word segments of a continuous passage of prose. The text was composed in such a way that at 16 selected points a transitive verb could be replaced by a complement verb (or vice versa) without substantially changing the meaning of the passage. The reaction times for the displays immediately following these critical verbs were recorded and it was found, against the hypothesis, that reading time was unaffected by the nature of the verb.

The evidence summarized above provides no support for the suggestion that people use the lexical access strategy when they are either reading or listening to sentences. Verb complexity may influence performance at some later stage in processing (see Foss and Hakes, 1978, p. 128), but it does not seem to be a factor in constructing the propositions that underlie the sentence.

The degree of support for the second important strategy suggested by Fodor *et al.* (1974) is equally uncertain. It will be recalled that they suggested that subjects use surface-structure cues such as relative pronouns to assist them in computing the underlying structure of the sentence. This hypothesis has generally been tested in experiments using sentences such as example 21 which contain words that can be deleted from the sentence without changing its meaning:

(21) The box (that) the man (that) the child liked carried was empty.

Fodor and Garrett (1967) showed that sentences of this kind tend to be paraphrased less adequately when the relative pronoun is deleted. However, phoneme-monitoring studies using similar materials have yielded somewhat contradictory results. In two studies (Hakes and Foss, 1970; Hakes and Cairns, 1970) it was found that phoneme-monitoring latencies were longer in the reduced condition (i.e. the condition in which the relative pronoun was deleted). In a third experiment, Foss and Lynch (1969) found that there was no difference at all between the conditions.

All of these studies can be criticized on the grounds that the materials (doubly self-embedded sentences) could easily have forced the subjects to use unconventional processing strategies. To date, only two investigations appear to have been conducted using less artificial sentences with singly embedded clauses, and neither of them provides unequivocal support for the hypothesis. Hakes, Evans and Brannon (1976) conducted two experiments, one employing object relatives and the other subject relatives. In the first case the hypothesis was confirmed by a phoneme-monitoring measure, but disconfirmed on a paraphrasing measure. In the second case there was no effect on either measure. In the other study using singly embedded clauses Mitchell and Green (1978) used the subject-paced reading task described earlier and found that deletion of the relative pronoun had no significant effect on reading time for the next three words in the relative clause.

These results and the results of the experiments on the verb complexity hypothesis provide no compelling evidence that the *perception* of sentences is facilitated in any way by perceptual cues in the manner suggested by Fodor *et al.* (1974). Some of the experiments based on memory techniques have yielded positive results, and so it may be that surface-structure clues can be used to improve the retention, reconstruction or retrieval of sentences. However, there is no reason to believe that they have any influence on performance while the sentence is being parsed.

The present discussion has been restricted to just two of the strategies suggested by Garrett and his colleagues but, as mentioned above, this reflects the emphasis of research to date. Very few experiments have been conducted on the remaining hypotheses and, at the time of writing, none of these studies has succeeded in providing unequivocal support for the notion that readers use a fixed set of perceptual strategies to parse sentences.

4.7 EVALUATION OF ATNs

Kaplan (1972) has shown that most of the perceptual strategies suggested by Bever (1970) can be incorporated into ATNs. Moreover, ATNs come closer to providing a full and detailed account of the perceptual processes, and in this sense they are preferable to the earlier approaches.

Recently a number of attempts have been made to test predictions derived from ATN models (Kaplan, 1974; Wanner & Maratsos, 1974; Kramer and Stevens, cited in Rumelhart, 1977b). Although these studies have not been published at the time of writing, some of them, particularly the paper by Wanner and Maratsos, are frequently cited and it is probably worth considering their evidence in favour of ATNs.

Wanner and Maratsos studied the way in which people process sentences like examples 22a and 22b:

(22a) /The admiral who proposed to / the countess left / the country/.

(22b) /The admiral whom the countess / proposed to left /the country /.

On the basis of an ATN analysis they argued that in both types of sentence subjects would have to retain the first noun phrase (i.e. 'The admiral') until they were able to determine its syntactic role in the following relative clause. This, they suggested, should occur after the word *who* in sentences like example 20a and after the word *to* in sentences like example 20b. In other words, at all points between the fourth and seventh words, the second kind of sentence should place more demands on memory than the first. Memory load was measured at four different points in the sentence by interrupting the presentation and displaying a short list of words to be recalled at the end of the trial. The authors predicted that at points 1, 3 and 4 the memory load would be comparable for the two types of sentence, but that at point 2 the load would be greater for the second type of sentence. An experiment was conducted with 20 subjects and the overall pattern of the results was in line with these predictions. However, the crucial effects failed to reach significance at the conventional levels. A related prediction was tested in a second experiment, but the results of this study were also inconclusive. Thus the Wanner and Maratsos experiments do not provide any compelling evidence in support of ATNs. In fact, it is difficult to see what kind of evidence could be regarded as supportive since, as Anderson (1976) has pointed out, the general ATN model is so flexible that it could probably be used to simulate almost any pattern of behaviour that might arise in the processing of sentences. If it is true that the model is incapable of making falsifiable predictions, then it is clearly unsatisfactory as an account of the way in which people parse sentences.

In conclusion, there are at present no adequate general theories of sentence parsing. Of course, there are a number of reliable empirical findings that would have to be taken into account by a successful model, but since these results do not in themselves provide any answers to the central questions the material will not be presented here. The interested reader may wish to follow up these issues by referring to reviews of the psycholinguistic literature (Johnson-Laird, 1974; Fodor *et al.*, 1974; Clark and Clark, 1977; Levelt, 1978).

Parsing a sentence is a necessary but not a sufficient condition for the construction of the propositions that underlie its meaning. After the syntactic functions have been assigned to the words, this information must be used to build up propositions. Even less is known about this process than about the parsing procedures used in the first stage. Woods (1973) and Kaplan (1972) have speculated a little about how the process might occur, but so far their ideas do not appear to have been submitted to any kind of experimental test.

4.8 WHEN ARE INAPPROPRIATE WORD-MEANINGS ELIMINATED?

In discussing sentence comprehension so far we have considered the process by which propositions are constructed from the string of words that appear on the page. Essentially the problem under consideration has been that of determining the appropriate relationship between the words in the sentence. Relationships of this kind represent only one of several determinants of the meaning of a sentence. Equally important is the contribution made by the meanings of the individual words themselves.

The cued recall studies discussed earlier in the chapter indicate that the semantic information which is incorporated in the final representation of the sentence is not the same as that made available by the mental lexicon. In particular, the data suggested that the precise meaning attributed to an individual word is strongly influenced by the remainder of the sentence. If this is true, it follows that the semantic specification of the word in the lexicon must be modified at some stage in the comprehension process.

In the case of an ambiguous word this means that all senses of the word that are inappropriate in the sentence must be eliminated from the representation. At what stage in the process might the alternative meanings of the word be removed? One possibility put forward by MacKay (1973) is that selection takes place so early in the process that the 'wrong' meanings are not even retrieved from the lexicon. This might occur if the context is used to select in advance which sense of the word should be retrieved. Foss and Jenkins called this the Prior Decision model. The main alternative to this view is that all meanings of the word are retrieved and that selection takes place at some later stage in the comprehension process (the Many Meanings model).

Most of the evidence seems to suggest that all senses of a word are retrieved at first, but that the inappropriate senses are suppressed soon afterwards. Some of the earlier work has been criticized on methodological grounds, but the results of more recent investigations suggest that the conclusions reached in these studies were substantially correct.

In one of the earliest studies, Foss and Jenkins (1973) used the phoneme-monitoring task to examine processing load immediately after the presentation of an ambiguous word. They argued that if a single meaning of an ambiguous word were selected in advance the word would be processed exactly as if it were unambiguous. In other words, the processing loads for ambiguous and unambiguous words would be equivalent. On the other hand, if both (or all) senses of an ambiguous word were recovered it would be necessary for the subject to handle irrelevant information and this additional processing requirement would tend to cause the phoneme-monitoring latency to be longer than it would have been for an unambiguous word in the same position. The results supported the second hypothesis. Response latencies were significantly longer following ambiguous words even when the prior context produced a strong bias in favour of one of the alternative senses.

Cairns and Kamerman (1975) replicated and extended this finding by testing the phoneme-monitoring latency at two different points: immediately after the ambiguous word and after the presentation of two further words. The results showed that the difference between ambiguous and unambiguous words was only evident in the first condition (i.e. the monitoring latency was equivalent in the two conditions when the target phoneme was delayed). This suggests that ambiguous words very quickly come to be processed like unambiguous words. The authors interpreted this as evidence that the appropriate sense of an ambiguous word is selected within a few hundred milliseconds after the word has been identified.

As mentioned above, the conclusions drawn from these studies have been queried on methodological grounds. In particular, doubts have been expressed about the interpretation given to the main dependent variable (Mehler, Segui and Carey, 1978; Newman and Dell, 1978). It has become apparent that monitoring latency is systematically affected by factors such as the length and frequency of the word preceding the target phoneme. Unfortunately, these factors were not adequately controlled in the studies just considered, and an experiment by Mehler et al. (1978) shows that when they are controlled the ambiguity effect disappears. This result can be interpreted in two ways. Either it means that the appropriate sense of an ambiguous word is selected in advance or, alternatively, it could be that although several meanings are accessed the phoneme-monitoring technique is not sensitive enough to detect this and is therefore unsuitable for investigating the phenomenon. Recent work using various cross-modal priming tasks suggests that the latter interpretation is more likely to be correct.

In cross-modal priming tasks a sentence (or series of sentences) is played on a tape and at some point in the sequence a single word is presented visually. The subject is required to respond to this word by naming it or by making a word/nonword decision about it. In either case the results indicate that the decision latency is reduced whenever the test word is semantically related to a recently presented auditory word.

In one of the studies using this technique Tanenhaus, Leiman and Seidenberg (1979) employed materials including ambiguous words that could either be nouns or verbs (e.g. She held a rose; They all rose). The test word was related either to the noun (e.g. flower) or to the verb (e.g. stand) and it was presented either immediately after the end of the ambiguous word or after a delay of 200 ms or 600 ms. There were also control conditions in which the ambiguous words were replaced by words that bore no relation at all to the test words. The subject's task was simply to name the test word as rapidly as possible. The results showed that when there was no delay both related and unrelated words were processed faster than they were in the corresponding control conditions. When the test word was delayed by 200 ms or 600 ms, however, the facilitation effect was restricted to the appropriate sense of the word. These results suggest that both senses of the ambiguous word were active at first, but that after a short delay only the appropriate sense was active. The interpretation of the data offered by Tanenhaus *et al.* (1979) was similar to that put forward by Cairns and Kamerman (1975)—namely that all meanings of ambiguous words are automatically retrieved but that the inappropriate readings are subsequently suppressed.

Swinney (1979) used an experimental technique that was broadly similar to the one just considered. Visual test words were displayed at two different intervals after the subject had heard an ambiguous word. There were several differences, however. The most important were (i) that the context materials consisted of 30–40 word paragraphs rather than short sentences; (ii) both senses of the ambiguous words were nouns; (iii) the auditory presentation continued while the test word was displayed; (iv) the subject's main task was lexical decision task and (v) in the delay condition the interval between the ambiguous word and the test word was three syllables (i.e. about 750–1000 ms). Despite these procedural differences the results were very similar to those obtained by Tanenhaus *et al.* (1979). In the immediate test both the appropriate and the inappropriate senses of the ambiguous word were facilitated and this happened even when there was a very strong bias in favour of the relevant word. After a three-syllable delay only the relevant sense of the word remained activated.

Taken together these results support the Many Meanings hypothesis. The evidence clearly suggests that both (or all) senses of an ambiguous word are accessed at first and that the inappropriate senses are eliminated within a period of about 200 ms after the information has been retrieved from the lexicon. Of course, in all of this work the ambiguous words were presented aurally and it may be that ambiguity is handled differently when the critical materials are presented visually. However, in the absence of any definite evidence that there are differences of this kind, it seems reasonable to assume that the present conclusions apply to reading as well as to listening.

4.9 HOW ARE PROPOSITIONS LINKED?

Up to now we have been concerned with the processes that occur as individual propositions are extracted from the text. Clearly, these propositions have to be combined before the reader can begin to grasp the overall meaning of the passage. How is this integration achieved?

It may not be possible to give a single, straightforward answer to this question because propositions and sentences can be related to one another in a variety of different ways, and it is conceivable that different linking strategies are used for different types of relation.

Halliday and Hasan (1976, p. 304) distinguish between three general kinds of relation: (i) relatedness of reference, (ii) semantic connection and (iii) relatedness of form.

Reference is the relation between an element in the current proposition and something else—usually an entity mentioned within the previous sentence or two of the text. In example 23 the words *zookeeper* and *he* are coreferential and so are the words *tiger* and *it*.

(23) The reporter asked the zookeeper where the tiger was. *He* said *it* had jumped out of a lorry while *it* was being transferred from Plymouth to London.

The second type of relation, semantic connection, is also used to indicate the way in which successive propositions or sentences are linked to one another. In this case, however, the relationship is usually specified by means of a conjunction such as *and, but, so, then,* etc. For instance, in example 24 the word *so* indicates that the second proposition is to be understood as a direct consequence of the first.

(24) He wore frilly garments. So they chose him as their leader.

In this kind of relation, substituting one conjunction for another drastically changes the meaning of the text. (For instance, consider the meaning of example 24 when *So* is replaced by *because* or *However*).

The third kind of link is different from the others in that the relation lies in the *form* of the preceding text rather than the identity of the elements mentioned. For instance, in example 25 the word *one* does not refer to the object mentioned earlier, but to another member of the same class of objects.

(25) Do you want this racquet? No, I want an expensive *one*.

This relatedness of form allows the reader to recover a word (or string of words) from the preceding text and use it (or them) to understand the current sentence. In other words, this kind of relation does not necessarily entail any link between the underlying propositions of the sentence. For this reason relatedness of form is less relevant for the immediate question than the other two kinds of relation.

A common feature of the three kinds of relation is that the second sentence contains a word (or phrase) which acts as a signal that further information is available elsewhere in the text. Typically, the reader has to recover the information before he can understand the sentence or appreciate the way in which it is connected to the prior material.

Haviland and Clark (1974; Clark, 1978) have suggested that readers and listeners compute the relations between sentences by using a problem-solving approach which they term the Given–New Strategy. According to this proposal the reader first constructs the propositions in the current sentence and then allocates each of these propositions to one of two categories depending on whether it contains presupposed information or information that has not previously been mentioned in the text. (These two kinds of information are referred to as Given and New information, respectively.) The process of analysing sentences can be illustrated by referring to example 13 on p. 82. In this example, the sentence presupposes that someone is stroking the cat and asserts that this someone is the girl. Thus, in this case the Given information is X *is stroking the cat* and the New information is $X = the\ girl$.

In the next phase of the strategy, it is assumed that the reader searches his internal representation of the preceding text for an antecedent that exactly matches the Given information. If such an entity can be located in memory this obviously provides a way of linking the current sentence to the material that has gone before it. According to the hypothesis, this link is established by storing the New information in the current sentence with the Given information that has just been located. Thus the existing copy of the Given information is used to provide an address for storing the recently received New information.

This strategy should be relatively easy to apply in cases where the Given information in the current sentence is mentioned explicitly in the preceding text (as in example 26).

(26) I met a man and a woman yesterday. The woman was a doctor.

However, explicit links of this kind are probably the exception rather than the rule in normal texts. What happens when the Given information is not mentioned explicitly, as in example 27—one of Clark's examples?

(27) I met two people yesterday. The woman was a doctor.

Here the Given information in the second sentence concerns the existence of a woman who is assumed to be identifiable to the reader. In fact, unlike example 26, no such person has previously been mentioned and so there is no way that this Given information can be located in the reader's memory.

According to the Given–New Strategy this problem is handled by the *invention* of the required information. That is, the reader makes up a set of propositions to provide the missing information. Thus, in the present example Clark suggests that the subject might add an assumption such as example 28.

(28) One of the two people mentioned is a woman and the other is not.

This would then allow him to locate an antecedent for the Given information in the second sentence and proceed with storing the New information as he would have done if the entity had been mentioned explicitly.

This refinement of the linking process serves a dual purpose. It not only offers an explanation of how linking might occur when the Given information is not mentioned explicitly. It also provides an account of how inferences (or 'bridging assumptions', to use Clark's term) might be introduced into the memory representation of the text.

An obvious implication of this suggestion is that the demands made by the process of identifying an appropriate antecedent should be greater when the reader has to invent an appropriate candidate than when a suitable antecedent is explicitly mentioned in the text. Haviland and Clark (1974) tested this prediction by presenting subjects with pairs of sentences like those in 29 or 30.

(29) We got some beer out of the truck. The beer was warm.
(30) We checked the picnic supplies. The beer was warm.

The subjects read the two sentences one after the other and the time taken to comprehend the second sentence was measured. As expected, the comprehension time was longer for sentences with direct antecedents like example 29 than for sentences like example 30 where the antecedent had to be reconstructed.

In discussing the Given–New Strategy so far we have considered two relatively extreme situations—one in which the antecedent is mentioned directly in the preceding sentence and another in which it is not mentioned at all. Recently there have been attempts to investigate what happens in the intermediate situation where there is an explicit mention of the antecedent which is located, not in the immediately preceding sentence, but at a point several sentences earlier. Does the introduction of a delay following the first mention of an antecedent cause problems similar to those that occur when it is not mentioned at all? The quick answer seems to be that it *can* cause difficulties but that it does not do so in all circumstances. The crucial factor seems to be whether the information associated with the antecedent remains in a state which is easily retrievable (i.e. *foregrounded*—Chafe, 1973). Lesgold, Roth and Curtis (1979) demonstrated this in a recent series of experiments. They constructed paragraphs in which reference was made to an entity mentioned up four sentences earlier in the text. In some of the conditions the intervening material was designed to keep the entity in the foreground while in others the interjected sentences were chosen so that the topic changed and the critical information was pushed into the background. Examples of the two conditions are given below:

(31) [Critical information foregrounded:] A thick cloud of smoke hung over the forest. [Initial mention of critical information.] The cloud was thick and black and began to fill the clear sky. Up ahead Carol could see a ranger directing traffic to slow down. *The forest was on fire* [test sentence].

(32) [Critical information backgrounded:] A thick cloud of smoke hung over the forest. Glancing to the side Carol could see a bee flying around the back seat. Both of the kids were jumping around, but made no attempt to free the insect. The relative quiet was broken by her children's piercing squeals. Carol had to pull off the road, stop the car and roll down the window herself. *The forest was on fire* [test sentence].

Subjects read the material sentence by sentence, using a procedure similar to that employed by Haviland and Clark (1974), and it was found that the reading time for the test sentence was significantly faster when the antecedent information was kept foregrounded than when it was allowed to slip into the background. Moreover, when it was kept active, the results showed that the subject's performance was not influenced by the number or type of intervening sentences. Similar results using anaphoric reference with pronouns have been reported by Anderson and Garrod (1979).

In a second experiment, Lesgold and his colleagues presented evidence that information that has been backgrounded can be reinstated again if there is a new reference to it. Subjects read paragraphs similar to those in the back-grounded condition of the first experiment, but in certain critical conditions part or all of the antecedent information was repeated just before the test sentence occurred. The results showed that the time taken to read the test sentence was shorter than that required in control conditions where there was no repetition of the earlier information. This result is consistent with the hypothesis that some of the information presented earlier was reinstated when it was mentioned again. However, it is also compatible with other, less interesting explanations. For instance, it could be that the second mention alone was responsible for bringing the information into the foreground and facilitating the processing of the test sentence. To eliminate this possibility the investigators conducted one further experiment along the same lines, except that in this study the information that was previously backgrounded was now completely removed from the text while the rest of the material was left relatively unchanged. Now, if the critical information in the earlier experiment had been foregrounded by the second mention alone the results of the modified experiment would have been comparable with those in the previous study. In fact, the difference in reading time between the foregrounded and backgrounded conditions was much greater when the earlier mention of the target information was removed than when it was kept in the paragraph. This suggests that the initial reference to the critical information must have made a contribution to the results of the first study, and it follows that it must have been reinstated (or recalled from long-term memory) during the course of reading the paragraph.

If there is some kind of reinstatement of earlier information it is clear that the representation of the earlier propositions must first be located. Presumably this is achieved by some kind of search process. There are various ways in which such a search might proceed. One possibility, suggested by Clark and Sengul (1979), is that readers might start by examining the immediately preceding sentence and work back from there to each of the earlier sentences in turn. Alternatively, they might start with the information that is currently active and then work systematically through the *propositional network* underlying the textual representation (Lesgold *et al.* 1979). At the moment there are no data that can be used to distinguish between these and various other viable accounts of the data. However, relevant experiments will almost certainly be completed in the near future.

Until now we have considered only one general way of linking propositions — that based on what Halliday and Hasan (1976) refer to as 'relatedness of reference'. It will be recalled that they identified another kind of relationship that can from ties between the underlying propositions of a text — that based on semantic connection or the relationship between 'facts' in a text (cf. Kintsch and van Dijk, 1978). Recently Haberlandt and Bingham (1978) have provided empirical support for a distinction of this kind by demonstrating that cohesive ties based on reference are not sufficient to make a text appear coherent. Subjects were required to read strings of sentences like example 33 or 34:

(33) Margaret punched Jim. Jim called the doctor. The doctor arrived.
(34) Margaret punched Jim. Jim liked the doctor. The doctor arrived.

The referential ties between the two types of sentence are identical, but the change of verb in example 34 appears to make the material less cohesive. This was confirmed by the time that subjects took to read the sentences in the two conditions. For the first sentence this was approximately the same in each case (which it obviously should have been since there was no difference), but for the other two sentences the reading time was significantly longer in the less cohesive sequences. It is not known in any detail how these nonreferential connections between sentences are established, but Haberlandt and Bingham suggest that readers automatically compute the prerequisites and the likely consequences of the action represented by the main verb in each sentence (cf. Schank, 1975), and that this additional inferred information is later checked against the content of subsequent sentences. In a sense this may be viewed as a kind of implicit use of reference. A sentence like *Jim called the doctor* presupposes that there is some reason for this action, and the reader may try to locate such a reason in the preceding text in the same way that he might search for the antecedent of a more explicit references. However, the 'action-consequence' relation is only one of several different types of connection between propositions (see Kintsch and van Dijk, 1978, for other possibilities) and the ideas underlying this kind of linking have not been worked out in enough detail to specify exactly how the process occurs.

4.10 CONSTRUCTING STORY HIERARCHIES

The discussion of proposition linking provides some idea of how local details of a text might be connected, but it gives no indication how certain propositions come to assume a greater importance than others in the passage—how the propositions are assembled into a hierarchical structure.

It seems clear that the process of constructing a story hierarchy must ential more than establishing the referential and semantic links between individual propositions. Indeed, the hierarchies considered by Thorndyke (1977) and Mandler and Johnson (1977) (see Section 4.2.4) were based explicitly on the *role* or *function* of the sentence in the text as a whole. Thus a sentence expressing an attempt to reach an important goal (i.e. one associated with the main theme of a passage) would normally be assigned to a higher level in the hierarchy than one describing an attempt to achieve a minor subgoal that is virtually irrelevant to the central theme.

How are sentences or propositions assigned to appropriate levels in the hierarchy? A general answer might be that this is achieved by parsing the passage using some kind of text grammar comparable with the 'story grammars' proposed by Rumelhart (1975) and Thorndyke (1977). This would allow the role of each new sentence to be determined and it would provide a basis for assessing its importance. While the exact details of this process are not yet known, there is clear evidence that readers can make accurate appraisals of the importance of individual sentences in a passage. In fact, they seem to be able to do this when the sentence first appears in the text. The evidence comes from a study reported by Shebilske (1978). Subjects were simply required to work through one of Thorndyke's stories, rating the importance of each sentence in turn. The results showed that the sentences that were high in the hierarchical structure tended to be judged to be more important than the others.

4.11 SUMMARY

Research based on memory techniques suggests that in comprehending a passage of prose readers construct the individual propositions expressed in the text and combine them to form an organized representation of the material. At some point (or points) in the process they tend to introduce information that is not expressed directly in the text.

Little is known about the processes by which propositions are constructed. However, it is generally agreed that part of the process involves sentence parsing. Two related 'theories' have been put forward to explain how this occurs. One of them, the Perceptual Strategies approach suggested by Fodor, Bever and Garrett (1974), is not comprehensive enough to provide a full account of the process. The other, based on Augmented Transition Networks, is almost certainly too general to be useful since it could probably be adapted to explain almost any conceivable pattern of data. Neither approach has received any clear empirical support.

A little more is known about the processes that are used to link propositions that are connected by cohesive ties. The evidence suggests that this may be achieved by a procedure referred to as the Given–New Strategy. That is, the reader appears to search the text base for a prior mention of the Given part of the current sentence, and when the information is located in memory it is used as an 'address' to integrate the New information into the text base. The evidence suggests that it is relatively easy to locate Given information which is close to the topic of the passage (i.e. information which remains foregrounded), but that a time-consuming reinstatement of the information becomes necessary if the topic shifts in such a way that the Given information is backgrounded.

In addition to providing an account of the way in which propositions might be linked, the Given–New theory also offers some suggestions about the way in which inferences are introduced into the text base. It is suggested that this occurs whenever the reader fails to locate any explicit earlier mention of the Given information. In an effort to overcome the difficulty it is argued that the reader constructs 'bridging assumptions' to establish a link with material which he *can* locate, thus enabling him to proceed with storing the new information in the normal way.

Finally, although the evidence from the recall of stories suggests that readers take account of the thematic function of individual sentences and that this influences the way in which the material is organized, there is little known about how this is achieved.

CHAPTER 5

Interaction of different processes in reading

5.1 PARALLEL PROCESSING IN READING

The previous chapters have described many of the processes that play an important part in reading, starting with the analysis of the most peripheral visual representation of the page and culminating with the processes that are used to construct textual representations of the material. For the sake of convenience we have considered each of these subprocesses in isolation and we have often treated the different operations as if they occurred in a strict sequence, totally independently of one another.

This is obviously a gross oversimplification. There is no reason why a reader should not be engaged in several processes at the same time, and if he is there is a strong possibility that the processes will interact with one another.

It is convenient to distinguish between two broad ways in which such interactions might occur. First, different operations might influence one another because they draw upon the same resources (e.g. both may require a certain amount of attention). With interactions of this kind the rate of progress in one part of the system may be influenced by any competing activity elsewhere in the system. Thus, if one process makes heavy demands on the shared resources others will be slowed or impaired in some way. In the second kind of interaction, the effects are caused not by the competing activity itself but by the *products* of this activity. That is to say, processing in one part of the system may be facilitated or inhibited by the *information* made available to it from another part of the system. (This distinction is similar to one drawn by Norman and Bobrow, 1975.)

This chapter will examine some of the interdependencies between the different subprocesses of reading. First we shall consider interactions caused by competing activity within the system, and later we shall turn to what might be termed data-sharing interactions.

5.2 INTERFERENCE CAUSED BY COMPETING ACTIVITY IN DIFFERENT SUBPROCESSES OF READING

Before reviewing the experimental evidence on interference effects of this kind it is important to consider a few methodological problems that are encountered in research on this issue. The basic difficulty arises from the fact that it is impossible to 'dissect' the reading process experimentally without destroying or at least distorting the process. This makes it very difficult to determine whether one subprocess is influenced by another. Most investigators have approached the problem in a roundabout way by instructing their subjects to perform two competing tasks, one of which (the *primary* task) is chosen to represent a particular subskill of reading and the other (the *secondary* task) to provide a measure of the processing demands of the first. If the two tasks truly represent concurrent subprocesses in reading then it seems reasonable to assume that any interactions that come to light in the experimental situation will also occur in normal reading. Unfortunately, the tasks that have been used to date bear no more than a marginal resemblance to the processes that occur in reading and so it is usually not safe to generalize the findings in this way. Admittedly, such generalizations could be made if it could be shown that a process which interferes with one secondary task will also interfere with any other secondary task. However, as Norman and Bobrow (1975) have pointed out, this is not usually the case. A process may have virtually no effect on one secondary task and a dramatic effect on another. In short, this means that most inferences about interference between subprocesses in reading have to be treated with considerable caution. Nevertheless, it may be useful to document some of the conclusions that have been reached to date.

There is certainly evidence that many of the main subskills of reading may be influenced by competing activities that are broadly similar to other concurrent operations in reading. Starting with some of the more peripheral operations, Posner, Boies, Eichelman and Taylor (1969) and Phillips and Christie (1977) have presented some evidence that Short-Term Visual Memory (STVM) is impaired when people engage in a concurrent arithmetic task (adding digits). It will be recalled from Chapter 2 that STVM plays an important role in the initial extraction of visual information from the page. Thus, it is *possible* that the extraction process becomes less efficient when there are heavy processing demands at other levels of the reading process. However, it would certainly not be safe to conclude that this does occur on the basis of present evidence. For one thing, the subjects in the interference experiments were required to maintain visual information over an interval which is considerably longer than that which would be required in normal reading (four seconds in the case of the Phillips and Christie study). If the effects of attention are restricted to tasks in which visual information has to be maintained for reasonably long periods (say, half a second or more) than processes such as visual extraction would not be subject to interference. A second reservation about the conclusion is that the arithmetic interference task does not resemble any of the subprocesses of reading, and so it is difficult to tell whether reading processes would have comparable effects. Thus the possibility that reading is impaired as a result of interference with STVM is no more than a speculative suggestion at the moment.

Turning to a slightly later stage in the processing sequence, there seems to be evidence that at least some aspects of the recognition process are automatic (i.e. that they are not influenced in any way by concurrent activity). Posner and Boies (1971) investigated the attentional demands of letter recognition by using a dual task technique. In this paradigm the subject's primary task was to indicate whether two successively presented visual letters had the same name. The secondary task was simply to press a button whenever they heard a brief burst of white noise. The time taken to respond to the auditory signal was taken as a measure of the processing demands of the main task. Using this technique, Posner and Boies found that provided the signal occurred during an interval of about 300 ms after the appearance of the first letter in the main task, the response latency was no longer than that in a control condition in which there were no competing demands on attention. Other results indicated that the letter was very likely to have been encoded during this interval, and so the data suggest that letter recognition does not require processing capacity. This conclusion might be criticized on the grounds that the secondary task may not be sufficiently demanding to provide a proper test of the hypothesis. However, the same conclusion has been reached using other techniques (e.g. Shiffrin and Gardner, 1972; Shiffrin and Schneider, 1977; Egeth, Jonides and Wall, 1972), and so there is some reason to believe that it is valid.

On the basis of research of this kind some investigators (e.g. LaBerge and Samuels, 1974) have assumed that familiar stimuli other than letters are also recognized automatically. However, experiments using words suggest that this is not the case. Becker (1976) conducted a study in which the subject's primary task was to indicate as rapidly as possible with one hand whether a string of letters spelt an English word. The secondary task was to respond with the other hand to an auditory signal which was presented either 90 or 190 ms after the onset of the visual stimulus. The signal was either a high-pitched or a low-pitched tone. In one condition the subjects were instructed to press different keys in response to high- and low-pitched tones, and in another they were required to press the same key whichever tone occurred. In both tasks it was found that the latency of the response to the auditory signal was slower when it was presented with a lexical decision task than when it was presented alone. Also, when the letter string was a low-frequency word the mean response time was longer than that for high-frequency words. Finally, the difference between the mean latencies in the choice and simple secondary tasks was larger for low-frequency words than for high-frequency words. Taken together these results provide fairly clear evidence that word recognition as represented by the lexical decision task is not an automatic process. As before, however, the distraction tasks in this study do not resemble any of the subprocesses of reading, and it is therefore a matter of speculation whether word identification is influenced by the kinds of concurrent processing that might occur in reading.

There has been little research on the attentional demands of the reading processes that occur after word recognition. In fact, the only real evidence comes from phoneme-monitoring studies (see Chapter 4) which, of course, are not based on reading at all. Experiments of this kind are only informative about reading processes to the extent that the operations of interest are shared by listening and reading. It will be recalled that, in the phoneme-monitoring task, subjects listen to a sentence and are required to press a button as soon as they hear a target phoneme. Several studies have shown that the monitoring latency is increased during sentences such as doubly self-embedded sentences in which it is particularly difficult to determine the syntactic structure (e.g. Foss and Lynch, 1969; Hakes and Foss, 1970). These results suggest that in listening, at least, certain parsing processes compete with other concurrent activity. If the processes in reading operate in a similar way, then it may be reasonable to generalize these findings to the reading task. However, as before, it is clear that the evidence available does not permit us to draw any firm conclusions at the moment.

To recapitulate, the experiments that have been conducted on the effects of attention on the subprocesses of reading have typically made use of secondary tasks that do not closely resemble any of the subprocesses of reading. For this reason it is difficult to draw any firm conclusions about interference between different subprocesses. There is some evidence that word recognition and certain parsing processes interfere with concurrent tasks that have relatively low attentional demands. It seems likely that many of the subprocesses of reading are just as demanding as these tasks and, if this is the case, it is reasonable to assume that processes beyond the level of word recognition interfere with one another to some extent.

5.3   INTERACTIONS CAUSED BY DATA-SHARING:
THE NOTION OF TOP-DOWN PROCESSING

The second kind of interaction considered in Section 5.1 was that in which the activity in one subprocess is influenced by information made available by another subprocess.

A rather trivial form of this might occur if the output of one process is the major source of raw material for another. In this situation the efficiency of the first process will almost certainly have a direct effect on the analysis that takes place in the next stage. A much more interesting type of interaction occurs when a process is influenced by information from some other source (i.e. information that does not come directly from the previous stage of analysis). The most widely discussed form of this occurs when early operations in the processing sequence are affected by previous (or concurrent) activity at higher levels in the system. As an illustration of this kind of interaction consider the sentence: *The service was conducted by the priest.* Here the recognition of the word *priest* might be facilitated by the fact that the semantic and syntactic analysis of the first six words of the sentence places strong constraints on the kind of word that can appear in the final position. If this does occur (and the evidence for this will be considered shortly) then it is clear that word recognition must be subject to influences derived partly from processing at higher levels in the system.

With the first kind of interaction the processing starts with the raw input and passes through increasingly refined analysis until the meaning of the text is eventually determined. This kind of processing is therefore known as *data-driven* or *bottom-up* processing (see Norman, 1976). (The term 'bottom-up' simply refers to the fact that the processing of a stimulus starts at the more peripheral levels and proceeds to 'higher' or more sophisticated levels in the system.)

The second kind of interaction is produced when decisions made at the higher levels in the processing system are used to guide choices at lower levels. This is referred to as *top-down* processing. In order to analyse the text in this way the reader has to draw upon his knowledge of the world and his knowledge of the structure of the sentences. For this reason this kind of analysis has also been termed *conceptually-driven* processing (Norman, 1976). It is obvious that bottom-up interactions make a significant contribution to processing during most if not all of the substages of reading. However, when it comes to top-down processing the position in much less clear. Do interactions of this kind occur often and do they have an important influence on reading performance? Answers to these questions will be outlined over the next few sections. To set the scene we begin by presenting a more detailed account of some of the top-down processes that might play a role in fluent reading.

5.4 TOP-DOWN PROCESSES POSTULATED IN THE LITERATURE

Over the last few years investigators have suggested that there are top-down influences at most levels of processing including the extraction of visual information from the page, the recognition of words and the processes that are employed to parse sentences.

Top-down effects at relatively peripheral stages of analysis have been proposed by Goodman (1967) and by Marcel (1974). According to Goodman, top-down processing may have an effect on operations as early in the sequence as those used to extract graphic cues from the page. Thus, he has argued that the reader uses graphic cues to form a 'perceptual image' which is 'partly what he sees and partly what he expects to see' (see Singer and Ruddell, 1976, p. 307). Presumably this perceptual image corresponds to the STVM trace that is used as the raw material for the recognition process (see Section 2.6). If this is the case, then Goodman's hypothesis appears to be that the reader's expectations affect either the read-out from the icon or the integration of visual information in STVM. Marcel's (1974) position is fairly similar. He argues that context might facilitate the process of extracting visual features from the page, and he speculates that this might allow processing capacity to be distributed away from the foveal region to the more peripheral areas of the visual field. If this happens it might allow information to be picked up at greater distances from the fixation point than would be possible in the absence of contextual effects.

The view that top-down processes influence the most peripheral stages in reading is not widely accepted, but a large number of investigators have concluded that the next process—word recognition—is influenced by the reader's expectations (cf. Huey, 1908; Morton, 1964, 1969; Smith, 1971;

Rumelhart and Siple, 1974; Stevens and Rumelhart, 1975, and many others). Detailed accounts of how these interactions occur vary from one investigator to another.

Huey (1908) has suggested that the reader expects a particular word or type of word at each point in the text and that 'there is a "set" or "predisposition" in its direction which may need but few supplemental signs to set off its proper perception' (p. 108). This proposal can clearly be considered as a form of top-down processing since expectations of this kind could only be set up by processes that draw upon the results of prior analysis at levels beyond that of word recognition (e.g. syntactic analysis).

Morton (1964, 1969) has put forward a more mechanistic account of the process. His suggestion, expressed in terms of his logogen model of word recognition (see Section 3.7), is basically that logogens are activated by context in exactly the same way as they are by visual information. Thus, if a word is highly predictable in a given context, the logogen count is incremented with the result that less visual information is required before the threshold is reached and the word is recognized.

Other suggestions about top-down processing in word recognition have been made by Rumelhart and his colleagues and by Smith (1971). Rumelhart's proposals are incorporated in a model of word recognition described by Rumelhart and Siple (1974). According to this model contextual information is used to choose between individual members of a class of words that are compatible with the visual information extracted from the display and, in the end, a decision is made to identify the stimulus as the item in the sample that was most to be expected given the context. According to the account offered by Smith (1971) the visual information is used to select a word from a range of possibilities that are compatible with the context.

In addition to these proposals about word recognition it has been suggested that top-down processes have an influence on parsing procedures (e.g. Fodor, Garrett and Bever, 1968). This suggestion has already been considered in detail elsewhere (see Sections 4.4 and 4.6), but it should perhaps be mentioned again for the sake of completeness. It will be recalled that Fodor *et al.* proposed that syntactic processing would be easier for sentences containing transitive verbs (for which only one structural hypothesis needs to be entertained) than for sentences containing complement verbs (which require two or more alternative hypotheses to be considered). In other words, it is suggested that syntactic processing is influenced by the reader's expectations.

In each of the proposals considered so far the author has specified quite clearly the level at which the contextual effects are assumed to operate. In a few cases researchers have placed strong emphasis on top-down processing without specifying which subskills are affected (e.g. Hochberg, 1970; Levin and Kaplan, 1970). Hochberg (1970, p. 85) claimed that reading is 'an active process, involving the continual generation and testing of hypotheses'. He argued that readers set up predictions about the contents of a passage before the relevant part of the text is reached, and that the new material is then processed in the light of these hypotheses. If the predictions are confirmed the material is processed easily and quickly. Otherwise the process of comprehension is somehow retarded. While the locus of the contextual effect is not spelt out, it is clear from Hochberg's account that a tentative meaning is assigned to the text *before* the words are fixated by the eyes, and so it is clearly implied that some kind of top-down processing is involved.

The suggestions outlined in the preceding paragraphs constitute a family of top-down hypotheses many of which emphasize effects at different levels of analysis. Clearly these hypotheses are independent of one another, and if any one of them were confirmed or rejected this would not necessarily have any implications for the rest. The evidence in favour of each of the hypotheses will be presented in the next two sections. However, before proceeding with this it may be useful to make some general observations concerning the circumstances in which top-down processing is most likely to influence performance.

A prerequisite for top-down processing is that the process of formulating hypotheses or expectations should be completed rapidly enough for the results to influence the outcome of the processes which are said to be facilitated. Clearly this would not occur if top-down processes were invariably slower than those employing raw material from lower levels of analysis. Unfortunately, virtually nothing is known about how long it would take to complete any of the putative top-down processes in reading and so there is no easy way of telling how feasible each of the suggestions outlined above might be. One thing is relatively clear, however, and this is that any manipulation which has the effect of retarding bottom-up processing will increase the likelihood that the top-down contribution will become available before the process is completed. It follows that top-down processing is most likely to influence performance under conditions where the quality of the print is poor or where bottom-up processing is held up for some other reason. In the next section we present evidence which supports the view that top-down processing occurs under these circumstances, and later we shall examine whether similar effects occur under conditions which are more typical of those in normal reading.

5.5 EVIDENCE FOR TOP-DOWN PROCESSING IN STUDIES WITH POOR STIMULUS QUALITY

There is a considerable amount of evidence that readers make use of contextual information when the visual quality of the reading material is poor. Much of the evidence is based on experiments in which the stimulus quality is reduced either by presenting the material very briefly or by obscuring or distorting it in some way. In a typical study using the first approach, Morton (1964) used a threshold technique to examine the effect of context on word recognition. In one condition the target word appeared in a highly predictive context (e.g. *At the sink she washed a* . . . [target word:] *cup*). In another condition the context was relatively unpredictive (e.g. *He hoped to win the* . . . *cup*), while in a third the 'context' consisted simply of a row of *X*s. The target word was flashed briefly in the appropriate position at the end of the context display and the subject was instructed to try to identify it. If he failed, the exposure duration was increased in a series of equal steps until the response was correct on two successive occasions. The results of the experiment showed that the recognition threshold was significantly lower when the word was easy to predict than it was in the other two conditions. This suggests that the subjects used top-down processes to anticipate the target word and to facilitate the processes entailed in identifying it. Other studies using slightly different techniques have shown that the probability of identifying a briefly presented word varies systematically as a function of its predictability (Tulving and Gold, 1963) and as a function of the proportion of the context sentence that is available to the subject (Tulving, Mandler and Baumal, 1964).

In the experiments outlined above the test stimulus consisted of a single word. Similar effects have been demonstrated in studies where several words appear together in the test display. For example, Marcel (1974) showed that the number of words that subjects are able to report from such a display increases with the degree of sequential constraint between the words and their preceding context (and between the words themselves). Contextual effects have also been shown in studies in which a text is suddenly obscured while the subject is reading aloud. For example, Levin and Kaplan (1970) have shown that the number of words that people are able to report after the disappearance of the text depends on the degree of sequential constraint between the words. A comparison between active and passive sentences, for instance, revealed that subjects tend to recall more words towards the ends of passives (where the material is relatively predictable) than at any point in actives or at the beginnings of passives where the material is less constrained. It is not clear whether effects of this kind occur as the material is interpreted or while the information is held in short-term memory prior to report (cf. Baddeley, 1964), but whatever the locus, the findings provide clear evidence that performance is influenced by contextual constraints under these conditions.

In each of the studies presented so far the stimulus quality was reduced by reducing the time for which the text was available. Contextual effects have also been shown in tasks in which the text was degraded or distorted in various ways. In one experiment conducted by Forster (1970), subjects were presented with blurred typewritten copies of strings of words and they were given an unlimited period of time to decypher the words. In one condition the strings of words formed ordinary English sentences while in another the words appeared in a haphazard order. As might be expected, the results showed that the proportion of words identified was significantly greater in the former condition. Presumably this result occurred because the subjects were able to use sequential constraints to choose between alternative possibilities. In another experiment using the same technique Forster and Olbrei (1973) showed that performance with plausible sentences such as *The hungry boy found some dry bread* was better than that for implausible sentences like *The clever fly made some tiny drugs.* Since both kinds of sentence were perfectly grammatical, this findings suggests that semantic factors play some part in the reconstruction process.

Contextual effects are also obtained when words are degraded in other ways. Perfetti and Roth (1981) conducted an experiment in which stimulus clarity was reduced by removing a proportion of the dots in a computer-controlled display of the target word. Subjects were required to read and pronounce each word either in isolation or in the context of a well-structured story. The results showed that for each of the four different degrees of degradation employed (ranging from 14 per cent to 35 per cent of dots removed) readers recognized a higher proportion of words when they appeared in context than when they appeared alone.

Finally, Kolers (1970) used geometrically transformed texts in one further series of experiments employing distorted materials. Eight transformations were used in all. These included materials in which the page was turned upside-down or laterally inverted, and in some conditions the individual letters were inverted as well. In one experiment the subjects were given a page of each type of transformed material and they were instructed to read the text aloud. All of the errors were recorded and it was found that they showed a marked sensitivity to the grammatical constraints in the text. In particular, Kolers observed that on the occassions when one word was replaced by another, the word substituted tended to belong to the same grammatical class as the original word. As in the previous studies this indicates that the subjects were probably using contextual information in their attempts to decypher the words.

In the investigations considered so far it is likely that the experimental conditions encouraged the subjects to make use of the context. In each case the stimulus quality was reduced and this presumably reduced the probability that identification processes reached completion before they could be influenced by contextual constraints. There are various other circumstances in which the emphasis would tend to be placed on top-down processes. In particular, a reader might employ this strategy if he has difficulty in recognizing a word in spite of the fact that the printing is perfectly clear. This kind of difficulty might occur quite frequently with inexperienced readers, and hence young children and other poor readers might be expected to show contextual effects even when the reading material is not degraded. Studies by Goodman (1967) and by Weber (1970) have confirmed that they do. In each of these investigations children read a passage of prose and their errors were noted for subsequent analysis. As in Kolers's (1970) study, it was found that the overwhelming majority of the substitution errors were grammatically correct. This indicates quite clearly that the children must have made use of contextual cues in their efforts to read the material.

To recapitulate, the results summarized in this section indicate that in reading situations where the visual quality of the reading matter is poor, people tend to make use of contextual information in their efforts to decypher the text. The evidence also suggests that the same thing happens when the reader is so inexperienced that he is frequently unable to decode the words using the visual stimulus alone. As pointed out above, this does not establish that top-down processes are used by fluent readers with legible materials in normal reading tasks. The evidence for top-down processing in these circumstances will be examined in the next section.

5.6 EVIDENCE FOR TOP-DOWN PROCESSING: LEGIBLE MATERIALS AND FLUENT READERS

Most of the work on this issue has concentrated on the effects that occur at the level of word recognition and so this aspect of processing will be considered first.

5.6.1 Effects on the word recognition process

There is a good deal of evidence that the recognition of undegraded words can be influenced by context in just the same way as it is when the words are degraded. This has been demonstrated using a number of different experimental techniques, all of which adopt the same broad approach. An experiment reported by Schuberth and Eimas (1977) is fairly typical of these studies and can be used to illustrate the approach and the general findings. Subjects were presented with an incomplete sentence which remained on display for 1.5 seconds and was then followed immediately by a frame consisting of a string of letters. The subject was instructed to indicate as quickly as possible whether or not these letters spelt an English word. In one condition all the strings that were, in fact, words fitted in well with the preceding context (e.g. *The puppy chewed the ... bone*). In another, they were incongruous (e.g. *The puppy chewed the ... hour*). In a third condition the context sentence was replaced by a blank, white field. There were several other experimental manipulations but these are not of immediate concern in the present discussion. The results of the experiment showed that there was a facilitatory effect for congruous words—the response latencies for these words were significantly shorter than those for isolated words. There was also a significant inhibition effect for incongruous words.

Broadly similar results have been obtained in a number of other studies. In a series of experiments very similar to the one reported by Schuberth and Eimas (1977), Fischler and Bloom (1979) were able to demonstrate both facilitation and inhibition effects, but the facilitation effects only occurred when the target word was highly predictable. Using a slightly different technique, Perfetti, Goldman and Hogaboam (1979) found that the time that subjects took to pronounce a visually presented target word was shorter if the word was shown immediately after they had read or heard relevant contextual material (in the form of a story) than when it was presented in the absence of any context. Comparable facilitation effects have also been reported by Roth, Perfetti and Lesgold (1979) and Perfetti and Roth (1981).

Stanovich and West (Stanovich, 1980, 1981; West and Stanovich, 1978; Stanovich and West, 1979, 1981) have conducted several experiments that are similar to the study reported by Schuberth and Eimas, except that in most cases the subject was required to *pronounce* the target word rather than to make a lexical decision about it. In almost every experiment if was found that a congruous context produced a strong facilitation effect. Unlike Schuberth and Eimas, however, Stanovich and West found no evidence of inhibition effects in adults when the interval between the incongruous context and the target word was short. The inhibition effect only became apparent when there was a delay of 750 ms or more before the critical word was presented.

Taken together these studies provide convincing evidence that, in suitable circumstances, the processing of undegraded words can be affected by the context in which they appear. An important question remains, however, and it is this: Are these effects likely to occur under normal reading conditions? To answer this question it is necessary to consider facilitation and inhibition effects separately.

As far as the facilitation effects are concerned, the answer is that they probably do not operate fast enough to influence fluent reading. In each of the experiments considered so far there was a short interval between the point at which the subject finished reading the context and the point at which the target word was presented. In many cases, a delay of half a second or more was deliberately introduced into the stimulus sequence (e.g. in experiments by Perfetti *et al.*, 1979, Expt I; West and Stanovich, 1978; Fischler and Bloom, 1979; Stanovich, 1980, Expts I–IV; Kleiman, 1980). In others, there was a delay while the subjects looked up from a card on which the context material was printed and waited for the target word to be displayed on a screen (e.g. Perfetti *et al.*, 1979, Expt 2; Perfetti and Roth, 1981; Roth *et al.*, 1979), or a delay while the subject pronounced the last word of the context before the experimenter initiated the target display (in the Stanovich and West experiments).

These delays may be crucial for demonstrating facilitation effects. It may be essential to have a pause which allows the subject time to formulate his predictions or expectations about the target word before the stimulus is actually presented. If this is the case then the facilitation effect should become less marked as the interval is reduced. The evidence suggests that this is exactly what does happen.

In a recent experiment Mitchell and Green (1980) examined facilitation effects by using a variant of the subject-paced reading task described in Chapter 3. The words of a passage of prose were presented individually in a computer-controlled display. Each word remained on display until the subject pressed a button, at which point it was replaced immediately by the next word in the passage. At ten points in the passage, strings of letters that did not spell English words were introduced into the stimulus sequence. The subject was instructed to work through the list of words, pressing the button as quickly as possible whenever the letter spelt an English word, but counting to ten before proceeding whenever a nonword was displayed. In a control condition the instructions were exactly the same, but the materials consisted of a random list of words rather than a passage of prose. This control list contained 20 of the content words and all of the function words that appeared in the experimental condition.

The remaining words were replaced by words of the same grammatical class and approximately the same length and frequency. The order in which the words appeared was randomized so that the sequence bore no resemblance at all to English text.

We predicted that if the subjects had time to use top-down processes they would be able to make their decisions more rapidly when the words appeared as part of the text than when they appeared in a random order. In fact, the mean viewing time for the critical words in the text condition (570 ms) was not significantly faster than that for the same set of words in the random condition (595 ms). Moreover, none of the common function words such as *the* or *and* revealed any differences.

The important difference between this study and the earlier investigations is that the target word was displayed as soon as the subject indicated that he had read the preceding word. The fact that there was less evidence of a facilitation effect under these conditions suggests that the duration of the pause may be important in making contextual effects possible. Of course, it could be argued that the subjects in this experiment were responding before making the lexical decision, or that there was no effect of textual structure because the subjects in the first condition were not processing the materials as a text. However, neither of these suggestions seems likely. If the subjects had responded before making the lexical decision they would have made quick responses to the nonwords as well as the words. In fact, this only occurred on about 12 per cent of the trials. It also seems unlikely that the subjects failed to take account of the structure because in constructing the materials for the text condition we had inserted two words that failed to fit in with the preceding context, and it turned out that the viewing times for these words were significantly longer than those for the same words appearing in the appropriate context elsewhere in the passage (i.e. there was an inhibition effect). This indicates that the failure to find an effect in the main part of the experiment cannot be attributed to the fact that subjects simply failed to take account of the textual structure of the materials.

While there was some evidence that subjects in this experiment read the materials as prose, it is clear that the task requirements were appreciably different from those in normal reading, and so it is conceivable that contextual effects would be obtained in more conventional tasks. However, other experiments employing the subject-paced reading task provided no evidence in support of this view. In one study (Mitchell and Green, 1978, Expt III) subjects were instructed to read a 1000-word passage based on an extract from Tolstoy's *War and Peace*. The materials were presented three words at a time and the subjects were told to expect a simple comprehension test at the end of the experiment. Distributed throughout the passage there were points at which alternative versions of the passage could be presented. In each case one of the phrases (the test phrase) was the same in the different versions. However, the material that came before this phrase was varied in the different conditions. The alternative versions were written in such a way that the text phrase was highly predictable in one case and neutral (but completely acceptable) in the other. The overall gist of the passage remained the same in both cases. Half of the subjects read each version of the text and the viewing times for the test phrases were compared in the two conditions. The results showed that predictable phrases were read slightly faster than the more neutral phrases (1864 ms compared with 1895 ms). However, as in the previous study, this difference did not approach significance. Again, the effect of reducing the pause between the context and the target word was to reduce the magnitude of a facilitation effect.

Independent support for these findings comes from a study conducted by Stanovich (1981). He responded to our observations about the relatively long pauses in his paradigm by attempting to eliminate as many of the delays as possible. The main change was that the target display was triggered by the subject himself as soon as he had read the last context word (rather than by the experimenter when he *heard* the subject pronounce the last word). The materials and the experimental apparatus were exactly the same as those used in an earlier study in which there were relatively long pauses (Stanovich and West, 1979, Expt II). The results of the modified experiment showed that the facilitation effect was reduced from 111 ms to a nonsignificant 16 ms.

In another recent study, McConkie and Zola (1981) went even further in eliminating artificial pauses by observing subjects' eye movements as they read more conventionally presented texts. They found that the duration of the fixations on highly predictable words were only 14 ms shorter than those appearing in more neutral contexts.

Overall, then, the data suggest that facilitation effects are reduced and become statistically insignificant as the timing characteristics of the experimental task approach those that occur in fluent reading. It is possible that some small facilitation effects remain under normal reading conditions, but if they do it is clear that they are not very important determinants of reading performance.

Turning to inhibition effects, the picture is rather different. As mentioned above, Stanovich (1981) has maintained that there are no inhibition effects when the interval between the context and the target word is less than about 750 ms. However, other investigators (e.g. Schuberth and Eimas, 1977; Fischler and Bloom, 1979; Mitchell and Green, 1978, 1980) *have* demonstrated significant effects within this range, and in the case of our own studies the anomaly effects were present despite the fact that the target word was displayed as soon as the subjects had indicated that they had read the context material. It seems likely that the discrepancies between Stanovich's findings and the rest can be attributed to the fact that there were different demand characteristics in the different studies. For example, it appears that the proportion of words presented in anomalous contexts was higher in the Stanovich experiments than in any of the other studies, and this may have led subjects to place less weight on context than they do under conditions when it is normally informative.

Whatever the explanation of the difference, it seems that inhibition effects *can* occur when the interval between the context and the target word is very short. If this conclusion is correct, it is important to explain how it is possible to obtain inhibition effects under conditions where facilitation effects do not occur. Clearly, if a subject's expectations or predictions do not become available early enough to *facilitate* word recognition they are unlikely to arrive early enough to *inhibit* the process.

One way out of the dilemma is to assume that the inhibitory effects occur *after* word recognition and that they have no influence at all on the identification process itself. This could occur if newly identified words are submitted to a post-access check to confirm whether they are compatible with the prior context (cf. Mitchell and Green, 1978, 1980). On trials with anomalous target words, the outcome of this test would reveal that there was some kind of inconsistency between the target and the preceding materials and it can be assumed that this information holds up the execution of the response for a short time. If this checking procedure is partially under strategic control this could explain the inconsistencies regarding the conditions under which inhibition effects occur. Subjects might apply the procedure when they expect all of the words in the text to be compatible with their contexts or when they expect this to happen frequently enough for the outcome of the test to help them make the required response in the experimental task.

This account of inhibition effects in reading would be strengthened if it could be demonstrated that the delays in processing anomalous materials are introduced in subprocesses other than those responsible for the identification of words. One technique for dealing with issues of this kind is a method known as the Additive Factor Technique (Sternberg, 1969). This approach is based on a number of arguments and assumptions that have to be spelt out before it is possible to show how the technique can be applied to the present problem. The first assumption is that processing is carried out in a series of stages with the completion of the first process triggering the second stage and so on. It is further assumed that by manipulating suitable variables it is possible to increase or decrease the duration of individual subprocesses without changing the end-product of the processing stage in any way. Under this kind of scheme experimental variables that influence distinct stages of processing should have additive effects. That is to say, any increases or decreases in overall latency produced by changes in one variable should not affect (or be affected by) changes in latency caused by other variables. (This follows because influences at an early stage of processing should merely hold back or bring forward the analysis tackled in the latter stages and this in itself should have no effect on the duration of any subsequent processing). When two experimental variables affect the *same* stage (or stages) a different pattern of results is expected. Here the most likely outcome is that the two variables should interact in some way.

Given these arguments it is easy to see that the Additive Factor Technique may provide a way of determining whether or not contextual effects are introduced during word recognition. If the inhibition effect occurs during the recognition process then context should interact with any other variable that influences identification time. On the other hand, if the effect occurs at some other stage before or after word recognition then the effect of the two types of manipulation should be additive.

The results of two recent experiments tend to favour the second alternative. Mitchell and Green (1980) conducted an experiment in which students were required to read a passage using the subject-paced reading task described a little earlier. At various points in the text were test phrases that could be rendered incompatible with the preceding context by changing a single word in the immediately preceding display. For each subject half of the displays were syntactically and semantically acceptable in context and half of them were anomalous. Also, in each condition half of the displays were overwritten by an irregular pattern of dots and the other half were left intact. The results showed that the time taken to read the critical displays was increased both by degrading the display (which presumably postpones or slows down the recognition process) and by removing a word from the context display (which produced the inhibition effect). However, the most important finding for the present purposes was that these two variables did not interact significantly and this suggests that they influence distinct stages of processing. If degradation has a direct effect on word identification this result can be taken to imply that the inhibition effect is introduced at some other stage in the analysis.

The second study was conducted by Schuberth, Spoehr and Lane (1981). In this case the subjects were required to make lexical decisions about degraded or intact words appearing in neutral or anomalous contexts (see Schuberth *et al.* 1981, Expt II). As before, there was no significant interaction between the two variables. In this experiment the target items also varied in word frequency—a variable which many investigators consider to affect word recognition. Like degradation, this manipulation also produced effects that were independent of the context effects. The results were therefore completely consistent with the view that contextual effects are not introduced during the recognition process. Since it seems most unlikely that context could have any influence *before* word recognition, the results can be taken to provide a certain amount of support for interpreting the inhibition effect as a phenomenon associated with post-access checking.

Summarizing, then, it has been argued that while contextual inhibition effects seem to occur under normal (or near-normal) reading conditions, they are not the result of top-down processing. Word recognition is not guided or influenced in any way by the contextual information. Rather, the identification process runs its course and produces a decision which is then checked against the earlier material. In other words, the results suggest that fluent word recognition can be characterized as a bottom-up process—a conclusion which is entirely consistent with the failure to find facilitation effects under conditions approximating those of normal reading.

Before accepting this conclusion it is necessary to consider the possibility that we have failed to demonstrate top-down effects simply because the kinds of context used were not suitable for this purpose. In all of the studies considered so far, the contextual information was presented in the form of an incomplete sentence. Two other kinds of context could also play a significant role in fluent reading: (1) contexts consisting of single words that are highly associated with the target word and (2) contexts that might have influences extending over sentence boundaries.

It is well-established that the processing of a word can be facilitated when it is preceded by another word that is semantically related. For instance, Meyer and Schvaneveldt (1971) showed that the time taken to decide that a string of letters like *nurse* is a word is faster when it is preceded by a word like *doctor* than when it is preceded by an unrelated word such as *bread*. This facilitation effect occurs even when the interval between the presentation of the two words is very small (Fischler and Goodman, 1978), and so there seems little doubt that it could have an effect under the timing constraints of fluent reading. However, there are reasons for believing that these priming effects make little contribution to the processing of normal English texts.

The main factor limiting the role of priming effects in reading is that the facilitation effect is grossly attenuated and perhaps even destroyed completely when one or more unrelated words are interposed between the context word and the target word (Gough, Alford and Holley-Wilcox, 1979). This means that in reading the facilitation could only occur at points in the passage where successive words are semantically related. As Gough *et al.* (1979), Forster (1979) and others have pointed out, this probably only happens very rarely and so it seems unlikely that lexical priming effects make any useful contribution to normal reading. In fact, if these facilitation effects are active when a person is reading text it seems that they would almost certainly be counterproductive. The reason for this is simply that the most likely candidates for a target word in the context of a sentence are words that are *not* associated in any way with the immediately preceding context and so, if semantically related words are facilitated at the expense of other possibilities, this would merely serve to misdirect the process of word recognition.

The second kind of context would be much more likely to have beneficial effects in reading because the facilitation effects would not be local and priming would not have to be directed rapidly from one class of words to another as the reader progressed through the sentence. This would tend to shift the balance in favour of top-down effects because, unlike the situation with local effects, there could easily be time for the reader's expectations to be formulated before the critical part of the text is reached.

What kinds of material could remain primed over one or more sentence of a passage? An obvious possibility is a set of props or actors associated with a familiar setting or activity (e.g. kitchen utensils in a kitchen, or candles, cake, guests, etc., in a 'birthday party' setting). As long as the textual setting remains unchanged there is a possibility that some of the associated terms will be mentioned. The relevant words could therefore be kept active over the course of several sentences and over this period the identification of these words might be facilitated.

This possibility has been put to the test in an experiment conducted by Noel

Sharkey, a research student at Exeter University. On each trial the subject was presented with a computer display containing one or two sentences which made it clear that an individual was in some familiar situation or 'script' (cf. Schank and Abelson, 1977; Bower, Black and Turner, 1979). For example, one pair of context sentences was as follows: 'Colonel Jones strolled on the railway platform. He sat down to wait for his train.' The subject was required to read this background material and press a button when he was ready to proceed. As soon as he did this the display was replaced either by an English word or by a nonsense word and the subject had to respond to this by making a conventional lexical decision. Half of the words were script-related props (e.g. *bench* in the current example) and the other half were unrelated words matched for length and frequency (e.g. *waste*). The results showed that the responses to the script-related words were significantly faster than those in the control condition. This finding shows that script-based predictions can remain active over at least one or two sentences, and while the task is a bit too artificial for us to conclude that comparable effects occur under more conventional reading conditions, there does not seem to be any reason why this should not be the case. If they do occur in normal conditions then this may be one of the few ways in which top-down processing occurs in fluent word recognition.

In conclusion, then, there is little reason to believe that top-down processing plays an important part in word recognition under fluent reading conditions. It is easy enough to demonstrate that context has an effect on performance but, with the possible exception of the script-based effect just considered, the only effects that occur with short intervals between context and target are *inhibitory* effects. Since these are most plausibly interpreted as bottom-up effects, it seems that top-down processing must be restricted to circumstances in which the normal recognition processes are held up in some way. In the next section we shall consider how contextual effects occur when this happens.

5.6.2 Theoretical accounts of contextual effects in word recognition

Before considering specific proposals on the nature of contextual effects it is important to decide whether or not all facilitation effects are produced by a single mechanism.

Stanovich (1981) has presented evidence which suggests that more than one kind of mechanism may be involved (see also and Stanovich, 1978; Stanovich and West, 1979, 1981; Stanovich, 1980, in press). Subjects were required to read a context sentence (or word) and then pronounce a target word that was congruous, incongruous or neutral in the context. The results of several experiments (e.g. West and Stanovich, 1978; Stanovich and West, 1979) showed that with short intervals between context and target word, fluent readers tend to show a facilitation effect (i.e. they read congruous words faster than those appearing in a neutral context) without any sign of a corresponding inhibition effect (i.e. a tendency to delay longer before pronouncing a word in an incongruous context than one in a neutral context). However, when the processing of the target word was held up in some way both types of effect were obtained. This occurred whether the response was delayed by increasing the interval before the presentation of the target word, by degrading the display or simply by using inexperienced readers as subjects. This suggests that there are at least two distinct kinds of contextual process: one that operates very rapidly and is capable of speeding up the identification of a few highly predictable words, and a second that takes longer to put into effect and acts in a manner that both facilitates likely words and inhibits unlikely words. Following a theory of attention put forward by Posner and Snyder (1975), Stanovich (1981) went on to argue that the first process may be an automatic one while the second is under the reader's conscious control. While this two-process theory provides a convincing account for Stanovich's own data, it faces one or two problems that have yet to be resolved. The main difficulty is that the argument for two distinct contextual processes ultimately rests on the demonstration that facilitation can occur without inhibition in some conditions but not in others. Without this distinction there would be no need to postulate more than one contextual mechanism. As mentioned above (see p. 114), other investigators have succeeded in demonstrating inhibition effects where Stanovich has failed and so at present we are not really forced to postulate more than one contextual mechanism in word recognition. In the following discussion we shall assume, for the sake of simplicity, that all facilitation effects in word recognition are produced by a single contextual mechanism.

How does a facilitatory context speed up the process of identifying a word? One possibility is that the context leads the reader to predict the target word before it is fixated. The evidence suggests that a correctly predicted word is processed more rapidly than an unanticipated one (e.g. Gough et al., 1979; Perfetti, Goldman and Hogaboam, 1979) and so the successful anticipation of individual words could easily produce a facilitation effect. However, there are several shortcomings to the suggestion that a particular word is predicted at each juncture in the text. The main problem is that there are costs to be paid for incorrect predictions: wrongly guessed words take longer to process than words that are not guessed at all (cf. Gough et al., 1979). Since fluent readers tend to make accurate predictions for less than a third of the words in a typical text (Gough et al., 1979; Perfetti et al., 1979), it has been argued that the facilitatory and inhibitory effects of predicting individual words would tend to cancel one another, so that overall such a strategy would not make a positive contribution to word recognition (see Gough et al., 1979). A second problem is that the data obtained in word recognition tasks do not appear to show the disadvantages that would be expected if this strategy were adopted. In particular, Fischler and Bloom (1979) have shown that the time taken to identify an unlikely but perfectly acceptable word is the same whether the word appears in context or follows a row of Xs. If a predictive strategy of the kind outlined above had been used, the unlikely words would almost certainly not have been guessed correctly on most trials, in which case they would have been processed more slowly than the same words presented out of context. These findings suggest that context is not used to specify any single candidate for privileged treatment. A more likely suggestion is that context influences a broad class of words.

It will be recalled from the discussion in Chapter 3 that there are two broad kinds of theory of word recognition—search theories and theories based on evidence-collecting devices (see Section 3.7). Ideally, any account of contextual effects should be compatible with one or other of these theories. As it turns out, the most plausible versions of each kind of theory can easily be extended to account for contextual effects.

The word-detector theory that was considered in greatest detail was the one based on Morton's (1969) logogen model. It will be recalled that this is based on a system of evidence-collecting devices (or logogens) associated with individual words. When a stimulus is presented the logogen counts for all of the words that resemble it are incremented. This process continues until one or other of the units reaches a given threshold. At this point the logogen 'fires' and the word is identified. Although contextual effects were not considered in our earlier discussion of the model they *were* provided for in the original statement of the model. It was suggested that contextual information causes the logogen count to be increased in exactly the same way as visual information does. More specifically, Morton (1970) suggested that immediately after the subject has read a sentence such as *He was a drunken* ————, syntactic and semantic attributes such as ⟨noun⟩, ⟨animate⟩ and ⟨male⟩ are used to activate the logogens of all words that share one or more of the attributes. The end result is that there is a reduction in the amount of visual information that is required to raise the count to the threshold level, and so the time taken to identify the word is less than that required to recognize the same word when it is presented in isolation.

Inhibition effects can be accounted for in two different ways. They can either be interpreted as effects which occur during the recognition process itself or, alternatively, they can be viewed as delays that are introduced during a post-access check on the material. Perhaps the most straightforward account of the first kind is one spelt out by Schuberth and Eimas (1977). As these investigators pointed out, one of the consequences of presenting a word in a misleading context should be that it raises the general level of activity in the logogen system as a whole without significantly increasing the activity of the target logogen itself. On the *variable criterion* version of the logogen model (see p. 59) this should have the effect of increasing the threshold of the target logogen and so it should take longer to identify the word than it does when there is a neutral context or no context at all. With the second kind of explanation it is assumed that logogen activation proceeds in exactly the same way in a misleading context as it does in other circumstances. However, problems occur when the word is checked to see whether it fits in with the prior context. Additional time is required to resolve these difficulties and this introduces a delay corresponding to the inhibition effect.

The basic contextual effects can be handled equally well by the *shortlist* or *verification* model (Becker, 1976; Forster, 1976). It will be recalled that in this type of model it is assumed that word recognition proceeds in two stages. A preliminary selection of a sample of candidates is followed by a detailed serial examination of these items to see whether the sample includes the target word. In the earlier discussion of this type of model (cf. Section 3.7) we only considered the contribution of one type of preliminary sample—shortlists based on the physical properties of the stimulus word. In order to account for contextual effects, Forster and Becker have proposed that semantic and syntactic constraints are used to generate a second shortlist. The items in this second set are treated in exactly the same way as those in the 'visual feature' shortlist. The stored orthographic description of each entry in turn is checked against the visual trace of the stimulus word. As soon as a suitable match is found the appropriate lexical entry is selected and the word is considered to have been identified. According to Forster's version of the model the detailed inspection of the contextual and orthographic shortlists proceeds in parallel and the availability of the first list speeds up processing because the target word is sometimes located in the context set before it is reached in the orthographic set. Variations in the facilitation effect are easily explained by assuming that the entries are arranged in order of decreasing predictability so that predictable words are located more rapidly than others. Inhibition effects can be attributed to the difficulty in reconciling a newly accessed word with an inappropriate prior context (as in the second suggestion above for the logogen model).

One or two additional contextual mechanisms are proposed in Becker's version of the model. For example, Becker and Killion (1977) suggest that, in certain circumstances, the context list might become available for processing before the shape list has been prepared. When this happens there will be an opportunity for the verification process to begin as soon as the stimulus word is presented. Under these conditions the search for an entry in the context list will have a head start over that for the corresponding item in the orthographic list and this could contribute to the facilitation effect. It could also provide an explanation for the inhibition effect since if the context list is searched exhaustively before a start is made on the orthographic list, this could have the effect of delaying the discovery of an item in this second list.

As this discussion shows, both the logogen and the shortlist models are capable of providing relatively straightforward accounts of the basic contextual effects. In fact, there is no reason to favour either type of model on the basis of any of the evidence presented so far. However, a more detailed consideration of contextual effects suggests a test which could potentially discriminate between the two approaches. This concerns the relative magnitude of the word frequency effect when the target word appears in predictive, neutral or misleading contexts.

The logogen model predicts that the word frequency effect should not vary with context whereas the shortlist model predicts that the effect should be smaller for highly predictable words than for words appearing in isolation or in a neutral contest. To see how the first prediction is derived, consider Morton's (1969) version of the logogen model. According to this account, word frequency influences only the resting level of activation in the logogens and contextual constraints subsequently cause these levels to be raised by an amount that is completely independent of the resting levels. Response latency is largely determined by the amount of (visual) activation required to raise this new level to the threshold value. Given these assumptions a predictable context should increase the counts of both low- and high-frequency words, thereby reducing response latency. However, the increase should have no effect on the *difference* between the levels of activation for low- and high-frequency words. Since it is this difference that is responsible for the word frequency effect, it follows that the magnitude of this effect should not vary with context.

In contrast with the logogen model, the Forster–Becker model predicts that there should be an interaction between word frequency and context. This follows because predictable words should often be accessed via the contextually derived shortlist rather than by the list based on the shape of the word. Since the entries in the list are assumed to be ordered on the basis of the predictability of the words and not on the basis of their frequencies, it follows that the frequency effect would be smaller than that for words accessed by using the orthographically derived shortlist.

Which of these two predictions is supported by the data? The evidence suggests that the effects of context and word frequency are additive.* In particular, the word frequency effect does not seem to be any smaller when the target word appears in the context of a predictive sentence than when it appears in a neutral or misleading context (Schuberth and Eimas, 1977; Schuberth *et al.*, 1981). This finding clearly favours the logogen model rather than the shortlist model.

Schuberth *et al.* (1981) have tried to reconcile the shortlist model with this evidence by modifying the model is such a way that the organization of the contextual list reflects the frequency as well as the predictability of the entries. They suggest that the entries are arranged into a series of groups ranging from the strongly predicted to the weakly anticipated possibilities. Within each group the entries are ordered on the basis of word frequency. With this refinement the model is capable of explaining the fact that there are word frequency effects even for predictable words. However, this development does not seem to be entirely satisfactory for two reasons. The first is that in order to explain the fact that the size of the frequency effect is the same whether or not there is a helpful context it is necessary to assume that each subgroup of the contextual shortlist contains about the same number of members as the orthographic list as a whole—which seems a rather unreasonable assumption. The second reservation about Schuberth's refinement of the model is that the process of setting up a shortlist ordered on two different criteria seems so complex that it is difficult to imagine that it would evolve as an efficient way of using context.

For these reasons, it seems appropriate to favour the kind of account of contextual effects offered by the logogen model: one in which the level of activation of numerous word detectors is somehow influenced by the contextual

---

* Becker (1979) has reported that there is an interaction between word frequency and the kind of context produced by word association. However, for the reasons outlined above (see p. 117) it does not seem likely that contextual effects of this kind are particularly relevant in normal reading.

constraints on the word about to be processed. If this argument is accepted, then it seems reasonable to conclude that the evidence as a whole marginally favours the logogen theory of word recognition. The evidence is too finely balanced to present this as a firm conclusion, but for the sake of convenience it will be accepted as a working hypothesis in the remaining chapters of the book.

5.6.3 Evidence for top-down effects in other processes in fluent reading

Most of the research considered so far was designed specifically to investigate contextual effects at the level of word recognition. It is worth giving some consideration to the possibility that there may be top-down influences in some of the other subprocesses of fluent reading.

Starting with the more peripheral processes, there does not seem to be any positive evidence that any of the processes that occur before word identification are subject to top-down influences under fluent reading conditions. Only a few studies have tried to investigate the effects of context on peripheral processing, and those that have all appear to have used degraded or impoverished stimuli (e.g. Marcel, 1974) and are therefore unlikely to give much indication about what happens with intact words.

Turning to parsing procedures, the picture seems to be equally vague. Most of the main theories of parsing assume that there is a strong element of top-down processing in deducing the structure of a sentence. Theories based on ATNs (see Section 4.5) assume that the alternative arcs of a network are tested in an order which depends partly on the preceding analysis. Theories based on perceptual strategies assume that hypotheses about the possible structure of a sentence may be influenced by the analysis of material that occurs earlier in the sentence (see Sections 4.4 and 5.4). However, there does not seem to be any empirical evidence to suggest that top-down processing plays an important part in parsing undegraded sentences. Indeed, it may be recalled that attempts to test some of these views directly, using intact materials, gave no indication that performance is affected in the manner that might be expected if top-down analysis were used (cf. Mitchell and Green, 1978; see Section 4.6 above).

Finally, it seems rather more likely that top-down effects have an influence on the process of linking propositions to form an integrated representation of the text. Up to now this process has been interpreted in terms of Haviland and Clark's (1974) Given-New Strategy which places strong emphasis on bottom-up processing (see Section 4.9). However, Sanford and Garrod (1981, Chapter 5) have recently presented evidence which suggests that the linking process might be facilitated by procedures that are carried out before the reader reaches the critical proposition (i.e. the one that has to be related to the previous material). The experiment was very similar to the one carried out by Haviland and Clark (1974) (again, see Section 4.9). Subjects were required to read a context sentence and then a test sentence that referred to an entity that was either implied or else mentioned explicitly in the previous sentence. The main departure from the Haviland and Clark study was that the information in the implicit mention condition was suggested much more strongly than it was in the earlier study (e.g. *Mary dressed the baby. The clothes were made of pink wool*).

In these circumstances the reading time for the second sentence was no faster when the given information (i.e. *clothes* in this example) was previously mentioned explicitly than when it was merely implied by the first sentence. Sanford and Garrod (1981) interpreted this as evidence that the subject sets up 'bridging assumptions' as soon as the first sentence is read. Thus, in the present example he might infer that a *transfer of clothes* is involved immediately after reading the word *dressed*. The ready availability of this bridging assumption then allows him time to process the next sentence just as rapidly as he does when the word *clothes* is mentioned explicitly. If bridging assumptions are set up before they are needed to establish the links between sentences this suggests that there is an element of top-down processing in this aspect of comprehension.

5.7 TOP-DOWN PROCESSING IN FLUENT READING: CONCLUSION

The main conclusion to be drawn from the work on contextual effects is that top-down processing palys a very limited role in fluent reading. It may influence word recognition when there are global contextual effects such as those that extend over sentence boundaries, and more local effects might come into play when bottom-up processes are held up for some reason (e.g. when the reader encounters a word that is visually unfamiliar); but generally it seems likely that in fluent-reading conditions the contextual information becomes available too late to have a significant influence on the identification process. The only other procedure that is at all likely to be affected by top-down processing is the proposition-linking process discussed in the previous section.

These conclusions contrast sharply with those reached by authors writing about a decade ago (e.g. Hochberg, 1970; Levin and Kaplan, 1970; Smith, 1971). Without exception the earlier writers characterized fluent reading as a process that is dominated by top-down processing. Hochberg (1970) argued that 'normal practiced reading ... is an active process, involving the continual generation and testing of hypotheses' (p. 85). Levin and Kaplan (1970) suggested that a fluent reader 'continually assigns tentative interpretations to a text or message and checks these interpretations. ... When a prediction is confirmed the material covered by that prediction can be more easily processed and understood' (p. 132). Similarly, Smith (1971) maintained that the fluent reader uses syntactic and semantic constraints to 'predict what the surface structure should be, and [that] he needs only a minimum of visual cues to provide a confirmation of that prediction' (p. 221).

How did these investigators reach the conclusion that top-down processing is so important in fluent reading? The answer seems to be that they placed undue emphasis on the results obtained in experiments using impoverished stimuli. As discussed earlier in the chapter (cf. Sections 5.6.1 and 5.6.2), readers do tend to make heavy use of top-down processing under these conditions, but it is not safe to conclude from this that they use the same strategies under normal reading conditions. Indeed, to reemphasize our own conclusions, much of the more recent evidence suggests that top-down processing makes a relatively small contribution to skilled reading under more conventional conditions.

A second reason for adopting the top-down view was given by Smith (1971). He argued that the subprocesses of reading could not be carried out rapidly enough to perform their function if they were not aided in some way by contextual facilitation. For example, he points out (on p. 203) that some people are capable of reading at the rate of a thousand words a minute 'which is four times faster than the probable speed if they were identifying every word' and he argues that redundancy must therefore be used to avoid the necessity of identifying all words. There are several problems with this argument. The first is that there is no generally agreed way of estimating the speed at which people would read if they were identifying every word. There are some techniques for estimating the time required to identify a single word (e.g. Sabol and DeRosa, 1976), but there is no easy way of converting such measures into estimates of reading rate since the maximum speed of reading obviously depends on the degree to which different words can be processed in parallel. Smith apparently assumed that the processing is strictly serial, but there does not appear to be any compelling evidence to support this assumption. If the successive words are identified in parallel then the 'probable speed' of reading may be much higher than the figure calculated by Smith.

Even if an estimate for the probable speed of reading could be agreed upon it is not certain that it would tell us anything about top-down processing. Proficient readers might exceed this rate simply by skipping parts of the text without making any effort to fill in the missing material. Smith has claimed that high-speed readers are able to understand much more than normal readers (p. 214), which would argue against such an interpretation. However, a review of the work on high-speed reading by Gibson and Levin (1975) provided no support for this claim, and so the argument is not very convincing. In short, the fact that people can 'read' as fast as several hundred words a minute does not appear to offer any reason for supporting a top-down rather than a bottom-up view of reading.

5.8 SUMMARY OF CHAPTER 5

It seems likely that the subprocesses of reading operate in parallel and there is some indication that they interact with one another. A few findings point to the possibility that processes such as word recognition and parsing might interfere with other subprocesses and perhaps with one another. However, the experimental tasks that have been used to examine these interference effects are not tasks that resemble normal reading very closely, and so the results have to be treated with caution.

Some of the subprocesses of reading also have facilitatory effects on each other. For example, there is clear evidence that word recognition can be influenced by the results of prior syntactic and semantic analysis and that proposition linking can be influenced by processing at other levels. However, these effects are only evident in certain circumstances. Word identification is usually only affected by prior context if the target word is presented in an impoverished form, if there is a short pause between the context and the target or if the reader is particularly backward or inexperienced (see Section 7.3.4 for more on this). It does not seem to be affected in any way under the conditions that occur in normal fluent reading.

The reason that contextual effects vary with the stimulus condition and with the reader's experience seems to be that it takes quite an appreciable time to set up the facilitation effects. If the target word is presented before this has been done there is nothing to prevent the reader from trying to identify the word without using contextual information. If he succeeds there will be little or no effect. However, if the context-free recognition process is held back relative to the facilitation effect, then this will increase the chance that the reader's performance is influenced by top-down processing (Perfetti and Roth, 1981; Stanovich, 1980, 1981). Clearly, experimental manipulations such as introducing delays between the context and the target word, and degrading the target word, will tilt the balance in favour of the kind of processing that is guided by top-down effects. Conditions will also favour top-down processing when the reader is unfamiliar with the target word and takes a long time to recognize it directly. This would explain the tendency for poor or inexperienced readers to show strong contextual effects (cf. Stanovich, 1980).

Two main kinds of models have been used to explain the contextual effects which do occur. One of them (the logogen model) proposes that context acts in such a way that it increments the level of activation in all of the word detectors that are suggested by the previous material. The second kind of model assumes that contextual information is used to set up a special list of word candidates which are then tested individually against the stimulus trace. The evidence available at the moment marginally favours the account provided by the logogen model.

CHAPTER 6

Models of fluent reading

6.1 ARE MODELS OF READING USEFUL?

The main purpose of this chapter is to draw together the conclusions reached in the first part of the book. One way of doing this is to present a detailed description or model of the reading process based on the evidence reviewed earlier. There are both advantages and disadvantages in trying to summarize the evidence in this way. One advantage is that the attempt to specify the details of the model often shows up its inadequacies. (This process will be disconcertingly familiar to anyone who has attempted to write a complex computer program. A program that initially seems to be quite straightforward will often present a number of unforeseen problems.) A second advantage of models, and one that is possibly more important in the present context, is that they can help in the communication of theoretical ideas. A model often contains a succinct and (relatively) unambiguous statement of the author's position on the main points under discussion and the discipline of presenting a theory in this way makes it difficult to fudge important issues.

The main disadvantage of models is that they invariably misrepresent the reading process by making it seem simpler than it actually is. This is inevitable if the model is to be kept manageable, but oversimplification may not be desirable. Gibson and Levin (1975) have argued that there can be no single model of reading; that 'there are as many reading processes as there are people who read, things to read, and goals to be served' (p. 454). They suggest that existing models ignore the complexity and richness of reading and that, in doing so, they fail to capture the essence of the process. While this view is contentious—in principle there seems to be no reason why a model should not handle the issues raised by Gibson and Levin—it is certainly true that is their efforts to describe the reading process in a manageable way modellers tend to leave out important aspects of the process.

Gibson and Levin try to avoid the problem of oversimplification by the simple expedient of refraining from engaging in the activity of model construction. Instead they spell out a number of 'general principles' of reading that apply in a variety of different tasks. As Massaro (1976), Coltheart (1977) and others have pointed out, this is somewhat unsatisfactory since it fails to retain the advantages of models. A better approach, suggested by Massaro (1976), would be to develop a model which allows different kinds of reading and specifies the conditions under which each of them occurs.

6.2 THE SCOPE OF MODELS OF FLUENT READING

A model of the reading process should specify the sequence of operations that occur in reading and the sources of information consulted during the course of each operation. Ideally, it should say something about how each operation works, but certain subprocesses such as word recognition are so complex that it would be cumbersome to specify all of their details in a model of the entire reading process. In cases like this, model builders often just mention the subprocess in their general description of reading and spell out the details elsewhere in a series of more specific models of the various subskills of reading.

A complete model of reading should specify the way in which the processing sequence can be modified by the reader in his efforts to achieve different goals (e.g. reading for enjoyment, skimming, reading to memorize material, etc.) and the way in which it is varied in response to processing difficulties that arise during reading.

A complete model should also cover all of the operations involved in reading, including processes such as comprehension and the control of eye movements. Models which stop short of comprehension are more accurately viewed as descriptions of word recognition than as models of reading.

In the next section we shall consider some of the more influential models in the literature.

6.3 MODELS OF READING

6.3.1 Goodman's (1967) model

Goodman (1967) presented a model of reading represented by the flow-chart reproduced in Figure 6.1 (from Goodman, 1970). The model was developed on the basis of the author's experience of oral reading in youngsters, but it is clear that he considers it to be a model of fluent reading as well. For example, he points out that the reading performances 'of other readers show similarities and differences, but all point to a selective, tentative anticipatory process' which is a central feature of the general model (see Goodman, 1970, pp. 263–264).

The processing sequence starts with an eye movement and a fixation on new material. After this the reader selects 'graphic cues' from the field of vision and uses this information to help in the formation of a 'perceptual image' of part of the text. The selection of visual information is guided by a number of factors including the reader's strategies, cognitive style, knowledge, and in particular it is guided by the contextual constraints imposed by the material previously analysed. The resulting perceptual image is made up partly of what the reader 'sees and partly what he expected to see' (see Goodman, 1970, p. 270, Step 4).

The next stage is somewhat obscure (to the present writer, at least). The reader 'searches his memory for related syntactic, semantic and phonological cues' and uses them to enrich the perceptual image. It is not clear how syntactic, semantic and phonological cues can be 'related' to a perceptual image unless

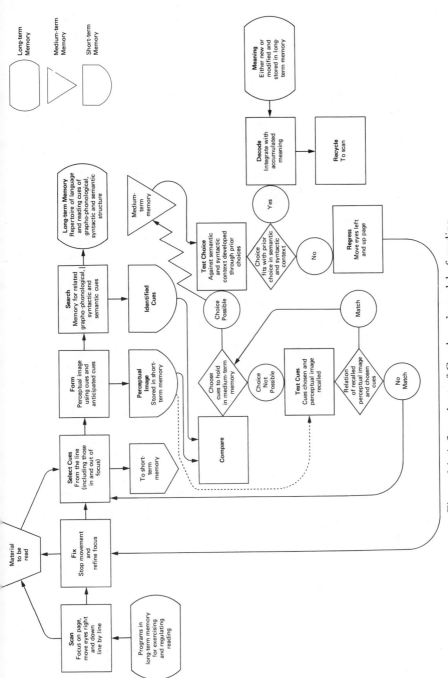

Figure 6.1 A flow-chart of Goodman's model of reading

this is first identified as a sequence of letters or a word. However, according to the model, identification occurs at a later stage. It may be that the new cues are 'related' to the contextual constraints rather than to the perceptual image, in which case the model is merely stating that information provided by the context is used again to modify the perceptual image.

At this point Goodman's reader tries to make 'a guess or tentative choice consistent with the graphic cues' and if he is successful he holds the resulting choice in 'medium-term memory'. If not, he tries again or, as a last resort, looks back at the earlier text. Although it is not made explicit in the model, the 'tentative choice' is apparently a guess about the identity of one of the words in the text.

Once this choice has been made it is tested against the prior context for grammatical and syntactic acceptability. If it fits in with the earlier material, its 'meaning is assimilated with prior meaning' and the results are stored in long-term memory. At this point predictions are made about the forthcoming text and the cycle is repeated. If the word is not consistent with the prior context the reader regresses and repeats the earlier operations until a suitable sequence of words is found.

This model has several shortcomings. The main problem is that, for all its boxes and arrows, it does not specify much about the reading process. It does not indicate how the various non-visual sources of information are drawn upon and used to modulate the formation of the perceptual image, and it does not say anything about how the system deals with the problem of graphic cues which are repeated in successive fixations. At the word recognition stage, it lists some of the sources of information that might be used to make a 'tentative choice' about the identity of the word, but it does not spell out *how* the extra information is used to facilitate the choice. Nor does it have anything to say about the relative importance of the contributions from the different sources. Are all of them used equally or is one source normally more informative than the others? Is the reader's reliance on different sources fixed or does it alter when he tackles different kinds of reading material or when he changes his reading strategy? If he fails to make an appropriate choice and tries again, what does he do to improve his chances of success on the second attempt?

A similar lack of detail is evident in the later stages of the model. For example, before checking that the new word is compatible with the prior context it is necessary for the reader to parse and interpret the portion of the sentence analysed to date, but Goodman's model makes no separate provision for procedures of this kind and it does not give any hint as to how they might operate. Nor does it spell out what is meant by the phrase: 'the meaning is assimilated with prior meaning' (see Goodman, 1970, p. 270). Does this refer to the process of interpreting individual propositions and sentences, or is it concerned with the process of linking propositions to form an organized representation of the text?

The lack of precision at different stages of processing means that it is difficult to determine exactly what claims the model makes about the process of reading.

However, the model is quite explicit in one respect. It maintains that reading is a predictive process; that the reader samples from the print 'just enough to confirm his guess of what's coming' (p. 266). It also suggests that prior context influences even the earliest stages in the processing sequence such as the selection of graphic cues, the formation of the perceptual image and the initial identification of words. The evidence summarized in the previous chapter (see Section 5.6) provides little support for these statements. It will be recalled that a detailed review of the literature yielded no firm evidence that any of the processes that precede word recognition are influenced by the reader's anticipations. Nor was there much evidence that the identification process itself is influenced by forms of context other than the script-based contexts discussed at the end of Section 5.6.1. There was some evidence in Section 5.6 that readers may adopt a strategy based on anticipation when they are in difficulty (e.g. when the text is unclear or when the words are unfamiliar), but the indications are that this is just one of many strategies that can be used by readers when the more direct recognition procedures fail to identify a word.

Goodman's (1967, 1970) emphasis on context, anticipation and guessing can probably be traced back to the fact that most of his work has been with inexperienced young readers whose reading strategies are different from those used by adults. This, and the other problems raised above, makes the model unsatisfactory as a description of fluent reading.

6.3.2 Gough's model

The next model to be considered is one that was presented by Gough (1972). It is actually a model of oral reading rather than fluent silent reading, but it seems likely that the two types of reading have several subprocesses in common and so it is worth giving some consideration to the model.

The flow diagram of Gough's model is given in Figure 6.2. In the first stage, visual information on the page is registered in the icon where it remains available until the reader makes another fixation. This information is used as raw material for the purpose of identifying the sequence of letters in the display. This recognition process is assumed to operate serially from left to right across the display and in the course of the operation the device responsible for the identification process (the Scanner) is assumed to consult pattern recognition routines held in long-term memory.

The string of letters read from the display is placed in a Character Register and immediately operated on by a mechanism (the Decoder) which maps the characters onto a string of 'systematic phonemes'—hypothetical entities that are systematically related to speech but are capable of being set up much more rapidly than speech itself. In the course of operation the Decoder is assumed to make use of a Code Book of grapheme-to-phoneme correspondence rules. The end-products of the process are stored temporarily in a form analogous to a tape recording.

The phonemic representation, supplemented by reference to the Lexicon, is

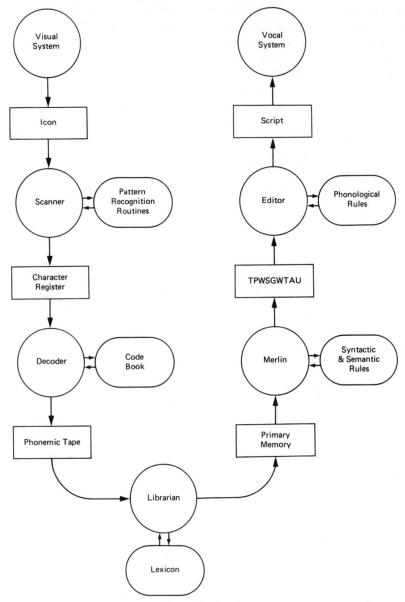

Figure 6.2 Gough's model of reading

used to identify the sequence of words in the sentence, and these words are held in Primary Memory until the sentence can be parsed and placed in another more stable form of storage termed TPWSGWTAU (for The Place Where Sentences Go When They Are Understood). The comprehension device draws upon syntactic and semantic rules in the course of analysing the sentence.

Gough was unable to offer any clear suggestion as to how it might achieve its purpose and nicknamed it Merlin to draw attention to its almost magical properties. The rest of the model deals specifically with the problem of reading aloud and these aspects of the proposal need not concern us here.

The model contains several weaknesses and omissions, many of which were recognized by Gough himself in a discussion which immediately followed the presentation of the 1972 paper. First, as with Goodman's model, there is no provision for dealing with letters that are encompassed in more than one fixation. Duplication of this kind would lead to great confusion if the model were interpreted literally. Secondly, the model pays no attention to the problem of integrating sentences and propositions although this operation obviously plays an important role in the comprehension process (see Sections 4.9 and 4.10). Thirdly, the model says little about the control of eye movements. The only suggestion that is relevant is the observation that difficulties in parsing might cause fixations to be prolonged and that they might eventually lead to regressive eye movements, and even these proposals are not represented in the flow diagram of the model. The model does not consider the possibility that eye movements may be influenced by other aspects of processing and it says nothing about how normal forward movements might by guided. Fourthly, the model is vague about the way in which the reading process is influenced by prior context. It is quite clear that Gough assumes that the processes up to and including lexical search are not influenced in any way by prior context (see Gough, 1972, p. 338), and after some discussion of lexical ambiguity he concludes that he has found 'no evidence that disambiguation takes place until *after* lexical search'. This is entirely consistent with the conclusions reached earlier in Sections 4.8 and 5.6 but, as the quotation suggests, disambiguation must take place at *some* point, and wherever this happens in the processing sequence there will be sentences in which the choice between alternative senses of a word can only be made by referring to prior context (e.g. *In the distance the escaped convict heard a* bark). This suggests that there must be some mechanism for making use of contextual information and, of course, there is a lot of other evidence suggesting the need for such a mechanism (e.g. Haviland and Clark, 1974, and other evidence summarized in Sections 5.5 and 5.6). Gough's model does not make any provision for referring to prior context and this seems to be a serious deficiency.

In addition to these problems, there are several aspects of the model that have proved to be incorrect in the light of subsequent research. For example, it is now clear that the phonemic route to the lexicon is not the only on that is available to the reader. In fact, it is doubtful whether this route is ever normally used by a fluent reader except when he comes across an unfamiliar word (see Section 3.3.3). Similarly, there is no strong evidence that the individual letters of a word are identified during reading (see Section 3.3.1), and even if they are it is very doubtful that they are processed in a serial left-to-right fashion (cf. Brewer, 1972).

A more general criticism of Gough's model is that it lacks flexibility. The reader has no choice of operations or strategies to deploy in different reading tasks and he has little freedom to vary the sequence of operations in any way.

In spite of all these difficulties Gough's model has made a significant contribution to research on reading. It has played a part in stimulating a large body of research (much of which, ironically, has highlighted the limitations of the model). The reason for this is partly that the statement of the model is bold and unambiguous. Gough was prepared to speculate about a number of issues in the absence of firm evidence and he was prepared to risk being proved wrong. His justification for this approach was that 'an analysis that can be attacked on detail can yield detailed knowledge' (p. 331) and this is precisely what has happened.

6.3.3 The LaBerge and Samuels (1974) theory of reading

This is really a theory about the relationship between attention and the subprocesses of reading and was not intended to be a comprehensive model of the reading process. It views reading as a process of activating internal codes corresponding to features, letters, spelling patterns, visual and phonological representation of words, etc., and is concerned primarily with the conditions under which successive codes can be activated, with or without the reader's attention. It makes little effort to specify what is entailed in activating the different types of code and it does not attempt to spell out the conditions under which various possible direct and indirect routes to the lexicon are used. (For example, it does not specify the circumstances in which a word is identified directly, using featural information, or indirectly, after prior identification of the constituent letters and/or spelling patterns and/or phonological represent-ation.) In its present (1974) version, the model says very little about comprehen-sion and nothing about the control of eye movements.

A central claim of the model is that while fluent readers can carry out certain operations without attention, this is the outcome of considerable practice. It is suggested that in the early stages of learning the processing of letters and words is not automatic. It is also suggested that attention might be used in different ways in different kinds of reading task. For example, in rapid reading processing in the visual system might receive no special attention, leaving the reader to concentrate on the meaning of the passage. On the other hand, for slower reading such as that associated with difficult or poorly printed text, attention might be directed more to the processes entailed in identifying letters, spelling patterns and other low-level units.

Since the theory does not attempt to present a comprehensive account of the reading process it will not be considered in further detail here. However, it is worth emphasizing the flexibility of the model since this is a desirable feature of any realistic description of reading.

6.3.4 Rumelhart's interactive model of reading

Of the models considered so far, Goodman's places strong emphasis on top-down processing while Gough's and LaBerge an Samuels's are based exclusively on bottom-up processing. Neither of these positions seems to be entirely satisfactory. As argued above, there is no compelling evidence that fluent reading is concerned exclusively (or even predominantly) with reader's attempts to confirm hypotheses about future material. Nor does normal reading always proceed without reference to prior context. In appropriate circumstances both the raw material and the readers's expectations can make significant contributions to the process.

Rumelhart (1977) has made a preliminary attempt to develop a model of reading in which both types of information are drawn upon before the reader eventually settles upon an interpretation of the text. A simple representation of the model is shown in Figure 6.3. In the first stage the information is picked up by the eye and registered in a Visual Information Store (VIS) or icon. Visual features are extracted from this store and made available to the central component of the model, the *pattern synthesizer*. This device draws upon a wide variety of different sources of information and uses them to work out the 'most probable interpretation' of the text. Sources of information that might be used in this way include information about letter-shapes and the orthographic structure of English, information in the mental lexicon, information about what is syntactically and semantically acceptable in the language and information about the contextual situation.

Information from all of the different sources is brought together in a store referred to as the *message centre*. Each knowledge source contributes a set of alternative hypotheses about the entities that might be present in the stimulus. The plausibility of each hypothesis is then evaluated by checking it against information (or hypotheses) in other parts of the system. This procedure reveals which classes of hypotheses are mutually compatible.

All of the hypotheses that are mutually consistent are strengthened while those that are incompatible with one another are weakened. Changes in emphasis at various levels in the system may lead to new hypotheses being entered into the message centre and these, in turn, are checked against other information in the centre. Eventually, after repeated checking carried out simultaneously

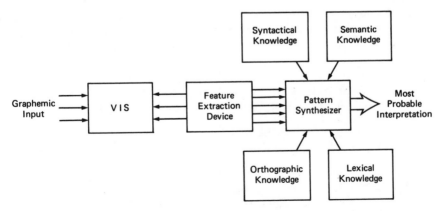

Figure 6.3 A representation of Rumelhart's interactive model of reading

at all levels, the selective strengthening of compatible hypotheses defines a set of hypotheses that are consistent both with one another and with the featural information. This set of hypotheses is accepted as the final interpretation of the text at each of the different levels of analysis.

This model gives a plausible account of the evidence which shows that context and reader's expectations can influence the reading process, particularly when the text is degraded (see Section 5.5). It is also capable of handling the evidence in Section 5.6 which suggests that context does not necessarily influence the initial selection of a word. When the print is clear, the lexical hypothesis derived from the featural information may reach an acceptable strength before the reader has had any chance to generate any hypotheses at the higher levels. If this happens, word recognition will be completely independent of context. At a later stage, when the syntactic and semantic hypotheses become available, the word just accepted could be reexamined in an effort to confirm that it is consistent with all of the information available. On rare occasions this test might fail, forcing the reader to reconsider the identity of the word, but in the main the results would confirm the initial choice and the sequence of operations would proceed as if the reader's expectations had played no part at all in the process.

While Rumelhart's model deals with contextual effects more adequately than earlier models of reading do, there are a number of other aspects of the process that are not handled in sufficient detail for it to be considered a comprehensive model of reading. It says nothing about the basis on which the various kinds of hypotheses are generated and it does not specify the relative importance of the contribution from each knowledge source. Nor does it indicate how the influence of each source varies with the reader's strategy and with the reading conditions. It has little to offer on issues such as the control of eye movements, the use of a phonological route and other back-up strategies in word recognition and problems in comprehension beyond the level of sentences. Some of these limitations are acknowledged by Rumelhart in his presentation of the model. He makes it clear that his main aim is to present a framework for the development of models which is an alternative to the conventional serial flow-chart and places more emphasis on highly interactive parallel processing. It seems likely that sophisticated models of this kind will make an increasing contribution to theoretical descriptions of reading in the future.

6.4 A DESCRIPTION OF FLUENT SILENT READING BASED ON THE EVIDENCE SUMMARIZED IN CHAPTERS 1–5

The research summarized in the first five chapters suggests that a model of fluent reading should reflect the following conclusions about the process:

(1) The fluent reader recognizes the majority of words in a text without pronouncing them implicitly or explicitly and without making use of contextual constraints. However, if for any reason he fails to recognize a

word directly he can fall back on a variety of strategies which use these and other sources of information to help in word recognition.

(2) Processing is carried out simultaneously at all different levels of the system. Although a particular portion of print may be subjected to a series of analyses (e.g. feature analysis, word recognition, sentence perception, etc.), it does not follow that the reader's attention passes from one subprocess to another. Instead, control is distributed throughout the system at all times.

(3) The processes that occur after word recognition make a significant contribution to the reading process as a whole and these higher-level procedures should be included in as much detail as possible.

(4) The control and guidance of eye movements is an integral part of the reading process. Provision for exercising this control should be incorporated in the model.

(5) Reading is a flexible process. A fluent reader can suspend the more routine operations while he imagines a scene (say) or works out the implications of what he has just read. He can also skip words, sentences or larger chunks of text if they do not seem essential to his immediate purposes.

A framework of one possible sequence of operations in fluent reading is presented in Figure 6.4. According to this simplified flow diagram the visual information is first transferred from the icon to STVM. Here it is used by an operation that attempts to identify the word represented by each cluster of features. If this process is successful, the words are delivered directly to a device that uses them to construct propositions. If it fails, other back-up strategies are used to identify the words and these are then handled as before. Following this, the propositions are integrated to produce the meaning of the text, and this is stored in a long-term representation of the text.

This description of the reading process is obviously grossly oversimplified and is merely intended to serve as an introduction to the more comprehensive flow-chart given in Figure 6.5. Here the sequence of operations just described — the operations that are central to fluent reading—are embedded in a much more detailed description of the process. Before working through the sequence it is worth spelling out a few of the conventions used in the diagram.* The most important of these are: (1) circles represent operations; (2) rectangles represent short-term stores that are re-used constantly throughout the process of reading. These might be referred to as working memories. In certain cases the form in which the information is assumed to be held is specified within the rectangle. Distinct rectangles are not necessarily intended to represent functionally different working memories. They might merely correspond to different forms of coding in a common store. (3) 'Curved' rectangles represent long-term sources of knowledge or information that are consulted in the course of reading. These stores might be updated or modified from time to time but they are not repeatedly overwritten in the way that working memories are. (4) In the course

* These conventions are derived from those used in Gough's (1972) model, and more generally the present description of reading can be regarded as an extension of this model.

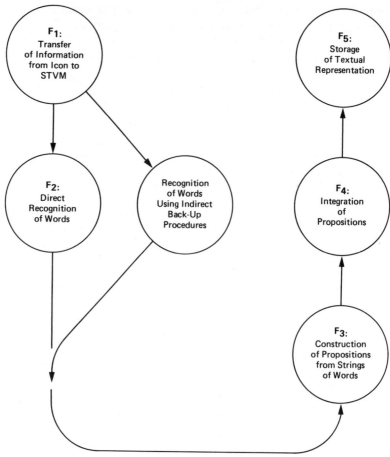

Figure 6.4 A possible sequence of operations in fluent reading

of performing their functions operations are assumed to draw upon various sources of information including both working memories and knowledge bases. The process of consulting a data base in this way is represented by a double-headed arrow between the operation and the base. (The arrowheads can be thought of as representing a request for information travelling *to* the data base and the information itself flowing *back* in the opposite direction.) When an operation reaches its goal its products are registered in temporary storage where they become available for use by other operations. The process of delivering the products to a working store is represented by a boldly-printed arrow. Operations can be triggered either by the arrival of new data in one of the source stores* or by instructions received from other operations. (An instruction of this kind is represented by an arrow with a single head.) However, in the normal course of events the operations are assumed to proceed autonomously. In the first stage of processing the graphemes on the page are

* As in a computer controlled by 'data-flow'.

registered in iconic storage where they remain available until shortly before the next eye movement occurs. This information is drawn upon by F_1, a subprocess that selects a sample of visual features from the icon and transfers the information to a non-maskable STVM which preserves the spatial relationships between the features. The position in which the features are entered into the representation in STVM is determined by reference to a register which holds information about the point at which the eye is currently fixated in the external framework. When the next fixation occurs a new sample of features is extracted from the (changed) icon and added to the existing representation in STVM in a position determined by the most recent information in the 'eye direction' register. This integrated representation is assumed to be the source of raw material for all subsequent processing. This assumption is based on arguments covered in Section 2.7. Analysis based on a composite representation derived from different icons is assumed to be more plausible than separate analysis based on individual icons for two related reasons. First, a system based on an integrated source of information would have no difficulty in dealing with information derived from two or more fixations that cover the same ground more than once. Duplicated samples of features would merely be overlaid one upon the other and, at most, the new information would merely confirm the presence of features already in position in STVM. Secondly, the pooling of information might improve the processing of words that appear in the periphery of successive fixations. In particular, the information in STVM may sometimes be detailed enough for a word to be recognized when features from two or more fixations are combined but not when any of these sources are considered separately. If these suggestions concerning the integration of visual information were shown to be incorrect, then alternative procedures would have to be devised for editing the visual input in the manner required.

For the next stage of processing it is convenient to assume that individual parts of the representation in STVM—namely the portions flanked on either side by spaces (i.e. words)—can be segregated in turn and used one by one as the raw material for subsequent analysis. Several different operations are assumed to draw upon this information and it is simplest to suppose that they proceed in parallel. The first (F_2) is the procedure for recognizing words directly from the array of features in STVM. By hypothesis, this operation draws upon only one long-term source of knowledge in the process of identifying a word and this is the file containing instructions (or productions) for visual access. Following the discussion in Sections 3.7 and 3.8 it is assumed that the identification of a word is achieved by the activation of a logogen. As the access instructions are executed the counts of various logogens are activated by differing amounts and the current tally of all counts is kept in the form of a working memory. When one of the logogens eventually reaches its threshold (and the word is thereby identified) the outcome is used to recover from the lexicon information about the word's pronunciation, its grammatical label(s) and its various alternative semantic specifications. A copy of this information is delivered to a short-term store where it is held while subsequent operations

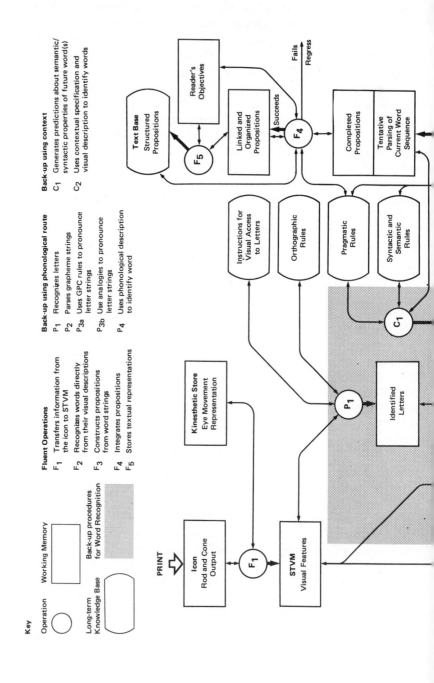

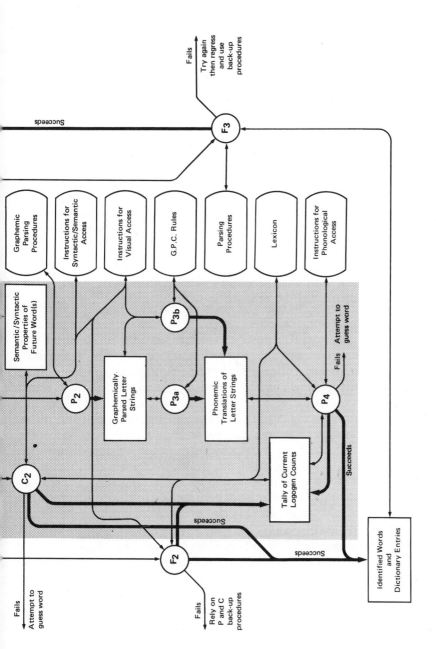

Figure 6.5(a) A diagrammatic representation of the main processes of fluent reading

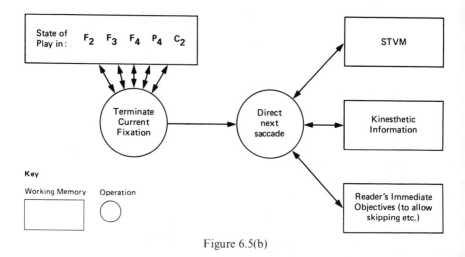

Figure 6.5(b)

take place. The assumption that the visual access file is the only source of knowledge drawn upon by the direct recognition procedure is made primarily for reasons of economy. The review presented in Section 3.3 yielded no convincing evidence that any other sources of information play a significant role in the process, so unless other sources can be shown to make a contribution it seems best to exclude them and by doing so keep the description as simple as possible.

The other operations which use the information in STVM are the initial stages of the phonological route to the lexicon ($P_1 \rightarrow P_2 \rightarrow P_3 \rightarrow P_4 \rightarrow$ identified word) and a route which makes predictive use of contextual information ($C_1 \rightarrow C_2 \rightarrow$ identified word). In order to account for the evidence that fluent word recognition is not influenced by the ease of pronouncing a word (see Section 3.3.3) or by most kinds of predictive processing (see Section 5.6), it is assumed that it almost always takes longer to gain access to the lexical entry by these alternative routes than it does by the direct route. On this hypothesis, the alternative procedures would only contribute to the flow of information if the direct recognition procedures failed to produce an output or if they were somehow slowed down. For this reason they are referred to as back-up procedures and, to emphasize the suggestion that they normally make no contribution to fluent reading, they will be considered separately at a later stage.

The next operation in the main processing sequence is the device for parsing sentences (F_3). This draws upon the ordered list of recognized words provided (predominantly) by F_2 and uses the information to construct the propositions expressed in the sentence. It will be recalled from the earlier discussions of sentence processing (see Sections 4.6 and 4.7) that there is presently no entirely satisfactory account of how this device operates. However, we can suppose that it proceeds in consultation with a source of knowledge about parsing procedures. This information might guide the operation in the manner prescribed by Augmented Transition Networks (see Section 4.5 for a description of ATNs and Section 4.7 for some doubts about the value of networks as a theory of parsing). In other words, the knowledge source might specify the range of lexical categories that could follow at each point in the sequence, together with the syntactic function to be assigned to the new word given each alternative continuation. As soon as a tentative function has been ascribed to the new word it may be checked against the preceding portion of the sentence to see whether it is semantically acceptable and plausible given the immediate context (for evidence on post-access checking see Section 5.6.1). This would normally be established by referring to preexisting sources of information pertaining to semantic and pragmatic combinations, but on occasion the word could be checked by comparing its syntactic and semantic features with those generated in advance by the predictive mechanism (C) (see below). If these checks reveal that the word fits in well with the preceding material (as they normally would with ordinary prose), the new word is added to a string of tentatively parsed words and the parsing device turns its attention to the next word. If the word is ambiguous and one of its alternative senses can be eliminated on the basis of semantic or pragmatic considerations, then this is done at this point and only the consistent sense of the word is carried forward to the next stage (see Sections 4.2.3 and 4.8). If there is no basis for rejecting either of the meanings both might be returned for further analysis. Generally, however, only the preferred meaning will be kept active. If the semantic and pragmatic checks reveal that the current word does not fit in with the beginning of the sentence (or if the syntactic class of the word is not one that was acceptable to the parsing procedure in the first place) then an attempt is made to parse the first part of the sentence in another way*. If this also fails, a regressive eye movement is triggered so that the reader can check whether the words in the sentence were correctly identified in the first place. If this fails to resolve the difficulty the reader can either skip the sentence without understanding it or he can consider the possibility that there are misprints or missing words (or lines) in the text. In principle, these problem-solving activities could draw upon any of the sources of information included in the model, but we are not in a position to say very much about how they might operate.

Presumably the strategies just described are not required very often in the processing of normal text. In the majority of sentences the parsing and checking procedures would probably run smoothly. Whenever this occurs the parsed clause or sentence may be used to construct propositions that are made available to the next operation, F_4, which links and organizes the propositions into a coherent text base.

---

* This kind of failure to integrate a word with the first part of the sentence is assumed to cause difficulties other than those associated with the parsing device. In particular, it is assumed to hold back the procedures that subjects use to indicate that they have identified the word. (See the discussion of inhibition effects in Section 5.6.1.)

It is assumed that the reader links propositions by using the Given–New Strategy described in Section 4.9. It will be recalled that according to this hypothesis the reader first distinguishes between presupposed and New information in the current proposition and then searches the text base (i.e. the organized long-term representation of the preceding text) for a previous mention of the presupposed information. If an earlier mention is located in a working memory containing recently integrated text, a set of 'linking' procedures (as yet unspecified) is used to integrate the current proposition with the relevant portion of the text base. If no relevant information is found in working memory a more stable (long-term) representation of the text base is searched. If the required information is eventually discovered in this second store it is reinstated in working memory so that the linking process can proceed as before. If no previous mention of the presupposed information is discovered in either long-term or in working memory the reader uses 'bridging assumptions' to create a link for himself, and in this case his inferences are incorporated into the representation (see Section 4.9 for further details of this process). If this also fails to produce an acceptable link, a regressive eye movement is initiated and the reader tries to solve the problem by re-reading earlier material. The extent to which a reader perseveres in his attempts to create a bridging assumption, and the detail with which he specifies the resulting inferences during the process, will depend on his purpose in reading the text and on the judged relevance of the current passage to the whole theme. If a person is reading for pleasure and the passage is marginal to the story line he may be inclined to skip on without understanding the detail, whereas in other circumstances he might dwell on the material until it makes some sense. To cover these possibilities the model assumes that the operation F_4 is free to refer to a short-term store in which the reader retains information about his present reading goals and to a long-term store which holds a set of heuristic procedures or strategies for achieving alternative aims.

The final operation in the reading process, F_5, takes the propositions that have just been linked and uses them to reorganize and update the text base in long-term memory. As with the previous operation, the detail in which the information is filed away depends on the reader's purpose and it is assumed that the type of material transferred to the text base can be modified in the light of the goals.

Having considered the 'normal' flow of processing in fluent reading, we can now return to the back-up procedures in word recognition. Although these procedures are assumed to be slower and less efficient than direct word recognition, it is reasonable to treat them as part of the process of fluent reading since they provide facilities that are sometimes required by even the most accomplished readers (e.g. the ability to identify a word that currently has no entry in the visual lexicon or the ability to read a word that is indistinct, mis-spelt or misprinted).

The phonological route to the lexicon will be considered first. The sequence of operations starts with the recognition of the individual letters of the word.

The process uses the visual features in STVM as raw material and draws upon a source of knowledge which links letter categories with their visual descriptions (i.e. an analogue of the visual access file described above). It may also make use of information about the legality and probability of particular strings of letters in the English language (i.e. orthographic rules). Once the letters have been recognized they are deposited, in order, in a temporary store where they can be worked upon by a graphemic parser which partitions the sequence into an appropriate string or spelling patterns. As with most parsing procedures it is not clear exactly how this device operates. However, it is clear that it must draw upon certain long-established principles in order to achieve its goals. These principles are referred to here by the (admittedly unenlightening) term *graphemic parsing procedures*.

Once the letter string has been segmented into spelling patterns it is converted into a phonemic form in one of two ways. The first method uses GPC rules to convert the sequence of spelling patterns directly into a string of phonemes. The second method initially consults the visual access file to find a word that is similar to the current stimulus, and retrieves the pronunciation of this word for use as an analogy in pronouncing the target word. Departures in the pronunciation of the target word are handled either by using a new set of analogies or by referring to GPC rules as in the first method. It is assumed that both methods work in parallel and the phonemic representation first delivered is taken as the raw material for the text process. This next process identifies the target word by using instructions for phonological access to increment the logogen counts for words until one of them reaches threshold. This process can be considered as a phonological analogue of F_2. If the process succeeds in identifying a word this word, together with any additional property returned from the lexicon, is then placed in temporary storage and the analysis proceeds as in fluent reading. If it fails, the information is passed to a device which controls eye movements and there it is used in conjunction with other 'progress reports' to prolong the fixation or to initiate a regressive eye movement (see below).

The second back-up route to the lexicon makes use of contextual information. The first operation in the sequence (C_1) uses previously analysed material to generate predictions about the properties of the next word in the sentence. This procedure takes account of the tentative parsing assigned to the sequence of words to date and consults pragmatic, syntactic and semantic rules to compute the likely features of the new word (e.g. its grammatical class and, if it is a noun (say), whether it is likely to be abstract or concrete, animate or inanimate, edible or inedible, etc.). These specifications are placed in temporary storage where they are later used by an interactive word recognition procedure (C_2).

C_2 draws upon the contents of two working memories and three long-term data bases. The two working memories are Short Term Visual Memory (STVM) and the store that holds the semantic/syntactic predictions considered above. The stable data bases are the lexicon itself, the files containing the instructions (or productions) for visual access and the instructions (or productions) for semantic/syntactic access. The visual information together with the visual file is used to carry out the instructions in that file. This causes the relevant logogens to be incremented and, as before, the tally of these changes is kept in working memory. Exactly the same kind of process occurs with the semantic information and the corresponding instruction file. If the combined effects of these two subprocesses eventually cause one of the logogen counts to reach threshold, the corresponding word is made available to C_2 which recovers any additional stored information on the word from the lexicon, and then places it in the temporary store for identified words. At this point the logogen counts are immediately returned to their resting levels and all the semantic/syntactic specifications tied to that particular word are dumped from working memory. After this the analysis proceeds as described above (i.e. $F_3 \rightarrow F_4 \rightarrow F_5 \rightarrow$ text base). If the logogen counts reach equilibrium without any of them exceeding the threshold then attempts are made to guess the word using whatever residual information is left over in the various working memories employed in the earlier stages of the process. No detailed consideration of these guessing procedures is included in the current description because it is very unlikely that they play an important part in fluent reading.

The major aspect of reading that remains to be covered is the control of eye movements and the duration of fixations (see Section 2.8 for a more detailed discussion of this issue). It is assumed that a fixation can be prolonged or curtailed marginally depending on the current state of any of a number of different operations including direct word recognition (F_2), sentence parsing (F_3), phonological access to the lexicon (P_4), context dependent word recognition (C_2) (and perhaps the integration of propositions, F_4) (see Figure 6.5 (b) for a diagrammatic representation of eye-movement control). If any of these operations fails to achieve its goal within a prespecified fraction of the mean fixation time, then it is assumed that the next saccade can be postponed fractionally. Conversely, if the analysis at all levels is completed rapidly the saccade can be brought forward by a few milliseconds. Note that the adjustments are not necessarily related in any way to the contents of the current fixation. The fixation durations are assumed to vary in line with the state of processing at a number of different levels in the system, and it is therefore quite conceivable that a fixation might be extended as a result of problems first encountered one or two fixations earlier.

The mechanism that guides the saccade itself must draw upon information in STVM (to direct the eye away from spaces, punctuation marks, etc.) and kinaesthetic information (to indicate where the eye is presently directed), and it must be sensitive to what might be called 'the reader's immediate objectives'. These objectives might change from moment to moment. At one moment the aim might be to gather information from a point further along the line of print. At others it might be to reconsider earlier material, to skip a paragraph or page or to stop reading completely and to pay attention to something else. Clearly, some of these objectives (e.g. re-reading the text) will be set up in response to the outcome of certain of the subprocesses considered above. Others, such as responding to a knock on the door, would be extraneous. We are not in a position to specify how the objectives are set up nor to spell out how they are translated into motor commands. The source of information is included merely as a way of recognizing that the problem exists.

6.5   SOME COMMENTS ON THE PRESENT DESCRIPTION OF FLUENT READING

This description of the reading process is based on the evidence summarized in the preceding chapters and should therefore be consistent with the conclusions reached earlier. It assigns an important role to non-maskable STVM, it presents fluent word recognition as a process that occurs directly without reference to contextual, phonological, orthographic or letter information, while back-up identification procedures can use any of these sources of information. It includes operations (such as the linking of propositions) that are not normally incorporated in models of reading but nevertheless seem to be demanded by the empirical data in the literature. It takes account of the fact that reading is a flexible process that can be varied in response to changes in the reader's strategies.

As a result of covering aspects of fluent reading that are not always considered explicitly, the description is more complex than the models summarized above. Obviously, it would be better if the description could be simplified. However, it is not easy to see how this could be done without merely ignoring crucial aspects of the reading process. In fact, numerous non-trivial details would have to be added before the model could be made viable as a computer program,* and so in this sense it could be argued that the description is not detailed enough.

Much of the present account of reading (e.g. the control of eye movements and most aspects of the comprehension process) is dealt with so imprecisely that it would be virtually impossible to reject the description offered. Procedures of this kind have been included in the overall description merely as a way of noting that they are crucial aspects of the reading process. Other aspects of the description, particularly those concerning the procedures up to and including word identification, are specified in more detail, and as a result they should be easier to falsify. For instance, the model states that duplicated information from successive fixations is edited out by integrating the visual features in STVM and this assumption could easily prove to be wrong. Similarly, it claims that familiar, clearly printed words are normally identified directly without reference to any sources of knowledge other than the visual lexicon, and that pronunciation rules, most types of contextual information and other similar sources of knowledge only influence the process when the direct procedure fails. Again, this suggestion could be falsified by showing that word recognition

---

* For example, it would be necessary to specify how slowly accumulating back-up information is prevented from misguiding the process of identifying words that appear later in the text, and it would also be useful to be able to spell out how the long-term memories are updated as the reader's vocabulary develops and as the various kinds of rules are learnt.

is influenced by one or other of these sources of information under conditions that are similar to those that occur in normal reading.

6.6 SUMMARY OF CHAPTER 6

The chapter starts by evaluating a number of well-known models of reading. These models seem to be deficient in a number of respects. The majority make no attempt to cover the process as a whole. They typically exclude any consideration of issues such as the control of eye movements, the integration of information from successive fixations and almost all aspects of processing beyond the level of word recognition. In most instances the models have no way of handling variations in the reader's strategies and in several cases they are unable to accommodate recent empirical evidence on issues such as the effects of context on word recognition and on the sources of information used to identify words.

In an attempt to overcome these problems we present a description of reading which follows the spirit of Gough's model. This description is summarized diagrammatically in Figure 6.5. In some respects it serves the function of a traditional flow diagram of the reading process (i.e. it spells out the substages of reading and the order of processing between input and output). However, it includes a wider range of procedures and options than is normally incorporated in such models and, more importantly, it makes an attempt to say something about the rate at which various kinds of computation proceed in real time and it tries to spell out exactly what sources of information are drawn upon by each of the operations.

The resulting summary appears to be capable of dealing with most of the important data and phenomena described in the earlier chapters. However, it suffers from several obvious deficiencies. One of its weaknesses is that certain aspects of the diagram are based on insufficient data (or even on speculation). A second deficiency is that certain parts of the description, particularly those associated with the higher processes, are much vaguer than I would like them to be. Indeed, there are few aspects of the specification that even remotely approach the detail which would be required if it were to be implemented in the form of a computer program. The present description of reading also lacks the directness and simplicity of some of the earlier models of reading. These deficiencies provide pointers as to how this account of reading could be developed into a more general and viable model of reading. In the meantime, I make no ambitious claims about the present description. It is merely intended to provide a reasonably compact statement of the conclusions reached in the preceding five chapters.

CHAPTER 7

Individual differences in reading

7.1 INTRODUCTION

The main aims of the preceding chapters have been to provide a cognitive analysis of fluent reading, to spell out in some detail how the individual subprocesses operate and to specify how they work together in normal circumstances. Unfortunately, the process probably only operates in this way for a very small proportion of the population. For the rest (e.g. for learners and for adults with reading difficulties) there may be significant differences in one or more stages of the analysis and it is important to know where these differences lie.

In this chapter we shall consider this question in relation to four broad groups of readers: (i) acquired dyslexics, (ii) backward readers at school, (iii) readers who are inexperienced and unskilled but not backward for their ages and (iv) slow (but effective) adult readers. In each case we shall try to determine which of the major subprocesses of reading show marked individual differences that are associated with differences in reading achievement. Before doing this it may be useful to list some of the main processes that may be reponsible for these differences.

(1) Backward readers may be less efficient at directing and controlling their eye movements. If they are, the quality of the visual information that is made available to the higher centres must presumably be lower than that available to better readers.

(2) Poor readers may be less effective at extracting visual information from the page during a fixation or in combining the information from different fixations (e.g. a deficit in the F_1 process in Figure 6.5).

(3) Poor readers may also be less accomplished in the subprocesses responsible for direct word recognition (F_2). This could occur either because there are differences in the access process itself or because of differences in the quality of information stored in the visual access file. On this second explanation, poor readers may encounter problems in understanding a passage because their access files contain visual discriptions for fewer of the words they might encounter in the text, or because some of the descriptions that *are* available are incomplete or inaccurate.

(4) They may also differ in their ability to use indirect routes to enable them to locate the lexical entry when the direct routes fail. Thus, they might be less efficient at decomposing words phonologically (using the P-route) or at

149

using contextual constraints (the C-route) or other sources of information to help them identify difficult words.

(5) Retarded readers might differ from better readers in their access to the lexicon or in the accuracy and completeness of the information available in this store.

(6) They may be slower or less accurate at constructing propositions from the sequence of words on the page or in combining these propositions in the manner discussed in Section 4.9 to derive the overall meaning of the text (i.e. there may be differences in subprocesses F_3, F_4, or F_5).

(7) Finally, backward readers may encounter difficulties associated with the way in which different processing stages interact with one another. For example, it is conceivable that the various subskills of reading do not work together efficiently in poor readers. Alternatively, the attentional demands of one subskill might detract from the performance in another (LaBerge and Samuels, 1974).

Any combination of these difficulties would presumably have a detrimental effect on reading performance and there is some evidence that almost every type of difficulty listed above can occur. Perhaps the clearest evidence comes from the detailed diagnostic investigations carried out with patients showing symptoms of *acquired dyslexia* (i.e. neurological patients who have lost the ability to read fluently following head injuries or cerebrovascular accidents). This small group of poor readers will be considered first.

7.2   ACQUIRED DYSLEXIA

Over the last few years several different forms of acquired dyslexia have been differentiated and some of them have been investigated in great detail. While it is not always possible to be precise about the source (or sources) of the reading difficulties experienced by these patients there is increasing evidence that deficits can occur in most of the major subprocesses of reading, including the extraction of visual information from the page, direct and indirect word recognition, and the retrieval of the meanings of words from memory. There is also some indication that certain dyslexics may differ from normal readers in the efficiency with which the various subprocesses of reading operate together. Evidence for each of these kinds of deficit will be considered in turn.

7.2.1   Deficits in extracting visual information from the page

Evidence for deficits in the early stages of visual processing comes from case reports and experiments by Martin (1954) and Warrington (1979). Martin observed that patients suffering from a syndrome called 'pure word blindness' have difficulty in basic visual skills such as following the lines on a page of text, while Warrington drew attention to a syndrome in which patients who are required to read a word tend to report not the target word itself but one that is physically similar to it (e.g. *yolk* instead of *milk*). Both of these reading problems obviously derive from deficiencies early in the visual system, and they can be taken as evidence that at least some dyslexics have difficulty in extracting visual information from the page.

7.2.2 Deficits in direct word recognition

Many dyslexic patients seem to have difficulties that are associated with the process of direct word recognition. Kinsbourne and Warrington (1962) described four patients whose performance can be accounted for in this way. These patients had great difficulty with any normal reading task, and when they did read their performances were inaccurate. Investigations of their recognition skills indicated that they had little difficulty in identifying letters (or other shapes) when they were presented alone, but were unable to recognize letters presented in pairs except when the duration of the display was particularly long. (Three of the patients made mistakes even when the display time was as long as 1600 ms.) It seems reasonable to suppose that their reading problems derived from this inefficiency in processing letter strings. Indeed, when faced with conventional reading material they tended to proceed by spelling out the words letter by letter. The fact that they were forced to adopt this unusual and inefficient strategy rather than treating each word as a unit in itself and identifying it directly strongly suggests that they were not capable of using direct recognition procedures.

More recently Marshall and Newcombe (1973) have described another patient with a syndrome dubbed 'surface dyslexia'. This patient was apparently unable to use direct procedures to identify words. His performance was characterized by the frequency with which he made phonological errors in the process of reading. On some occasions he would produce meaningless utterances while on others he merely mispronounced the words in the text. In either case the result of the mistake was usually that he was unable to identify or define the word in question. The fact that he was unable to ignore a mistake in his initial pronunciation of the word suggests that he recognized words exclusively by using a phonological route to the lexicon and this in turn suggests that, like the patients studied by Kinsbourne and Warrington, he was unable to recognize words directly from their visual descriptions.

7.2.3 Deficits in indirect word recognition

There is considerable evidence that certain dyslexic patients experience difficulty in using indirect routes to access the meanings of words. In particular, there have been several reports of cases in which patients apparently have great difficulty in using the phonological route to identify words. This condition has been given various names including 'deep dyslexia' (Marshall and Newcombe, 1973), 'phonemic dyslexia' (Shallice and Warrington, 1975) and, more recently, 'deep phonemic dyslexia' (Shallice and Warrington, 1980). Its main characteristic is that the patients are virtually incapable of translating strings of letters into a phonological representation. For instance, they are often unable to pronounce regular nonwords such as *fleep* or *wid* (Marshall and Newcombe, 1973; Patterson and Marcel, 1977; Saffran and Marin, 1977).

Evidence that deep-phonemic dyslexics have difficulty in converting the stimulus into a phonological form also comes from the finding that they fail to show a normal pseudohomophone effect (see Patterson and Marcel, 1977). It will be recalled that the pseudohomophone effect occurs when normal fluent readers make lexical decisions about letter strings (see Section 3.3.3 for further details). It is the tendency for the decision latencies for nonwords to be longer than usual whenever the string sounds like an English word (e.g. *frute*). The effect is usually explained by referring to the fact that the phonological representation of the stimulus and the letter string itself provide conflicting evidence about the lexical status of the stimulus. The finding that deep-phonemic dyslexics have no special difficulties in classifying these stimuli suggests that they fail to derive the phonological description that causes the problem in normal readers, and consequently it provides further support for the view that they are inefficient at recoding information in this way.

In addition to the inability to pronounce words and nonsense syllables there are a number of other symptoms which tend to be associated with deep/ phonemic dyslexia. First, it is often found that the patient's ability to read a word varies as a function of the syntactic class of the word. For example, Shallice and Warrington (1975) found that their patient was more successful at reading nouns than adjectives and that both of these classes of words were reported better than verbs. Other investigators (i.e. Marshall and Newcombe, 1966; Shallice and Warrington, 1975; Gardner and Zurif, 1975; Saffran and Marin, 1977) have reported that their patients have particular difficulty in handling function words such as *on* and *how*.

A second symptom which is sometimes apparent is the tendency for deep/phonemic dyslexics to read concrete words more accurately than abstract words (Richardson, 1975; Shallice and Warrington, 1975; Patterson and Marcel, 1977). Thirdly, it has been observed that when phonemic dyslexics misread a word they frequently respond by giving a word which is related to the target either semantically (e.g. *little—small*) or visually (*charm—chair*) or by common derivation (*heroic—hero*) (Marshall and Newcombe, 1973; Shallice and Warrington, 1975; Patterson, 1978).

These detailed symptoms of deep/phonemic dyslexia are difficult to account for solely in terms of failures to make efficient use of the phonological route to the lexicon. This means that patients in this category must have certain other difficulties in processing words.* Additional deficits are also suggested by the

---

* There has been a great deal of discussion in the literature about strategies patients might use to overcome these deficits and there have been several attempts to explain how the various symptoms are produced. These issues are not pursued here since we are presently concerned with the *loci* of individual differences rather than with the details of performance in deep phonemic dyslexia. However, the interested reader is referred to a stimulating collection of papers on deep phonemic dyslexia edited by Coltheart, Patterson and Marshall (1980).

fact that deep/phonemic dyslexics tend to have fairly general difficulties in reading. General reading problems of this kind would not be expected if the damage to the system were restricted to the phonological route. Fluent readers appear to get by without relying on this route (see Section 3.3.3) and so there does not seem to be any reason why a person with a damaged phonological route should not do the same. The fact that with a few isolated exceptions (see, for example, Beauvois and Dérouesné, 1978; and Shallice and Warrington, 1980) deep/phonemic dyslexics are unable to do this suggests that their reading performance must be impaired in other ways. There has been some discussion about the nature of these additional deficits (see, for example, Shallice and Warrington, 1980). Among the possibilities, one of the more important suggestions is that patients have difficulty in accessing the full meaning of the word once it has been recognized. The evidence for this is considered in the next section.

7.2.4 Deficits in accessing word meanings

Evidence that reading difficulties may occur as a result of deficits in retrieving word meanings comes from a case of deep/phonemic dyslexia studied by Warrington and Shallice (1979). This patient seemed to be able to retrieve only part of the meaning of many of the words he was capable of identifying. In one test he was presented with 25 words from each of five categories (animals, plants, parts of the body, foods and objects) and was instructed to try to define them. In 87 cases he was unable to indicate the precise meanings of the words. However, further tests showed that he had access to at least some information about them. In particular, when he was asked to which of two categories the word belonged (e.g. Is it an animal or a plant?) he was correct in 68 of the 87 cases—which is well above chance. Thus, it seems clear that he achieved partial comprehension of at least some of the words.

In another test he was able to classify words like *knock, hum* and *throw* as actions rather than objects but was unable to mime the actions referred to.* In a third test he was presented with the names of 100 well-known authors and politicians. Detailed probing indicated that he had failed to identify 86 of these public figures and yet he was subsequently able to identify the occupations of 69 of them correctly.

These and several other tests indicated that this patient was often unable to retrieve all of the semantic information associated with the words he was asked to read. It seems clear that the failure to retrieve detailed semantic information must inevitably result in some degree of reading difficulty, in which case this study illustrates that such difficulties can potentially arise form inefficiencies in recovering the meaning of words.

---

*The copy editor queried whether *anyone* could mime a hum. After testing a couple of colleagues I doubt it. The instruction merely elicits inane expressions and tightly-closed mouths. Still, the main point of the test remains unchanged.

7.2.5 Deficits resulting from inadequate interaction of subprocesses

Finally, there are certain cases of acquired dyslexia whose reading problems can be attributed to the failure of different subprocesses to work together efficiently. One specific syndrome of this kind was investigated by Shallice and Warrington (1977).

The two patients in this study had little difficulty in recognizing words presented individually but their identification performances fell when two or more words were presented together. This led one of the patients to hold a piece of paper over parts of the page he was not looking at. The reduction in performance was not restricted to words: it was also evident when the stimuli consisted of letters, line drawings or silhouettes.

The fact that the identification of individual forms was almost perfect indicates that both the processes which recognition depends upon (e.g. the extraction of visual information from the page) and the recognition process itself were intact. However, the breakdown in performance with multiple arrays suggests that the procedures are impaired when they have to operate in conjunction with others.

There are almost certainly other categories of acquired dyslexia in which reading difficulties are caused by different kinds of inadequacies in the interaction of subprocesses. However, this particular case is sufficient to establish that difficulties of this kind can occur.

To recapitulate, the work on various forms of acquired dyslexia shows that relatively local deficits can occur within most of the main subprocesses of reading. A patient might find it difficult to read because the visual information extracted from the page is inadequate in some way, because he is unable to recognize words either directly or by pronouncing them, because he has difficulty in retrieving the meanings of individual words or because, for some reason, he is unable to integrate subprocesses so that they work together effectively. If each of these deficits can arise when reading difficulty occurs as a result of brain damage it seems reasonable to suppose that exactly the same kinds of deficiency can occur in other groups of poor or backward readers. The evidence suggests that one or two of them do occur frequently enough to be responsible for major problems in reading, but that others are extremely rare.

7.3 SOURCES OF DIFFICULTY IN BACKWARD READERS NOT DIAGNOSED AS ACQUIRED DYSLEXICS

Perhaps the most direct way of discovering which subprocesses cause particular difficulties for backward readers is to examine the reader's performance on tasks designed to test his capabilities on each of the subskills individually. If the performance for a particular subskill is markedly worse than that for a control group of normal readers then it seems reasonable to hypothesize that the problems with this subskill may be a source of reading difficulty. On the other hand, if there is no clear deficit in a subskill under examination it is difficult to argue that it could be responsible for holding back the progress of reading.

The difficulty with this direct approach is that neither of the inferences above is completely watertight. In the first case, differences in the performance of normal and backward readers could easily be the *result* rather than the *cause* of the backward child's reading difficulties or, alternatively, the two forms of deficiency could be produced by differences in IQ or by some other general difficulty. In the second case, a child may have difficulty with a particular subcomponent of the reading process during the early phases of learning and the problem might subsequently be overcome. On this account the early problem might cause lasting difficulties in other aspects of reading without itself showing up as a potential source of difficulty in a later test. Another problem with the second argument is that it is only valid for common forms of reading deficiency. The deficit will only be apparent if it is shared by a reasonable proportion of the subjects in the experimental sample. If it is only present in one or two cases the effect is unlikely to show up in the average performance of a large group of subjects. In these circumstances the problem would appear to be insignificant even if it was actually an important cause of reading deficiency in certain isolated cases.

In spite of these methodological difficulties it should be possible to use variations in subskill performance to draw some tentative conclusions about the components of the task that are most likely to be responsible for backwardness in reading, and so we shall proceed with this relatively limited purpose in mind.

In the present discussion we shall concentrate on the performance of children whose reading achievements are worse than would be expected on the basis of their age, intelligence or socio-economic background. Different investigations use slightly different definitions of backwardness but the main criteria are generally similar. A typical definition is that used by Stanley and his colleagues who restrict their investigations to subjects who meet the following criteria (Stanley, 1977, p. 226): (i) specific reading deficit of 2.5 years or greater on standard reading tests, (ii) average or better performance on other subjects, (iii) average or better performance IQ, (iv) absence of gross behavioural problems and (v) absence of organic disorders. Rigorous preselection of this kind ensures that the subjects' problems are specific to reading and not general perceptual, cognitive or emotional problems. Subjects isolated in this way are sometimes said to be suffering from 'dyslexia' or 'developmental dyslexia'. However, these terms have connotations (e.g. neurological causes, irreversibility, etc.) that are not accepted by all researchers and for this reason these particular labels will be avoided in the remainder of the present discussion. We shall simply refer to the less accomplished readers as 'poor' or 'backward' readers and to the rest as 'normal' or 'good' readers. There is no suggestion that backward readers constitute a single, well-defined group with a common set of problems. On the contrary, they may fall behind in their reading for any of a large number of different reasons.

Following the kind of analysis carried out at the beginning of the chapter (see Section 7.1), reading backwardness could be caused by problems arising in a variety of subprocesses ranging from the inability to control eye movements to difficulties in constructing and integrating propositions. The potential role of each of these components will be considered in turn.

7.3.1 Deficits in eye movement control

There is good evidence that at least some cases of reading difficulty can be traced back to difficulties in oculomotor control. For example, Ciuffreda, Bahill, Kenyon and Stark (1976) reported a case in which severe reading difficulty was apparently caused by congenital jerk nystagmus and several other investigators (e.g. Zangwill and Blakemore, 1972; Pirozzolo and Rayner, 1978) have noted that individuals with particularly poor eye movement coordination tend to be backward readers as well. These studies suggest that lack of oculomotor control may lead to reading problems in some circumstances, but they do not tell us whether it is a common source of reading difficulty. One way of assessing the likelihood of this suggestion would be to compare preselected samples of good and poor readers to see whether they differ on measures of eye movement coordination. Indications that there could be substantial differences of this kind come from a study by Pavlidis (1978, 1979) and from a series of experiments conducted by Nodine and his colleagues (Nodine and Lang, 1971; Nodine and Steurle, 1973; Nodine and Simmons, 1974). In the Pavlidis experiment the subjects (poor and normal readers) were simply required to fixate a sequence of five lights as they flashed from left to right across a display. The results showed that, in their attempts to do this, poor readers made more forward eye movements and many more regressions. This suggests that the poor readers may have had greater difficulty in controlling their eye movements. In the studies reported by Nodine and his colleagues, 3rd-grade readers and kindergarten non-readers were required to compare pairs of letters, letter-like shapes or pairs of letter strings and their eye movements were monitored while they did so. The results showed that the older children made fewer redundant fixations and that their eye movements were more systematic and deliberate than those made by non-readers (see also Lefton, 1978). On the basis of these findings, Nodine and his colleagues argued that readers have greater cognitive control over their eye movements than non-readers do. Unfortunately, this is not the only interpretation that can be given to these data nor to the results reported by Pavlidis (1979). The important difference between the two groups of children may have been in the way they tackled the experimental task rather than in their ability to control their eye movements.

Evidence that the nature of the task can have a significant effect on variations in eye movement patterns comes from a recent study reported by Stanley (1978). The patterns of eye movements of good and poor readers were compared in two kinds of task—a reading task and a task in which subjects had to locate the picture of an object within a scene. In the first task there were substantial differences between good and poor readers on most of the major measures of eye movements (e.g. number and durations of fixations, number of regressions, etc.). However, these differences did not show up in the search task (which yielded equivalent performances in the two groups). Since the execution of the search task required the subjects to make relatively complex eye movements, it seems most unlikely that the poor readers had any difficulty in controlling their eye movements. If their problems did not derive from poor oculomotor control then the variations in the pattern of eye movements shown in the reading task, and in the earlier studies by Pavlidis and Nodine, must presumably have been caused by the fact that these tasks created other kinds of difficulties for the poor readers. If this is true, it seems likely that unusual patterns of eye movements are the *result* of a poor reader's difficulty in performing a task rather than the *cause* of these difficulties.

Support for this conclusion comes from Tinker's (1936, 1946, 1958) thorough evaluation of studies that have been carried out in various attempts to use oculomotor training to improve reading efficiency. The general outcome of this work was that, while certain procedures were effective in altering subjects' eye movements, they were no more successful in improving reading performance than other techniques based on completely different kinds of training. Tinker argued that since training which led to improvements in eye movement strategies did not improve reading performance, the initial disabilities of the poor readers could not have been caused by deficiencies in eye movement control and this confirms the earlier conclusion that oculomotor differences *per se* are not responsible for major differences in reading ability in the general population.

If these differences are not an important cause of backwardness in reading it is possible that differences in the visual information extracted from the page are. This suggestion will be considered next.

7.3.2 Deficits in visual processing

Good and poor readers may differ in several different aspects of visual processing. Following the sequence of processes described in Chapter 2, they could differ first in the quality or duration of their iconic persistences. Secondly, they could differ in the quality of the visual information extracted from the icon and transferred to STVM. Thirdly, they could differ in their capacity to retain information in STVM. Finally, they could differ in their capacity to integrate visual information from successive fixations. Each of these possibilities will be examined in turn.

7.3.2.1 *Iconic memory*

There is a certain amount of evidence that the iconic persistence of poor readers differs from that of good readers. Stanley and Hall (1973a) measured the duration of the icon for samples of backward and normal readers by using a technique similar to the 'composite image' technique developed by Eriksen and Collins (1968) (see Section 2.5). The subjects were briefly presented with two simple stimuli, one after the other, and the interval between them was increased until they judged that the stimuli no longer formed a composite image. This interval was taken as a measure of iconic persistence and the results showed that it was 30–50 ms *longer* in the sample of backward readers. Similar results were obtained by O'Neill and Stanley (1976) and Ellis and Miles (1978a) (but see also Arnett and Di Lollo, 1979).

A recent experiment reported by Riding and Pugh (1977) has yielded a slightly more complicated pattern of results. In this study iconic persistence was measured using a method similar to that introduced by Haber and Standing (1969). A visual display was switched off and then switched on again after varying intervals. The subject was required to indicate whether or not the stimulus disappeared at any point, and the largest interval at which the gap went unnoticed was taken to be the duration of the icon. On the basis of these measurements the subjects (9–10-year-olds) were divided into subgroups, with short, moderate and long icons and their scores for reading fluency, reading accuracy and comprehension were compared. It was found that children with short and long icons both fared worse on each of the reading tasks than those with average persistences. The implications of these results will be considered later.

7.3.2.2 *Quality of visual information extracted from the icon*

The investigation of this potential source of difference between good and poor readers is hampered by the fact that it is probably not possible to obtain a pure measure of the quality of visual information extracted from the icon. The information has to be tested in some way and this process of interrogation may introduce further sources of individual variation into the data. There are three main types of task which a subject can be made to perform to demonstrate the quality of the visual information available to him. One is simply to draw a copy of the stimulus. Another is to match the stimulus to a long-established prototype in memory (i.e. to identify it) and the third is to compare it with another recently presented form. In each case it is likely that the stimulus information is retained momentarily in STVM and so there is a possibility that performance will be affected by individual differences in the *retention* of the information as well as by differences in its quality. Also, if the subject makes more than one fixation on the stimulus (or on his own reproduction of it or on a comparison form) the data may be distorted by differences in the ability to integrate visual information from different fixations. However, as we shall see later, these two potential sources of difficulty do not turn out to be important.

Numerous studies have used reproduction techniques to test the possibility that good and poor readers differ in their visual processing skills. Some of these investigations give no indication that there is any relationship between a subject's reading performance and his ability to copy a stimulus shape (e.g. Werner, Simonian and Smith, 1967; Lovell and Gorton, 1968; Vellutino, Pruzek, Steger and Meshoulam, 1973; Vellutino, Steger, Kaman and DeSetto, 1975). However, in the majority of cases it has been found that good or average readers perform better at copying tasks than poor or backward readers (e.g. Goins, 1958; Koppitz, 1958; Lachmann, 1960; Smith and Keogh, 1962; de Hirsch, Jansky and Langford, 1966; Crosby, 1968; Larsen, Rogers and Sowell, 1976, and many others). Assuming that this relationship is a real one, we are faced with the problem of how it should be interpreted. The difference between good and poor readers could reasonably be attributed to the fact that poor readers are less proficient at visual discrimination, but there are several plausible alternatives to this interpretation. Poor readers might be less efficient at analysing the stimulus into its components. They might be worse at planning the operations required for the drawing or they might be worse at executing this plan (i.e. producing the drawing itself). The limited evidence available suggests that the differences between good and poor readers disappear if the subjects are allowed to indicate which stimulus was presented without actually having to draw it (see Owen, Adams, Forrest, Stolz and Fisher, 1971, and Zach and Kaufman, 1972). This suggests that whatever difficulties poor readers might have, they do *not* lie in their ability to discriminate shapes.

The second technique for examining the quality of the information extracted from the icon—matching it with information stored in long-term memory—is equally open to alternative explanations. Suppose it were shown that good readers are better at categorizing stimuli in this way. This could mean either that the raw visual data available to them in STVM are richer or that the categorization process is more efficient or that they are more effective in reporting the categories that are activated. It would clearly be difficult to use this technique to test hypotheses that are based exclusively on the first interpretation, and so this approach is of limited value for investigating individual differences in the quality of STVM.

Perhaps the most fruitful way of tackling the problem is to compare the way in which good and poor readers match pairs of visual stimuli or search for a target in an array of shapes. This approach cuts out some of the problems associated with reproduction techniques since it eliminates differences due to variations in the subjects' ability to plan and execute drawings.

Many of the matching and search experiments that have been conducted have made use of stimuli that are easy to name (e.g. letters, digits or words). The use of familiar stimuli gives rise to difficulties in interpreting the results since, if good readers are found to perform better than poor readers, the result can always be explained away by assuming that the difference lies in their coding ability and not in differences in the quality of the visual information extracted from the icon. This interpretative problem arises in at least two studies comparing good and poor readers. In one of these studies, Spring (1971) found that poor readers take longer to match pairs of simultaneously presented letters than good readers do. In the second study, Lahey and Lefton (1976) showed that poor readers make more errors in selecting a target string of 4, 5, 6 or 7 letters from a page containing the target string and six other strings of letters. In each of these experiments the good readers might have performed better than the others because they were more efficient at using strategies based on naming or identifying the stimuli. Hence it is impossible to tell whether or not there were differences in visual processing.

Other experiments seem to show that good and poor readers do not differ in their matching skills. These studies present fewer problems since, if there is no difference overall between the levels of performance of the groups, it seems unlikely that there is a marked difference in the quality of the visual information extracted from the icon. If there *were* such a difference in favour of good readers, it would have to be counterbalanced by an opposing effect at some other stage in the processing sequence, otherwise the effect would show up in the data. In one study in this category, Lahey and Lefton (1976) found that poor readers made no more errors in picking out short strings of 1–3 letters from a page containing seven alternative strings. Similarly Lahey and McNees (1975) found no differences in letter discrimination ability while Katz and Wicklund (1972) and Mason (1975) found that there was no difference in the time taken for good and poor readers to locate a target item in a random string of letters. Again, Leslie and Calfee (1971) found no difference between good and poor readers in the time taken to locate a word in a list of ten alternatives, while Ellis and Miles (1978b) found no difference in the time taken to say whether pairs of letters were the same or different.

While the results of these studies suggest that poor readers do *not* suffer from any kind of visual deficit, it would clearly be more convincing if the conclusion were based on data which are less likely to be distorted by the subjects' use of labelling strategies. The obvious way of obtaining such data would be to use stimulus materials that are difficult to name or identify. Most studies that do this show no differences between good and poor readers. For example, Vellutino, Steger, DeSetto and Phillips (1975) presented subjects with targets consisting of 1, 2- or 3-character strings of Hebrew letters. Immediately after seeing these stimuli they were shown a column of 20 alternative items and instructed to pick out the target strings. The results showed that there was no difference in the number of mistakes made by good and poor readers. In a more recent study, Gupta, Ceci and Slater (1978) showed subjects stimuli consisting of 1–6 Gibson forms. The subjects (7–8-year-old children with a range of reading ages) were then presented with a display containing the target together with three alternative strings, and they were instructed to point to the stimulus that was exactly the same as the original one. The results showed that the correlation between the number of mistakes in this task and reading ability did not approach significance. Another aspect of this study demonstrated some of the dangers of using nameable stimuli. The task was repeated using random letter strings, and again using pronounceable letter strings, and under these conditions there *was* a correlation between errors and reading ability.

In neither of these experiments was there much pressure on subjects to respond rapidly, and so it could be argued that the techniques were insensitive to variations in the ease with which the task was executed by good and poor readers. However, an experiment conducted by Mason and Katz (1976) suggested that there may be no differences even when there is time pressure. In this study, subjects were timed as they searched for a target shape in a random string of unfamiliar shapes (predominantly Greek letters). The results showed that the response latencies for good readers were no shorter than those for poor readers.

Not all studies employing unfamiliar shapes have shown matching performance of poor readers to be as good as that of good readers. Trieschmann (1968) found that when 7–9-year-olds were shown a Gibson form which they were subsequently required to point out in a line of alternatives, the backward readers made significantly more errors than good readers. A comparable result was obtained by Whipple and Kodman (1969) in a study in which 34 test alternatives were presented in succession. However, it is likely that the test conditions in both of these experiments encouraged the subjects to name or describe the stimuli, so there is no way of being certain that the differences originated in visual memory. In Trieschmann's study the subjects were shown the stimulus form for 10 seconds—a stimulus duration which would have given them ample time to liken it to more familiar shapes in the way adults tend to do (see Mitchell, 1972b). This could easily have produced a coding strategy which would favour the better readers. In Whipple and Kodman's study each of the test alternatives was presented for 3 seconds which means that the subjects had to retain the target shape for over 100 seconds. Since it is difficult to retain accurate visual information for so long (see Section 2.5) the experimental conditions almost certainly provided a strong incentive for subjects to make use of coding strategies of some kind. Similar criticisms may be levelled at other studies that purport to show that good and poor readers differ in their visual matching or recognition performance (e.g. Samuels and Anderson, 1973).

To summarize, good and poor readers tend to differ in their capacity to handle tasks that involve drawing or naming visual stimuli. However, there is no evidence of any difference in visual tasks which minimize the contribution of these two activities. Thus, there does not seem to be any convincing evidence that good and poor readers differ in the quality of the visual information extracted from the page. Similar conclusions have been reached by Audley (1976), Vallutino, Steger, Moyer, Harding and Niles (1977), Vellutino (1977) and Ellis and Miles (1981). However, the consensus on this issue is not complete. Other authors (e.g. Vernon, 1971, 1977) have argued that good and poor readers *do* show differences of this kind. Yet an examination of the studies reviewed by these authors reveals that most of them suffered from one or other of the methodological problems considered in the last few paragraphs and so, on present evidence, there does not appear to be any reason to qualify the conclusion that good and poor readers do not differ in the quality of the visual information extracted from the page.

7.3.2.3 *Non-iconic visual memory*

If there are no important differences in the information initially extracted from the page, the difference between good and poor readers may lie in the efficiency with which this information is retained.

Several studies have tried to examine this possibility. However, many of them suffer from the methodological problems considered above. Some of the investigators (e.g. Lyle, 1968a; Lunzer, Dolan and Wilkinson, 1976) have made use of drawing tasks to examine individual differences in visual memory. As pointed out above, differences in reproduction skills may themselves be responsible for the results obtained in such studies and so it is not easy to draw any inferences about possible differences in visual memory. Numerous other studies (e.g. Lyle, 1968b; Lyle and Goyen, 1968; Guthrie and Goldberg, 1972; Cummings and Faw, 1976; Lunzer et al., 1976) have used highly codable stimulus materials such as simple geometrical shapes, drawings of animals and so on. In these experiments it is clear that any differences between good and poor readers could be attributed to differences in the subjects' ability to use coding strategies. In fact, Torgesen and Goldman (1977) have conducted a study that provides positive evidence that coding differences account for a major part of the effect. In the first part of this study the investigators used a recognition procedure to test immediate memory for line drawings of simple objects. As expected, the results showed the good readers performed better than poor readers. However, the investigators noticed that the good readers also showed a greater tendency to verbalize the materials, suggesting that the difference in this experiment might have been wholly or partly due to differences in coding strategy. To test this possibility they conducted a second experiment designed to encourage poor readers as well as good readers to use coding strategies. The subjects were required to name the object aloud before tackling the recognition task. The result of this procedural change was to reduce the difference between good and poor readers, which tends to confirm the notion that the original advantage was largely due to verbalization.

The results of this and other experiments suggest that the ideal way of testing the possibility that there are reading-related differences in visual memory would be to use a task in which the possibility of verbalization is completely eliminated. This is probably impossible in practice, but the effects of coding can be minimized by using unfamiliar stimulus materials. Several experiments of this kind have been conducted and the results show no evidence of any differences between good and poor readers. In an experiment described in the previous section, Vellutino, Steger, DeSetto and Phillips (1975) tested subjects' ability to recognize short strings of Hebrew letters and found that poor readers performed just as well as good readers whether they were tested immediately, after 24 hours or after 6 months. The finding that good and poor readers do not differ in their immediate recall of Hebrew letters has been confirmed in other studies by Vellutino and his colleagues (Vellutino, Steger and Kandel, 1972; Vellutino, Smith, Steger and Kaman, 1975). It is also supported by the results of the experiments by Gupta, Ceci and Slater (1978) and Mason and Katz (1976) in the previous section, since the matching and search tasks employed in these studies almost certainly call for the use of visual memory. The absence of any differences between good and poor readers suggests that visual memory (as well as the quality of the information initially extracted from the icon) must be comparable in these two groups. Further evidence that good and poor readers retain unfamiliar shapes equally well has been reported by Clifton-Everest (1974), Stanley (1977), Ellis and Miles (1978b, Expts III and IV) and many other investigators.

In short, the evidence presently available suggests that while poor readers tend to be worse at retaining visually presented material, this can probably be attributed to the fact that they are less effective at using verbal coding strategies. There do not appear to be any differences between good and poor readers in visual memory *per se*.

The discussion of visual memory so far has concentrated on subjects' ability to remember the *identity* of shapes and patterns. However, it is sometimes suggested (e.g. by Vernon, 1971, 1977, and by Clifton-Everest, 1976) that good and poor readers differ in their ability of perceive and remember the *order* in which a sequence of shapes appear. There is a good deal of evidence to show that there are such performance differences in sequential memory tasks (e.g. deHirsch, Jansky and Langford, 1966; Bakker, 1967; Doehring, 1968; Zurif and Carson, 1970; Corkin, 1974, and Mason, Katz and Wicklund, 1975). However, it is not clear whether there are any differences in the *visual* retention of order information since, as before, the majority of the studies in the literature have used nameable stimuli* and this leaves open the possibility that the differences lie in the *verbal* retention of order information.

More definite evidence that verbal labelling could have been responsible for the differences comes from investigations carried out by Bowen, Gelabert and Torgesen (1978) and by Hicks (1980).

One of the few experiments which avoids the potentially confounding effects of verbal labelling was conducted by Bakker (1967). In this study good and poor readers were shown a sequence of visual stimuli and immediately afterwards the same stimuli were presented together on a card in a random order. The subject was required to indicate which of the stimuli had been presented first, second, third and so on, and the response was considered correct only if all of the items were in the correct order. In the condition which is crucial to the present discussion the stimuli were meaningless figures and were therefore difficult to name or describe. With these materials, the results showed that there was no difference between the performance of good and poor readers. In three other conditions employing drawings of familiar objects, letters and digits, it was found that good readers performed better than poor readers. These results suggest that the differences in order retention are associated primarily with tasks that involve labelling the stimuli. Further support for this conclusion comes from a similar experiment conducted by Done and Miles (1978). Like Bakker, these authors found that good and poor readers did not differ in their ability to remember the order of nonsense shapes. However, the

---

* De Hirsch *et al.* (1966), Doehring (1968) and Mason *et al.* (1975) used materials such as letters and digits. Other investigators used visual stimuli that can easily be converted into a verbal form. Zurif and Carson (1970) required subjects to match pairs of three or four flashes of light with short ($\frac{1}{2}$-second) or long (1-second) pauses between them, and Corkin (1974) produced visual stimuli by tapping small wooden blocks in various sequences.

subjects were tested again after they had been given an opportunity to learn a set of names for the shapes, and in this condition the performance of the good readers turned out to be superior. Again, the differences in performance seem to be associated with the use of labelling strategies. On present evidence, therefore, there does not seem to be any reason to believe that good and poor readers differ in their capacity to perceive the order of visual stimuli or to retain this information in visual memory.

7.3.2.4 *Integrating visual information from successive fixations*

Perhaps good and poor readers differ in their ability to integrate visual information over different fixations. At the time of writing no experiments appear to have been carried out specifically to test this possibility. However, in some of the experiments on visual discrimination and visual memory considered above (e.g. Vellutino, Steger, DeSetto and Phillips, 1975; Gupta, Ceci and Slater, 1978), the test materials were arranged in such a way that subjects could not have avoided making several different fixations in order to extract the information necessary to make a response. It will be recalled that these experiments showed no difference between readers of differing ability and so it seems unlikely that there are marked differences between good and poor readers in the integration of information over fixations.

7.3.3 Differences in direct word recognition

Before examining potential differences between backward and normal readers in relation to direct word recognition it is obviously important to establish whether young readers systematically use this kind of strategy to identify words. Some investigators (e.g. Mason, 1976; Doctor and Coltheart, 1980) have suggested that young and inexperienced readers tend to use phonological rather than visual information to access the lexicon. However, there is a certain amount of evidence that they do not always use this strategy. Barron and Baron (1977) carried out an experiment in which children ranging in age from 6 to 12 were shown a picture and a word (e.g. a picture of a loaf of bread and the word *butter*) and instructed to indicate whether they 'went together'. In one condition the subjects performed a vocal interference task (repeating the word *double*) at the same time as making the decision. In the other they performed the linking task alone. The results showed that the decision latencies were unaffected by the interference task. This suggests that even the youngest children did not use phonological coding to identify the word presented in the stimulus display. A potential problem with this conclusion is that phonological coding is not always impaired by suppression tasks of the kind used in this study (cf. Besner, Davies and Daniels, 1981). However, the results obtained in another part of the study suggest that phonological coding *was* interfered with under the conditions prevailing in the Barron and Baron experiment. Subjects were presented with a picture/word pair as before, but their task was modified so that they were required to indicate whether the word and the label for the picture rhymed with one another. Under these conditions, were phonological coding is obviously quite important, decision latencies *were* increased by the interference task, and so it seems that the children's performance would have been affected if they had been using phonological coding in the first task.

Another experiment which suggests that children do not use phonological information in identifying familiar words was reported by Golinkoff and Rosinski (1976). They found that while good and poor readers differ in their phonological decoding skills as measured by the speed with which they are able to pronounce nonsense words, the difference does not seem to affect their performance in a picture/word interference task. In this task the subjects were shown a picture of a familiar object and they were required to name the object as quickly as possible. Superimposed upon the picture was a string of letters. This was either the name of the object in the picture (the 'appropriate' word) or the name of some other object (an inappropriate word) or a nonsense syllable. The results showed that the time taken to identify the picture was longer when the superimposed word was inappropriate than when it was appropriate. This indicates that the subjects identified the word and that this interfered with the main task. However, the crucial finding was that the magnitude of the interference effect was the same for good and for poor readers (see also Guttentag and Haith, 1978). If the subjects had used a phonological coding strategy to identify the words then, given the difference in decoding skills, poor readers would presumably have been less efficient at this process than the more skilled readers. If this had been the case, they would have been less likely to recognize the word soon enough for it to influence their performance on the picture-naming task. Consequently, if phonological coding had been important, poor readers would have been expected to show a smaller interference effect and so the fact that the effect was approximately the same for both groups suggests that the subjects used direct access for the words employed in this study.

Given that there seems to be some evidence that direct access word recognition does occur in young readers, it is reasonable to return to the original question. Do normal and backward readers differ in this process?

Unfortunately, there does not appear to be any clear evidence on this issue. An ideal test would be restricted to a small sample of highly familiar words—if more difficult words were used the subjects might not use a direct access strategy (cf. Pace and Golinkoff, 1976). The test would also have to be based on a measure that does not involve pronouncing the word since less skilled readers may find that the problem of pronunciation itself causes difficulty, and so a response of this kind might distort the data.* The issue could potentially be resolved by comparing the response time for good and poor readers in a lexical

* This rules out evidence from several studies that appear to show that skilled readers are quicker at the direct recognition of high-frequency words than less skilled readers are (e.g. Perfetti, Goldman and Hogaboam, 1979).

decision task using common words. However, no experiments of this kind appear to have been carried out to date, and so no legitimate conclusions can be drawn.

The present discussion of individual differences in word recognition has concentrated almost exclusively on the processing of highly familiar words and, while there is no direct evidence that good and poor readers differ in the way they handle these materials, there may be differences in the way they tackle unfamiliar words.

7.3.4 Differences in word-attack skills

It will be recalled from Chapters 3 and 5 that when fluent readers are confronted with unfamiliar or indistinct words they tend to try to analyse them by using orthographic rules, phonetic recoding or semantic or syntactic constraints. Do less skilled readers do the same thing, and if they do, are they effective at using this strategy?

7.3.4.1 *Use of orthographic constraints*

It is conceivable that good and poor readers differ in their ability to make use of orthographic constraints in word recognition. Certainly, there is some evidence that good readers are able to make effective use of such constraints in a variety of tasks that may have some bearing on word recognition. They are more successful at identifying the character positions in which individual letters occur most frequently in English words (Katz, 1977). They are more effective at guessing material which is missing from the display (Lefton, Spragins and Byrnes, 1973). And they also benefit more from a orthographic constraints in tasks which entail matching pairs of letter strings (Seymour and Porpodas, 1980) and searching for a target item in an array of letters or unfamiliar symbols (Mason, 1975; Mason and Katz, 1976). If good and poor readers differ in their ability to use orthographic constraints in tasks that vary as much as those just cited, it is not unreasonable to suppose that they differ in the efficiency with which they use this information in word recognition itself. Unfortunately, however, there does not seem to be any direct evidence to support this suggestion and so at the time of writing it remains no more than a strong possibility.

7.3.4.2 *Phonetic recoding*

A second strategy which subjects might use to tackle unfamiliar or indistinct words is to recode the string of letters phonetically and use the resulting representation of the word to access its lexical entry. There is evidence to suggest that this is a strategy that is widely adopted by young readers and, in contrast with most of the possibilities considered up to now, there is strong evidence to suggest that good and poor readers differ in the efficiency with which they apply the strategy. Perfetti and Hogaboam (1975) presented young readers with regular nonwords and instructed them to pronounce each stimulus as rapidly as possible. The results showed that the response time for poor readers was slower than that for good readers. Similar results have been obtained by Golinkoff and Rosinski (1976), Hogaboam and Perfetti (1978), Perfetti, Finger and Hogaboam (1978) and Seymour and Porpodas (1980), while Calfee, Venezky and Chapman (1967, cited in Perfetti and Hogaboam, 1975), Firth (1972, cited in Rozin and Gleitman, 1977) and Snowling (1980) have all shown that good and poor readers differ in the *accuracy* with which they execute pronunciation tasks of this kind. (For further evidence on decoding differences see reviews by Barron, 1978, 1980; Jorm, 1979, and Ellis and Miles, 1981.)

While there is strong evidence that there are individual differences in decoding skills it is not entirely clear which aspects of the process are responsible for most of the problems. The process can be analysed into at least three stages. First, the graphemes comprising the stimulus have to be classified in terms of stored letter representations. Presumably information recovered from each entry is then used to generate a phonetic representation of the letter (or perhaps a variety of alternative representations—different tasks might require a subject to say the name of the letter (e.g. 'see' for *c*) or to generate various different phonemes it might represent (e.g. the initial phonemes in *cost* and *certain*)). Finally, the individual phonemes have to be combined or 'blended' in accordance with the rules of English pronunciation to produce an acceptable pronunciation of the string as a whole.

The evidence suggests that at least part of the difficulty must lie in the first two stages since the differences between good and poor readers are evident in tasks which are unlikely to involve any blending of phonemes. In one study, Audley (1976) found that good readers were more effective at coping with a task in which they were required to indicate whether the name of a picture rhymed with that of a simultaneously presented letter. Similarly, Ellis and Miles (1978b) showed that good readers performed better in an experiment in which subjects were required to indicate whether pairs of upper- and lower-case letters had the same name. Finally, Spring and Capps (1974a, 1974b) and Denckla and Rudel (1976a, 1976b) found that poor readers were slower at naming series of visual stimuli such as digits, letters, colours or line drawings. These studies suggest that poor readers may hit problems well before they try to blend the phonemes of a word. In fact, the last series of experiments suggests that they may suffer from a generalized deficiency in naming visually presented objects (see also Jackson, 1980; but see Stanovich, in press, for a dissenting view).

These studies do not tell us whether the difficulties are associated with the process of accessing the internal representation of the stimulus or in generating its name from this information, and it may be impossible to resolve this issue given the evidence presently available. However, the results of an experiment reported by Stanley and Hall (1973b) suggest that the first process is responsible for at least part of the difficulty. Subjects were required to identify a single letter followed after varying delays by a pattern mask. The interval was increased until the letter was correctly named on three successive occasions and the results showed that the critical interval was longer for backward than for normal readers. It is difficult to see why the process of generating a name from the internal representation of a letter should be affected by masking and so it seems likely that this difference must have arisen in the initial identification process.

If poor readers suffer from general difficulties in naming visual stimuli, as these studies suggest, then it might be expected that they would tend to avoid information-processing strategies that depend heavily on recoding the stimulus materials. Evidence in support of this suggestion has been reported by Liberman, Shankweiler, Liberman, Fowler and Fischer (1977). Good and poor readers were required to write down the material in briefly presented (3-second) arrays of rhyming or non-rhyming letters. The results showed that the good readers recalled significantly fewer letters when they rhymed, suggesting that they tended to tackle the task by recoding the letters acoustically. However, for poor readers the corresponding difference was considerably smaller, which presumably indicates that they make less use of the recoding strategy.

Generating the successive phonemes of a word is not the only part of the process which seems to cause problems for poor readers. There is evidence that they also have difficulty in blending phonemes to form the sound of the word. This has been shown in a number of studies employing tests in which subjects are presented with a sequence of phonemes and instructed to respond by saying the word they form. Golden and Steiner (1969) found that the level of performance in the task was better for good readers than for poor readers of the same age and intelligence. Also, several investigators have reported significant correlations between sound blending and various measures of reading achievement (Dykstra, 1966; McNinch, 1971: for a detailed review see Richardson, DiBenedetto and Bradley, 1977).

Summarizing then, the evidence suggests that good and poor readers differ markedly in their capacity to pronounce unfamiliar words. Part of the difference may lie in the speed and ease with which they identify individual letters, but the major problems are likely to be associated with the use of GPC rules or analogies to generate the sounds of individual letters and in blending these sounds to pronounce the word as a whole.

It is sometimes suggested that these difficulties are symptomatic of certain rather general problems that poor readers have in analysing acoustic stimuli. In support of this suggestion it can be noted that there seems to be a correlation between children's decoding skills and the difficulty they have in the phonetic segmentation of words. In a typical demonstration of this, Bradley and Bryant (1978) compared the analytic skills of normal and backward readers by using an 'oddity' task in which subjects were read a series of words (e.g. *nod, red, fed, bed*) and were then required to say which was the odd word out. The results showed that backward readers made significantly more errors than normal readers. Relationships between backwardness in reading and various measures of phoneme analysis have also been reported by Bruce (1964), Rosner and Simon (1971), Savin (1972), Calfee, Lindamood and Lindamood (1973), Fox and Routh (1975, 1976), Calfee (1977), Rozin and Gleitman (1977) and Wallach,

Wallach, Dozier and Kaplan (1977). Moreover, Liberman (1973) has shown that the segmentation performance of pre-readers can be used to predict their reading achievements a year later. These results seem to confirm that reading progress is somehow dependent upon the processes of phonemic analysis. However, no one, as yet, has specified exactly how this might occur.

7.3.4.3 *Use of semantic or syntactic constraints*

The third way in which readers might improve their chances of identifying a (visually) unfamiliar word is by using contextual constraints to narrow down the range of alternatives. It will be recalled from the material reviewed in Section 5.5 that there is a considerable amount of evidence that the accuracy of word information can be improved if readers make use of information of this kind. It is conceivable that good and poor readers differ in their ability to draw upon such contextual information and use it to help them identify new words.

Good readers certainly seem to have *some* advantages when it comes to handling contextual information. For example, Perfetti, Goldman and Hogaboam (1979) have reported an experiment which shows that good readers are more effective at using context to predict a future word. The subjects in this study were required to read or to listen to a passage word by word, stopping at each point to predict what they thought the next word would be. The results showed that the good readers made significantly more correct predictions than the poor readers did (32 per cent correct compared with 22 per cent for the less skilled readers). Comparable results have been obtained in a study by Guthrie (1973a) in which subjects were required to use contextual information to select the most appropriate word from sets of alternatives presented at various points in the passage and in a variety of experiments in which good and poor readers were required to fill in words that were missing from the text (Cromer and Wiener, 1966; Neville and Pugh, 1976–1977; Willows, 1980).

Can good readers capitalize on these advantages and use them to help in the process of identifying new words? Some of the evidence suggests that they can, but other studies suggest that good and poor readers do not differ in the degree to which they use context. An experiment in the first category was reported by Marcel (1974). In this study fast and slow readers were presented with brief visual displays containing strings of words that conformed to various different degrees of sequential constraint. The subjects were required to report as much of the stimulus material as possible. The results showed that, while both groups performed better with the more predictable materials, the advantage was less marked for the poor readers, suggesting that they might have been less efficient at using the contextual information.

A similar result was reported by Klein, Klein and Bertino (1974). In this study subjects were required to mark the beginnings and ends of words typed in a sequence without spaces between them. In one condition the sequence of words was in the form of connected prose and in the second condition the order was randomized. The results showed that the number of words correctly marked within a period of 90 seconds was greater in the prose condition and that this advantage was more marked for the accomplished readers. In a third study suggesting that good readers make greater use of context, Isakson and Miller (1976) instructed subjects to read materials that violated various syntactic and semantic constraints. The results showed that poor readers make fewer mistakes in this task which suggests that they may be less sensitive to the anomalies introduced by the contextual constraints.

More recent investigations conducted by Perfetti and his colleagues point a different conclusion. Perfetti, Goldman and Hogaboam (1979) carried out an experiment in which good and poor readers were required to read a number of target words presented in the context of a passage of prose. Vocalization time was plotted as a function of the predictability of each word and the results showed that the slope was almost exactly the same for the two groups of readers, suggesting that the poor readers may have used the contextual information just as effectively as the good readers did.

One difficulty with this conclusion is that the good readers may not have had as much opportunity as the less skilled readers to make use of context. The reason for this is simply that contextual processes can only influence performance if they can be put into effect rapidly enough to 'beat' the processes that are used to recognize the words in isolation. With good readers the identification of isolated words is typically faster than that for poor readers, and so in the study under consideration there may have been fewer trials on which performance could potentially be influenced by context. If this is the case, there is no way of telling from these data whether good and poor readers differ in their use of context.

One way of overcoming this problem would be to degrade the stimulus words presented to the more skilled readers so that the recognition time for words in isolation is approximately the same as that for undegraded or less degraded words presented to poor readers. In these circumstances, the opportunity to use contextual information would be roughly the same in the two groups and so the amount of contextual facilitation could be interpreted as a measure of the effectiveness with which contextual information is used to improve word recognition. An experiment of this kind has been reported by Perfetti and Roth (1981). The results showed that when recognition time was equated in this way, the degree of contextual facilitation (as measured by the difference in the latency to identify critical words in isolation and in context) was almost exactly the same for skilled and less skilled readers. In other words, the results tended to confirm Perfetti's earlier suggestion that the two groups do not differ in their ability to make use of context.

The inconsistencies between these findings and the earlier evidence that good readers are better at using context to facilitate word recognition are perhaps most plausibly explained in terms of differences in the degree to which subjects succeeded in mastering the material leading up to the critical test words. In the earlier studies it seems likely that the background material itself was difficult to read and understand. Thus, it may be that the good readers made better use of context because they had a sounder basis on which to make predictions. In the studies by Perfetti and his colleagues it is likely that these differences were minimized and in these circumstances the good readers showed no advantage. If this argument is accepted we can conclude that good and poor readers probably do not differ in their ability to facilitate word recognition by using linguistic constraints *per se*.

7.3.5 Differences in knowledge of word meanings

It is quite plausible that part of the difference in performance between good and poor readers is due to the fact that the poorer readers are able to identify fewer words than good readers and know less about the words they do succeed in identifying. It is easy to see that incomplete knowledge of word meanings could reduce reading speed and lower the reader's level of comprehension. Indirect evidence that differences of this sort might be significant comes from a study by McFarland and Rhodes (1978). Skilled and unskilled readers of various ages were required to carry out a task in which they rated a series of words as 'good' or 'bad', and they were subsequently tested to see how many of these words they were able to remember. Now, performance in 'incidental learning' tasks of this kind is known to depend on the use of semantic elaboration of the word meanings, and the level of recall can be taken as a measure of the child's tendency to retrieve detailed semantic information when he reads the word. The results showed that a higher proportion of the words were recalled by the skilled readers which suggests that these readers must have processed the words more elaborately than the others. It is conceivable that they did this simply because they had *access* to more information about the word meanings.

7.3.6 Differences in constructing and combining propositions

There is reason to believe that backward and normal readers might differ in their ability to retain information in short-term or working memory (Baddeley, 1978; Miles and Wheeler, 1974; Nelson and Warrington, 1980; Stanley and Hall, 1973b). If this is so, it might lead to more general differences in the processing of sentences. More specifically, if poor readers are relatively inefficient at retaining unintegrated strings of words then it is conceivable that there may be occasions on which the storage capacity falls short of that required for efficient sentence processing.

Direct tests of this 'post-identification' difference between good and poor readers have been carried out in various experiments reported by Cromer and his colleagues and the results seem to indicate that there is at least a small group of backward readers (dubbed the 'Difference' group by Wiener and Cromer, 1967) whose major problems lie in their inability to combine and organize the words in the test. These readers are distinguished from other poor readers by the fact that they have normal vocabulary skills as well as adequate language skills and adequate intelligence. In one study by Cromer (1970), subjects were required to read texts presented in four different ways: (1) normal presentation in the form of a page of prose; (2) presented one word at a time on a roll of paper; (3) presentation of words in 'meaningful' groups (i.e. groups consistent with the syntactic divisions in the text) and (4) partitioned into relatively meaningless segments of text. The comprehension performance for a 'difference' group of poor readers was compared with that for a control group of normal readers. As expected, the difference group performed worse in the three conditions where the material was not explicitly organized into meaningful units. However, in the meaningful phrase conditions their comprehension scores were as high as those for normal readers. This suggests that for this particular kind of backward reader the difficulty lies not in the identification of individual words but in integrating these words into meaningful units. A subsequent study by Oakan, Wiener and Cromer (1971) has shown that these organizational problems are not confined to reading tasks. A group of difference readers and a control group of normal readers were required to listen to a passage that was either read normally or read in a disorganized way (by a poor reader). The results showed that in the latter condition, when the material was not preorganized, comprehension performance was worse for the difference group, while in the former condition there was no difference.

These investigations do not pinpoint the processes which are responsible for the reading problems in the difference group. However, insofar as the difficulty is removed by grouping the words grammatically, it seems fairly likely that the difficulty is associated with the use of parsing procedures. Whether or not this is the case, the results suggest that at least some of the differences between good and poor readers may be introduced during the processes that follow the identification of individual words. Other studies that point in the same direction have been reported by Smiley, Oakley, Worthen, Campione and Brown (1977) and by Di Vesta, Hayward and Orlando (1979).

7.3.7 Differences associated with the interaction of reading subskills

It seems plausible that poor reading might sometimes occur when the individual subprocesses fail to mesh smoothly. On this hypothesis, good and poor readers might be equivalent in the efficiency with which the separate subskills of reading operate. The differences between them might be attributed entirely to the fact that the processes work together more efficiently in good readers.

There do not appear to be any studies that examine this issue directly. Guthrie (1973b) has shown that the intercorrelation between the performance on the different subskills of reading is much greater for normal readers than it is for disabled readers. Arguably, this result could be interpreted as evidence that the subprocesses are less interdependent in poor readers. On this assumption there would be less opportunity for the development of individual subskills to influence one another and this would account for the low correlation between the subskills. However, this is not the only reasonable interpretation of Guthrie's data. It could be that the processes intermesh to the same degree in good and poor readers, but that poor readers are less effective at using these relationships to develop the subskills in which they are deficient. It follows that Guthrie's data do not provide convincing support for the suggestion that good and poor readers differ in the efficiency with which the subprocesses of reading operate together.

There is a second way in which interactions between various subprocesses of reading might be responsible for part of the differences between good and poor readers. The more fluent readers may be capable of completing some of the subprocesses relatively automatically (i.e. without allocating much attention to them—LaBerge and Samuels, 1974). If so, they may be free to devote more processing capacity to other critical aspects of the task. Backward readers, on the other hand, may not achieve the same degree of automatic processing, in which case it can be assumed that they would not be in a position to attend so closely to other processes. Performance on these subprocesses (and therefore reading performance overall) could easily suffer as a consequence of this kind of diversion of resources.

LaBerge and Samuels (1974) suggest that automization plays an important part in fluent reading and they speculate that the capacity to process information in this way distinguishes fluent readers from learners. It is conceivable that similar differences are responsible for the different levels of performance in good and poor readers. However, it remains for this conjecture to be supported by empirical evidence.

7.4 SUMMARY OF THE DIFFERENCES BETWEEN GOOD AND POOR READERS

There are differences in the patterns of eye movements made during reading by good and poor readers. It seems likely, however, that except in a very small proportion of cases, this difference is the *result* rather than the cause of the differences in reading achievement.

Differences in visual processing capabilities also appear to be rather unimportant as causes of reading difficulty despite the fact that several investigators claim to have shown such differences. Many of the experiments designed to examine this question are difficult to interpret because of the possibility that the results may be influenced by non-visual factors (e.g. verbal coding strategies, differences in drawing skills, etc.). Studies in which these methodological problems are handled adequately suggest that there are no marked differences between backward and normal readers in the extraction of visual information from the page or in the retention or integration of this information prior to word recognition. There *do* appear to be some small differences in the duration of iconic persistence, but since it is unlikely that this kind of visual persistence plays an important part in reading (see Chapter 2) there is no reason to believe that these differences are responsibile for any of the differences in performance between backward and normal readers.

It is not known whether there are any differences between good and poor readers in the direct recognition of familiar words. The appropriate experiments have yet to be carried out. However, there *is* strong evidence that there are differences in word-attack skills used to analyse unfamiliar words. Good readers are certainly better at decoding words phonetically and at blending phonemes to produce the sound of words. They also seem to be more effective at using semantic and syntactic constraints to guess a missing word although it is not yet clear whether they are able to use this information to improve identification when a word is actually presented.

Turning to the processes that occur after word recognition, there is evidence that at least some poor readers encounter difficulties in combining words into sentences or in integrating successive sentences to derive the overall meaning of text. However it is not yet entirely clear how widespread these problems are.

Finally, while it has been suggested that the various subskills of reading might be poorly integrated in retarded readers, this possibility remains to be demonstrated empirically.

Taken together these results suggest that the most obvious weakness shown by poor readers as a group is that they have marked difficulty in identifying new or unfamiliar words. It is easy to see how problems of this kind could lead to more general difficulties in reading. The failure to identify a new word during the first few encounters may cause a number of subsequent problems for the reader. It may hold up the process of learning to identify the word directly and, if reading vocabulary is restricted in this way, it may also lead to deficiencies in understanding sentences or passages of prose. Indeed, it is conceivable that for many poor readers these problems with indirect word recognition are the source of *all* of their difficulties in reading. This is not to suggest that there are not other ways in which children can end up as poor readers. As the work on acquired dyslexia shows, deficits can and do occur in most of the important subprocesses of reading. These deficits are probably responsible for a certain amount of reading difficulty by they cannot contribute to more than a small proportion of cases because if they had done they would presumably have shown up as major sources of individual differences in the general population of good and poor readers used in the investigations covered earlier in this section.

7.5 DIFFERENCES BETWEEN READERS AT DIFFERENT STAGES IN LEARNING TO READ FLUENTLY

In the last few sections we have tried to pinpoint the difficulties encountered by children who do not read as well as might have been expected on the basis of their age, intelligence and social background. We now turn to the changes that take place normally during the course of learning to read. The approach adopted is similar to that employed in the discussion of backward reading. We shall attempt to determine which of the subprocesses of reading are responsible for the main differences between inexperienced and fluent readers. The subprocesses will be considered in the same order as before, starting with the control of eye movements.

With respect to eye movements there are, of course, gross differences between the saccadic patterns shown by fluent readers and those shown by learners. Inexperienced readers tend to make more fixations on each line of the text and a higher proportion of their saccades tend to be regressive (see, for example, Taylor, Franckenpohl and Pette, 1960). It is conceivable that these differences are attributable to differences in oculomotor control. Unpractised readers may be less efficient at organizing eye movement sequences appropriate to the reading task in hand and they may also be less skilled in the way they control the placement and duration of their fixations. However, there is little reason to believe that there are gross differences in oculomotor control *per se*. As pointed out in the discussion of eye movements in the previous section, the most likely interpretation of the data is that changes in eye movement patterns are the *result* and not the *cause* of changes that occur in other aspects of the reading process. For instance, inexperienced readers may make more regressive eye movements simply because they more frequently encounter words which they fail to recognize or material which they are unable to relate to the prior text. Direct experimental support is needed before we can be completely confident that this hypothesis is correct, but in the meantime the evidence that extensive training in oculomotor control does not improve reading performance (see Tinker, 1958) obviously suggests that this kind of control is not particularly important as a determinant of reading performance.

The next hypothesis to be examined is that experienced readers are more efficient in handling visual information. They may be better than learners, for example, in extracting visual information from the page or in combining the information from different fixations. In order to evaluate the possibility that there are differences in visual processing skills it is necessary to compare the performance of readers at different levels of achievement in tasks that provide a reasonably uncontaminated measure of visual processing. For reasons discussed at length earlier (see Section 7.3.2), it is important not to base any conclusions on data from experiments based on drawing tasks or tasks in which the subjects are able to name or describe the stimuli. Unfortunately, of the studies that remain none appears to compare the performance of readers who differ merely in the amount of reading experience they have had, and so there is no basis on which to draw any conclusions. However, given that differences in visual processing do not appear to be an important cause of reading difficulties, it seems reasonable to assume that mastering these processes is not an important stumbling block in learning to read.

In fluent readers the visual information extracted from the page is normally used for direct word recognition (see Section 3.3). Indeed, there is evidence that inexperienced readers use direct recognition as well—at least they seem to do so for common words (see Section 7.3.3). It may be hypothesized that the proportion of words the reader can identify in this way increases as skill develops. Furthermore, it is conceivable that the more practised readers are able to identify such words more rapidly.

Some support for the first suggestion comes from a study by Pace and Golinkoff (1976). The investigation was based on Golinkoff and Rosinki's (1976) finding that children take longer to name a picture if it is presented in conjunction with an inappropriate word than if it appears with the name of the object in the picture (see Section 7.3.3 for further details). It will be recalled that this result was attributed to the fact that a high proportion of the experimental words were recognized so rapidly that they interfered with the picture-naming task. Other evidence suggested that the recognition process tapped in this study was direct rather than mediated by phonological coding. If these conclusions are correct the interference effect should be restricted to words that can be read rapidly (i.e. words that belong to the reader's sight vocabulary). If the size of the sight vocabulary increases as the child gets older then it follows that the interference effect should steadily be extended to an increasing number of words. To test this possibility Pace and Golinkoff repeated the interference experiment using words that were less familiar than the (very common) words employed in the original study. As expected, the results indicated that the older children tended to show the interference effect with the new set of words but that the effect tended to disappear with the younger, less proficient readers. This suggests that there may be a restricted range of words that can be identified rapidly enough to interfere with picture naming and that the number of such words increases with reading experience.

The second suggestion—that proficient readers are able to identify familiar words more rapidly than less experienced readers can—finds little support in the literature. In fact, in one of the few studies which ensured that all subjects were familiar with the stimulus words, the older (5th-grade) children were, if anything, *slower* at pronouncing the words than the younger (3rd-grade) comparison group (Perfetti and Hogaboam, 1975, p. 464). While it seems unlikely that we should conclude from this study that readers actually get slower at identifying words as they gain experience, the results certainly provide no support for the hypothesis that recognition latency decreases as the reader becomes more proficient.

Turning to indirect word recognition skills, it seems likely that these processes improve steadily as the reader gains experience. Certainly, there must be *some* improvements in these operations since it is obvious that non-readers do not possess the skills at all, while it can be assumed that fluent readers are reasonably efficient at tackling new and unfamiliar words.

There is little direct evidence about the nature of these skills, their development or the sources of information they depend upon. Following the discussion of word-attack skills in backward reading, it might be proposed that with experience young readers increase their capacity to use orthographic constraints, phonological recoding and semantic/syntactic constraints in word recognition. With respect to the first suggestion, there is some evidence that *knowledge* of orthographic rules increases with experience although it is not clear whether there are any changes in the way that these constraints are used. Lefton, Spragins and Byrnes (1973) conducted an experiment in which subjects of different ages (Grades, 1, 3, 5 and adults) were presented with letter strings which contained blanks. Half of the strings conformed strongly to English spelling patterns but the rest were virtually random sequences of letters. On each trial the subjects were required to guess the identity of the letter which was missing from the string. Overall the results showed that subjects were more likely to guess the missing letter in orthographically constrained sequences than in random sequences. However, this advantage varied as a function of age. In the youngest groups there was no difference between the conditions, but the older children performed better with redundant strings and this advantage increased progressively with age.

While these results do not establish that experienced readers make greater use of orthographic constraints in *word recognition* they do show that this occurs with at least one type of task employing letters as stimuli. Given this evidence it seems reasonable to assume that there may be corresponding developmental changes in the use of orthographic constraints in the recognition process itself.

Developmental trends in *decoding* skills may be investigated by examining the speed and accuracy with which children of different ages pronounce unfamiliar words or strings of letters. In general the results show that performance improves with reading experience. Venezky (1974) carried out an investigation in which readers of various ages were required to pronounce selections of nonsense words. The results showed that the tendency to conform to the normal pronunciation rules increased with reading experience and the effect was quite marked with materials based on the more complex rules (e.g. those involving the letter *c*). More recently, Snowling (1979) has investigated developmental changes in pronunciation by using a matching task. In one of several different conditions children of reading ages 7, 8, 9 and 10 were shown a nonsense word followed by an auditory stimulus which was either the correct pronunciation or a slight deviation from the correct pronunciation of the word. The subjects' task was to indicate whether the two nonsense words were the same or different. As in Venezky's study, the results showed that the level of performance increased systematically with reading age and this provides a reasonably clear demonstration that pronunciation skills improve with reading experience.

The third type of word-attack skill considered earlier involved the use of syntactic or semantic constraints to facilitate the recognition process. Young readers may improve the accuracy of their word identification if, as they gain experience, they improve the efficiency with which they use contextual information. Evidence that this does indeed happen comes from studies by Guthrie (1973a) and Klein, Klein and Bertino (1974). In Guthrie's experiment, which has already been referred to in connection with the discussion of the differences between backward and normal readers, there were two groups of 'normal' readers differing in chronological age (mean ages: 7.42 and 10.12 years respectively). The experimental materials consisted of a passage of prose with sets of three alternative words printed at various points in the text. The subjects were required to select the correct alternative in each case. The results showed that the older groups performed this task significantly more accurately than the younger readers. This suggests that the older children were more effective in making use of the constraints imposed on the words by the body of the text. In the study conducted by Klein *et al.* (1974), children of different ages were required to mark the beginnings and ends of words typed on a piece of paper without spaces. In one condition the sequence of words comprised a passage of prose and in the second the words appeared in a random order. The results showed that in test periods of 90 seconds the subjects in each group were able to mark more words in the prose condition than in the random condition. However, the finding which was more important for the present purposes was that the size of this advantage was greater for the older children. This suggests that the older children are better at using contextual information in a task which requires them to decipher printed words. It seems possible that they may also be better at using this kind of information in identifying words in conventional reading.

Up to now we have been considering the development of the skills required for the identification of individual words. There remain a number of other changes that could potentially be important in the process of learning to read. In particular, there may be developments in the child's ability to combine the successive words to obtain the meanings of sentences or of larger portions of text. Such changes might occur because the child's detailed knowledge of the word meanings (and thus his ability to derive the meanings of sentences containing these words) improves with his general linguistic experience. Alternatively there could be developments in parsing or linking strategies used by older readers.

The first suggestion seems quite plausible and, indeed, there is a good deal of specific experimental evidence that children aged 8 or more sometimes misunderstand sentences because they do not know the meanings of some of the individual words. This evidence comes from studies in which children are given various instructions in terms which include complex words like possession verbs (e.g. *give, take, buy* and *sell*) and verbs of communication (e.g. *ask, tell, allow* and *promise*). In many cases the children make systematic mistakes in attempting to carry out the instructions. For example, Chomsky (1969) found that, up to the age of about 8 children tend to respond in exactly the same way to sentences containing the words *ask* and *tell*. Thus, given the instruction 'Ask Linda what her teacher's name is' the child tends to respond directly by giving the teacher's name herself instead of following the instructions and asking the third person (Linda) to provide the information. This suggests that young children do not understand exactly what the word *ask* means and this shortcoming obviously leads to difficulties in comprehension. Similarly Gentner (1975) has shown that many 8-year-olds have not mastered verbs such as *buy, spend* and *sell* and that they often have problems in understanding sentences containing these words.

Although the instructions in these studies were presented verbally there is no reason to believe that the findings would be any different if the subjects read the materials instead of hearing them. Thus the results illustrate that there are circumstances in which older children might perform better in a reading task simply because they have a more detailed knowledge of word meanings than younger children have.

There might also be developmental differences in reading because the older children are more effective in combining individual words to construct the meanings of sentences and texts. Differences of this kind are probably restricted to the most complex types of linguistic structure since the vast majority of linguistic rules are mastered by children long before they start learning to read (see, for example, Brown, 1973). Nevertheless, there are a few conventions that are not typically mastered until the child is 8 or 9 years old. One example concerns the problem of making appropriate use of the Given and New information expressed within a sentence (for a discussion of Given and New information see Section 4.9).

There is good evidence that adults distinguish between Given and New information and that they tend to take account of the fact that different degrees of confidence can be placed in the two kinds of information. For example, Hornby (1974) found that subjects are more likely to notice a misrepresentation in the New information than in the Given information. Obviously, these conventions about the trustworthiness of Given and New information have to be learned, and Hornby (1971) has presented some evidence which suggests that this process is not completed until some years after children start learning to read. This evidence comes from a study in which 6-, 8- and 10-year-old children were read sentences and required to indicate which of two pictures each sentence referred to. In each case, one of the pictures misrepresented the Given information while the other misrepresented the New information (e.g. for the sentence *It is the boy that is riding the horse* one picture might show a boy riding a bicycle and the other a girl riding a horse). The results showed that while the older children tended to behave like adults and place more trust in the Given information, the younger children showed some tendency to choose the picture which matched the New information.

This is one aspect of linguistic processing that may still have to be learnt by 6–8-year-olds. Another potentially important age-related difference in comprehension is that younger children may be less effective at picking up information that is implied rather than stated explicitly in a text. It will be recalled from our earlier consideration of comprehension (see Sections 4.2.5 and 4.9) that fluent readers tend to draw any inferences that are implied by a passage and then store them in memory in the same way as they would if they were stated explicitly. Experiments conducted by Paris and his colleagues (e.g. Paris and Upton, 1976; Paris and Lindauer, 1976) suggest that young children do not behave in the same way. Paris and Upton (1976) presented children aged between 5 and 11 with a series of stories and questioned them immediately about explicit and implicit aspects of the text. The results showed that the recall of both types of information increased with age, but that the magnitude of the effect was more marked for the implicit material, suggesting that there is a developmental improvement in the processing of implied information. Similar conclusions were drawn from the study by Paris and Lindauer. Children aged 7, 9 and 11 were read a list of sentences in which the use of an instrument was either implied or mentioned explicitly. Shortly afterwards they were required to recall the sentences and in each case they were given the name of the instrument as a cue to aid recall. The results for the older children showed that the prompt was equally effective whether or not the instrument had been mentioned explicitly. However, with the younger children it was found that implicit information was less helpful for recovering the sentence. This finding suggests that while the older children tend to handle inferred information in much the same way as adults do, younger children apparently fail to work out the full implications of the material they read.

Summarizing the evidence on the effects of reading experience on the performance of normal readers, the most marked changes seem to lie in the development of the skills used to identify words indirectly. In particular, there are progressive improvements in the ability to pronounce unfamiliar letter strings and to use contextual information to identify words. In addition, there is a steady increase in the number of words that a child can recognize directly (i.e. without using these indirect identification strategies), and there are probably gradual improvements in the child's ability to extract the full meaning from sentences or texts.

7.6 DIFFERENCES IN MATURE READING SKILLS

In the discussion of individual differences so far we have concentrated primarily on the characteristics of inexperienced readers. It need hardly be pointed out that these are not the only differences that can be demonstrated. There are remarkable differences between the levels of skill attained by people with many years of practice in reading. For example, it is not uncommon to discover reading speeds ranging from 200 to 800 or more words per minute in randomly selected samples of university students.

How is it that some people are able to read so much faster than others? What stages in the processing sequence are responsible for these kinds of difference?

From the limited amount of work that has been carried out on this topic it seems that the main differences may again be associated with the process of word recognition.

Jackson and McClelland (1975) have presented evidence which suggests that differences in reading speed cannot be attributed to the fact that the slower readers are less effective at extracting visual information from the page during a fixation. In a threshold experiment it was found that the time required to identify a single foveally presented letter was almost exactly the same for slow and fast readers. A second study showed that the probability of identifying letters briefly presented at points up to about 3° on either side of the fixation point was equivalent in the two groups. Neither of these results would have been obtained if the quality of the visual information available to the slower readers had been worse than that for the fast readers.

In contrast with these results there *is* evidence that highly skilled and less skilled readers differ in the time they take to identify individual words. Mason (1978) instructed subjects to vocalize words presented on a screen and recorded the interval between the presentation of the word and the initial vocal response. The results showed that the skilled readers responded more rapidly than the others. This particular result could have occurred because the skilled readers were faster at *articulating* the words and not because they were quicker at *identifying* them. However, the data from a second experiment showed that this is probably not what happened. In this experiment subjects were instructed not to respond to the word immediately, but to wait a couple of seconds until a signal appeared on the screen before doing so. In these circumstances the difference between the two groups disappeared, suggesting that articulation time *per se* was not responsible for the original difference. Thus the results suggest that fast readers actually identify the words in a passage more rapidly than slow readers do (see also Stanovich and Bauer, 1978; Butler and Hains, 1979).

One possible explanation for this difference in recognition time may be that slow readers tend to gain access to the lexicon by using a phonological code while fast readers tend to use direct visual access. However, Mason (1978) found no support for this suggestion. In fact, she presented evidence that both groups used direct visual access. This evidence was based on a comparison of vocalization times for regular words (e.g. *swoop*) and exception words (e.g. *sword*). If either group of readers had been using phonological recoding to identify the words, they would have been expected to encounter more difficulty in processing the exception words than the regular words. In fact, the latency difference between these two classes of words was negligible in both cases, suggesting that both groups of readers used direct visual access.

The differences between fast and slow readers do not seem to be associated exclusively with word recognition. Jackson and McClelland (1975, 1979) found that fast readers were more accurate in identifying a briefly presented string of unrelated letters (1975) and faster at indicating whether or not two letters have the same name (1979). Mason (1978) showed that highly skilled readers are faster at pronouncing nonwords. These results suggest that the differences in word recognition may be symptomatic of more general variations in recognition skills. However, given the evidence that words are identified directly on the basis of information in STVM, it seems unlikely that these more general differences are directly responsible for variations in reading skill.

In addition to these differences in recognition skills, there is some evidence that fast and slow readers may differ in some of the higher-level comprehension skills that are not associated exclusively with reading. Jackson and McClelland (1979) administered a battery of 15 different tests to groups of fast and slow undergraduate readers and found that the strongest predictor of reading speed was the student's score on a listening comprehension test. While the investigators were unable to specify exactly what aspects of processing were tapped by this test, it seems likely that the procedures used to construct and link propositions are implicated in some way. More direct evidence that mature readers may differ in the effectiveness with which they carry out the second of these processes comes from a study carried out by Daneman and Carpenter (1980). Subjects were required to read a series of paragraphs, and immediately after each one they were asked to identify the referent of one of the pronouns that appeared in the last sentence. The results showed that the readers who performed best on a standardized reading test tended to be more successful at locating the referent, particularly when several sentences were interposed between referent and pronoun. This suggests that part of the difference between accomplished and less accomplished readers might lie in the efficiency with which they are able to link propositions.

7.7 INDIVIDUAL DIFFERENCES IN READING: AN OVERVIEW

The evidence summarized in this chapter shows that it is not reasonable to suppose that there is any *single* cause of reading difficulty or of other individual differences in reading. The detailed analysis of a variety of syndromes in acquired dyslexia reveals that there are patients who have deficits in most of the individual subskills of reading and it would be most surprising if readers with comparable patterns of deficit could not be found in the general population. Having said this, however, it must be observed that there is one class of deficiency that seems to predominate as a source of reading difficulty and this is the group of problems associated with word recognition. Whether one is trying to trace the difference between 'dyslexic' and normal readers, between young learners and older, more fluent readers or between fast and slow adult readers, the largest and most reliable difference among the subskills invariably seems to be the difference in the effectiveness or speed with which individual words are identified. As we have already observed, this correlation between word recognition and reading achievement can be interpreted in a variety of different ways, but the most likely interpretation of the results is that the reader's skills at identifying words somehow influences his more general performance in reading. A plausible hypothesis is that the problem of mastering word recognition skills a major stumbling block in the process of learning to read. This possibility will be examined in more detail in the next chapter.

CHAPTER 8

Learning to read

8.1 INTRODUCTION

The analysis of reading carried out in the first part of the book has emphasized the fact that fluent reading comprises a number of different subprocesses. It seems clear from this that learning to read cannot be a single, unitary phenomenon. It must entail a variety of distinct types of learning—perhaps a different one for each of the individual subskills. Given this situation in seems reasonable to treat learning to read as a combination of more elementary learning tasks.

What are the main types of learning involved in the acquisition of fluent reading? Which of the subskills are particularly difficult to master? How are the more critical subskills acquired?

A partial answer to the first two questions can be obtained by considering the major subskills of fluent reading, viz. extracting visual information from the page, direct word recognition, indirect word recognition, and the extraction and combination of propositions. Clearly, the reader has to learn how to carry out each of these operations. However, not all of them are likely to present the same amount of difficulty, and from a practical point of view it makes sense to concentrate on the operations that are difficult to acquire rather than the subskills that are mastered so easily that they do not normally hold up the process of learning to read.

Presumably the easier processes are mastered early in the learner's career while the more difficult subskills improve gradually over a number of years. If so, it should be possible to identify the more troublesome subskills by examining the developmental changes that occur in reading. These changes were considered in the previous chapter (see Section 7.4). Briefly, the conclusions were as follows:

(1) In the early stages of learning to read there is no evidence that there are any appreciable changes in the control of eye movements.
(2) There is no evidence of improvements in the handling of purely visual information.
(3) There is no firm evidence that the *process* of direct recognition becomes more efficient as reading develops. Even the youngest readers seem to be capable of recognizing words directly, and in the absence of suitable evidence it is impossible to say whether the process speeds up as they gain experience.
(4) On the other hand, there *is* a change in the number of words that can be recognized directly. Older children can obviously process more words in this way.

(5) There is also an improvement in indirect word recognition skills, particularly those associated with decoding and blending the sounds of the words.

(6) Finally, there may be developments in the construction and linking of propositions and in other aspects of comprehension such as drawing inferences from the text, but there is no reason to believe that the changes that have been demonstrated would be of much significance in normal reading since they are associated with complex linguistic structures that are not normally used in children's books.

These findings suggest that the most important developments that occur during the early stages of learning to read are those associated with direct recognition and with word-attack skills. The remaining subskills do not show any major developmental changes in the first few years of learning to read. For this reason the remainder of the discussion of the learning process will concentrate predominantly on the processes of direct and indirect word recognition.

8.2 PREREQUISITES FOR LEARNING TO RECOGNIZE WORDS DIRECTLY

Before a person can learn a complex skill it is often essential for him to master a set of more basic contributory skills. Thus, in order to gain a full understanding of the process of learning to recognize a word directly it is important to know whether the process depends in any way on prior learning. Gagné (1965, 1970) has given a considerable amount of thought to the question of the interdependency of different kinds of learning and has put forward a convenient way of describing the relationship between different aspects of learning a skill. In essence, Gagné's approach to analysing a learning task is to construct a hierarchy of the different kinds of learning that are required before the final goal can be achieved. At the top of the hierarchy is the final skill itself. On the next level are the immediate prerequisites for learning this skill and, below this, the preconditions for these new, lower-level skills. The addition of new levels continues until an arbitrary set of fundamental skills is reached. The end result, which is referred to as a *learning hierarchy*, is a description of all the direct and indirect prerequisites for learning the skill.

In the case of recognizing a word directly an obvious prerequisite is that the learner should have an internal representation of the word (i.e. something like a logogen unit). If there were no such representation, recognition itself would clearly be impossible. In most cases this would present no problem because readers tend to understand and use the majority of words in normal conversation before they make any attempt to deal with them in their printed forms. A second prerequisite for direct recognition is that the reader should be able to analyse and extract the visual features which form the basis for the recognition process. Finally, the reader should be capable of setting up and refining the procedures for using the visual input to activate the internal representation (i.e. he should be able to modify the contents of the file of instructions for visual access—see Section 6.4). Presumably, such modifications are only useful if the reader receives new information about the relationship between the internal representation of a word and its visual description. This would normally occur when he comes across the word in the course of reading, but it is important to note that there is no way of making these refinements unless the reader has some independent procedure for identifying the word. If he is unable to do this, then it is impossible to specify which set of access instructions should be changed. It follows that a prerequisite for setting up and modifying the contents of the access file is that there should be some way for the reader to arrive at the identity of the word. In normal circumstances he could either be given the information by another person (e.g. a teacher) or else he could work it out for himself using indirect recognition procedures. If it is pointed out by someone else then there may be no other important preconditions for learning to recognize the word. However, there is reason to believe that the majority of words are not learnt in this way, and there is certainly evidence that the process of extending sight vocabulary depends to some extent on the efficiency of learning word-attack skills. For example, Valentine (1913, cited in Chall, 1967) found that children who were specifically trained in word-attack skills were much more successful at identifying words they had not previously encountered than were children who had not been given special training of this kind.

If, as this result suggests, the acquisition of sight vocabulary depends partly on word-attack skills it becomes important to consider the prerequisites of learning to use these procedures for indirect word recognition. It seems likely that mastery of these strategies depends on the reader's knowledge of linguistic rules, on knowledge of the relationship between graphemes and phonemes and on the use of phonic blending skills. Specific evidence that phonic skills influence the process comes from studies by Williams (1976) and by Farmer, Nixon and White (1976). Williams monitored the word-decoding performance of 64 children over their first three years of schooling, and he charted the development of their phonic skills over the same period. The word-decoding scores showed that most of the children showed a dramatic improvement in their performance at some stage during the study. For some of the subjects this occurred at a very early stage while for others the improvement was only beginning to show itself towards the end of the investigation. However, the crucial observation made by the author was that for an individual child the period of rapid improvement in word recognition did not occur until the child had mastered most of the phonic skills. This finding seems to suggest that rapid progress in word identification is largely dependent on the application of decoding skills.

Unfortunately, this study suffers from the fact that the interference with the children's learning was kept to a minimum. This means that it is difficult to rule out the possibility that the blending and decoding skills develop independently, producing a fortuitous correspondence between the two kinds of development. The more recent study by Farmer et al. (1976) provides stronger evidence that decoding skills are actually influenced by the development of blending skills, and that the two skills do not simply develop in parallel. Matched groups of 5–6-year-old children were submitted to two different training programmes. The experimental group practised sound-blending skills using a device that plays recordings of letter combinations (Bell & Howell Language Master), while the control group received an equivalent amount of training in naming words in response to pictorial prompts. After training both groups carried out a test to assess their word pronunciation performance, and it was found that the group who practised blending skills had improved more than the control group had. This provides reasonably clear evidence that indirect word recognition is influenced by the development of the skills that are required for pronouncing short strings of letters.

8.3   A TENTATIVE LEARNING HIERARCHY FOR DIRECT WORD RECOGNITION

The evidence considered so far provides some basis for constructing a tentative learning hierarchy for direct word recognition. The outcome is represented in Figure 8.1 (for an alternative suggestion see Gagné, 1970, p. 271). At the top of the hierarchy is the capacity to recognize words by direct visual access. It is suggested that the development of this skill depends on the prior establishment of internal word units, on the ability to extract featural information from the stimulus and on the ability to modify the stored visual descriptions that are used to access the words. This last facility depends on being able to identify the words in one of two ways—either by referring to the teacher for help or by working out the intended word by using indirect recognition procedures. It is assumed that the latter process is of overriding importance once the child progresses beyond the earliest stages of reading, and that this route is ultimately responsible for the development of most of the child's sight vocabulary. If this is correct the success of this type of learning will clearly depend on the child's ability to recognize words by indirect procedures. This, in turn, relies on his ability either to pronounce the word or to guess it using pictorial information or linguistic constraints. Pronunciation depends on the capacity to apply GPC rules to a novel string of letters* and, of course, one precondition for this ability is that he should previously have learnt the rules. Another is that he has acquired the necessary procedures for parsing letter strings into units for pronunciation (i.e. graphemic parsing procedures). The process of learning the GPC rules presumably depends on the ability to identify individual letters and to pronounce all of the potential sounds of these letters.

   This is by no means a full learning hierarchy for the reading process: it excludes the skills of combining words into sentences and all of the other 'higher-level' processes in fluent reading. It also gives an unsatisfactory account

---

* The 'analogy' strategy is not considered in detail here since it seems to be used more extensively by readers who have progressed beyond the early stages of reading under consideration here (see Section 8.5).

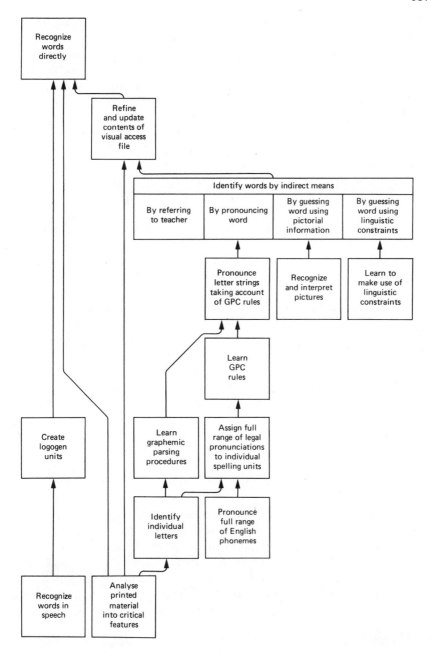

Figure 8.1 A tentative (and partial) learning hierarchy for direct word recognition

of the use of contextual constraints and pictures in the identification of words. However, given the profound effect that deficiencies in decoding skills seem to have on the acquisition of reading, it seems plausible that it forms a crucial part of the complete hierarchy of learning to read. If this is correct, and if much of reading depends on the prior acquisition of skills such as the use of pronunciation in recognizing words, letter recognition and the application of GPC rules, then it seems justifiable to examine the acquisition of each of these subskills separately. This will be the primary goal in the next few sections.

8.4 LEARNING TO RECOGNIZE WORDS AND LETTERS BY DIRECT VISUAL PROCEDURES

At first sight the obvious way to examine this issue seems to be to proceed by referring to the extensive psychological literature on paired associate learning. In this kind of task the subject has to learn to make a distinct response to a number of different stimuli, and it seems clear that to do this he must first learn to identify each of the stimuli. If pattern learning is a prerequisite of the task, then it is conceivable that the work on paired associate learning could throw some light on the acquisition of pattern recognition in reading. However, in practice it turns out that the conditions in most paired associate studies are quite different from those that are likely to occur in learning to read, and consequently the literature is not very useful for the present purposes. The two main differences are, first, that paired associate tasks often employ a very small number of responses—often only two (see Kintsch, 1977)—while in direct recognition in learning to read there may be hundreds and, second, that most paired associate studies deliberately minimize the problems introduced by the pattern-learning component of the task by employing highly discriminable stimuli. This means that the data emphasize the effects of processes such as response learning and stimulus-response hookup and it is difficult to use them to infer anything about the process of learning to classify stimuli.

A start can be made in investigating the problem of pattern learning by considering some of the operating principles built into a computer program designed to 'learn' to classify handwritten letters. This program, known as 'Pandemonium', was written by Selfridge (1959) (see also Selfridge and Neisser, 1960), and although it was not intended to be a model of the way in which human beings acquire the capacity to recognize letters, it provides a convenient starting point for considering the procedures which might be used by human learners.

In its final state, when it has 'learnt' the letters, 'Pandemonium' proceeds by extracting visual features from the stimulus form and using this information after various intermediate computations to activate a collection of devices (called *cognitive demons*) that accumulate evidence about the possible presence of each of the letters. The cognitive demon that is activated most strongly is taken to be the one most likely to correspond to the letter on display.

The extent to which a cognitive demon is activated by an individual feature is a quantity which changes as the program 'learns'. After every attempt to recognize a letter a note is made of the features that were found to be present and a cumulative record is kept of the number of times each feature is associated with each of the letters. This information is then used to determine the extent to which the relevant cognitive demon is activated when the feature is encountered on subsequent trials. For example, if a feature corresponding to a vertical line is regularly extracted by the program in its attempts to recognize the letter *l*, this would progressively increase the degree of activation of the cognitive demon for *l* whenever the feature is subsequently picked up. On the other hand, a curved or closed feature rarely associated with the letter in the past would lead to minimal activation of the *l*-demon.

If human beings learnt to recognize letters by using procedures of this kind, this would have a number of implications for the learning process. One particular characteristic of the system is the relatively unintelligent way in which it uses previous experience in its subsequent operation. According to the proposal, the process of building up the links between individual features and letters is no more than an actuarial procedure. Learning occurs independently for each and every letter and there is no mechanism for noticing the dimensions on which letters differ from one another or for making use of this information to improve the efficiency of the learning process.

Contrary to this view, Gibson (1965) has argued that human beings *can* learn by noticing how forms differ and transferring this information to help them to learn other shapes. She supports her case by citing an experiment conducted by Pick (1965).

In this study 60 kindergarten children were trained to pick out particular target shapes (Gibson forms) when they were displayed alongside a set of distractors consisting of three transformations of the form (e.g. 45° rotation, form turned upside-down, etc.). The same three transformations were used throughout the training session. When they had learnt to do this, one third of the children were trained to distinguish the *same* set of Gibson forms from a new set of distractors—three *new* transformations of the forms. A second group were confronted with a novel set of Gibson forms but in this case the transformations used for the confusion items were the same as those used in the first part of the experiment. The third and final group were required to deal with a new set of transformations as well as a new set of shapes.

As might be expected on almost any theory of pattern learning the results showed that the subjects in the first group made fewer errors in learning to criterion than those in the second group. This indicates that subjects acquired information about the features of individual shapes in the first part of the study and were able to use this information profitably when the same set of target shapes was used in the second discrimination task. Of more direct relevance to the present discussion, the data also showed that the subjects learnt something more than the visual description of individual shapes. This can be deduced from the fact that the performance in Group Two was better than that in

Group Three. Since the only difference between the groups lay in the use of new or old dimensions of variation for the confusion items, this result suggests that subjects are capable of learning the kinds of features that are relevant for the purposes of discrimination and paying special attention to these particular features when faced with a new set of stimuli.

These data suggest that it may be possible for a child to learn to distinguish shapes in a more systematic way then that used by 'Pandemonium'. However, before concluding that this is what actually happens during the normal process of learning to identify letters, it is perhaps worth observing that the characteristic differences between letters are not as clear-cut as the transformations employed in Pick's experiment and the letters are not usually presented with such a systematic set of a alternatives. This means that while subjects may be able to concentrate on important types of feature in idealized experimental conditions, we do not have any indication whether they can do this under the normal conditions of learning to read. Thus further studies are needed before this issue can be fully resolved.

Up to now we have been considering the process of learning to identify letters, and none of the discussion has been directly concerned with the identification of words. It seems likely that learning mechanisms similar to those described above could be used to build up visual descriptions or access instructions for words. In addition, it is conceivable that such a system could take account of features that are not relevant in the discrimination of letters (e.g. word length). It would also be more efficient if any excitation of a word demon (or logogen) by a particular feature were made conditional upon the position of the feature within the graphemic representation as a whole. This would allow, for instance, the descending vertical line and curve in the letter *p* in *top* to activate the logogen for the word *top* without greatly affecting that for *pot*. This could be achieved if the degree of excitation caused by a feature were determined by the number of previous occasions on which the presence of the feature *in that particular part of the array* was associated with the word in question. However, it should be emphasized that at the time of writing there is no clear evidence that the information required for the direct recognition of words is acquired in this way. It remains possible that it is based on a simpler procedure of some kind and it is even possible that it is based on an entirely different set of principles.

8.5 LEARNING TO PRONOUNCE WORDS

As pointed out in Section 8.1, the ability to pronounce new words is probably one of the most important skills that has to be acquired by a child in the process of learning to read. Reasonable pronunciation of a word can be produced in a number of different ways, and so it is probably best to regard pronunciation as a set of different skills that might be applied in various circumstances.

As mentioned in Section 3.6, there are two main strategies that tend to be used in pronouncing words. The first involves synthesizing the pronunciation directly from the string of letters using GPC rules. The second, more sophisticated strategy, consists of deriving the sound of the word by referring to the pronunciation of other familiar words that are spelt in a similar way. For example, a learner might work out a pronunciation for the word *tread* by using the information he has about the sound of the word *bread*. It will be recalled that Baron (1977) has referred to these two strategies as the *correspondence* and *analogy* strategies respectively.

There is some evidence that most readers use both strategies on occasion (see Baron, 1979), but there seems to be an increasing tendency to use the analogy strategy as reading experience increases. Marsh, Desberg and Cooper (1977) investigated the pronunciation strategy used by 5th-grade, 11th-grade and college students by asking them to read letter strings that were similar to words that are exceptions to the more general pronunciation rules (e.g. *tepherd*, cf. *shepherd*). With materials of this kind the correspondence strategy would lead to one pronunciation (in this case $ph \rightarrow /f/$) while the analogy strategy would lead to another ($ph \rightarrow /p//h/$), and this provides a technique for identifying the strategy used by each subject. The results of an experiment with ten test words showed that the correspondence strategy was used on 50 per cent of trials for 5th-grade learners and that this figure fell to 30 per cent for college students. The corresponding figures for the analogy strategy were 39 and 59 per cent respectively. (For the remaining trials the pronunciation used was different from that expected on either of the strategies is question.) These results suggest that both of the strategies may play a significant part in reader's attempts to pronounce new words, and the relative importance of the strategy may increase with reading experience.

How do readers learn to use these two pronunciation strategies? At the time of writing no one appears to have carried out any detailed investigation of the processes entailed in developing the analogy strategy. However, a certain amount is known about the prerequisites for employing the correspondence strategy. As pointed out earlier (Section 8.2), it is clear that the child must have a working knowledge of a large number of GPC rules before he can decode the majority of the words he encounters while reading. Before considering how the GPC rules might be learned it may be useful to say something about the rules themselves.

In the case of English the rules have been analysed and described in detail in monograph by Venezky (1970). In this book Venezky sets out to enumerate all of the ways in which more than 60 identifiable spelling patterns (e.g. *a*, *b*, *ai*, *ph*, *wh*, etc.) can be pronounced. In some cases these spelling-to-sound correspondences cover such a small set of cases or are so arbitrary that it is not reasonable to consider them rule-governed (e.g. the first *l* in *colonel*). Venezky refers to these correspondences as *unpredictable* patterns. In most other cases, the correspondences that occur in English follow one of 100–200 rules. In a small number of cases the relationship between the spelling pattern and the pronunciations is invariant (e.g. *r* is always pronounced /r/). However, most of the spelling units can be pronounced in several different ways and in these cases the rule is used to specify the conditions under which each of the alternative pronunciations is employed.

As an example of a variant rule consider the letter *c*. Here the pronunciation is governed by two main rules:

(1) $c \rightarrow$ /s/ if it is followed immediately by the letters *i*, *y* or *e* (e.g. *circus*, *ceiling*, etc.)

(2) $c \rightarrow$ /k/ in most other circumstances*

In order to apply this kind of variant rule a person not only has to know all of the potential pronunciations of the spelling unit, he also has to be aware of the conditions under which each pronunciation is used. Venezky (1974, Venezky and Johnson, 1973) has studied the way in which the application of such rules improves with experience. School children and students of various ages were shown strings of letters and asked to pronounce them as well as they could. The strings were nonwords but were constructed in such a way that they would be easy to pronounce if the subject had mastered the relevant GPC rules. For instance, in the case of the *c*-rule, strings such as *cipe*, *comp*, *jic* and *necy* were used.

The results for the *c*-rule showed that when the letter appeared at the beginning of the string before *a*, *o* or *u* it was pronounced correctly by 82.4 per cent of the youngest children tested (2nd graders). This figure improved to about 90 per cent for 4th graders and remained at approximately this level for more experienced readers. However, when a *c* in the initial position was followed by an *i*, *e* or *y* only 22.4 per cent of the 2nd graders pronounced it correctly as /s/ and, while there was a steady improvement with age, even college students mispronounced more than 30 per cent of the stimuli.

Two main points emerge from these results. First, the rules are not applied perfectly even by fluent readers. (And this was true of most of the rules studied by Venezky.) Second, different rules are acquired by readers at different rates. In the case of the $c \rightarrow$ /k/ rule there was no further improvement after the 4th grade, while with the other part of the *c*-rule subjects continued to show an improvement until the 8th grade (see Guthrie and Seifert, 1977, for further evidence on variations in acquisition rate).

The second finding raises the question of why some rules are learnt more rapidly than others, and since a satisfactory answer to this question would throw some light on *how* these rules are learnt it seems worthwhile to dwell on this issue for a while. In the particular case of the two parts of the *c*-rule, Venezky (1974) has suggested that the reason for the difference in acquisition rate might be that words in which *c* appears before *i*, *e* or *y* make relatively few appearances in the readers used by children, and so there might simply be fewer opportunities to learn this subrule. In fact, in other discussions of the

---

*In certain conditions a *c* in the middle of a word is pronounced /š/ (e.g. *social*) and there are other exceptions to the two rules given above (e.g. *cello*). However, the two main rules account for about 96 per cent of all pronunciations of the letter in English (see Venezky, 1970, p. 124).

issue (e.g. Venezky, 1978) he seems to interpret all differences in acquisition rate in terms of variations in the frequency with which the rules are encountered by the child, and to argue against the suggestion that some rules are intrinsically more difficult to learn than others.

Other authors, particularly those associated with the development of reformed orthographies for teaching reading (see Section 8.7.1), have based their work on the assumption that such differences *do* exist and that it is possible to simplify the learning process by replacing difficult rules with simpler ones. A central assumption made by these investigators is that variant rules are more difficult to learn than invariant rules, and on the basis of this assumption the reformers have normally tried to construct alphabets with one-to-one GPC rules.

Venezky (1978) has criticized some of the arguments traditionally used in favour of reformed orthographies and has presented two lines of evidence against the assumption that complex GPC rules are more difficult to learn. However, the case he makes does not seem to be particularly persuasive. His first argument is that no relationship 'has ever been established' between the orthographic regularity of a language and the ease with which children learn to read in that language. If invariant rules were easier to learn then regular languages like Finnish and Spanish should present fewer problems for the beginning reader and the failure rate in reading should be lower than it is in other countries. However, as Venezky himself has pointed out, it is almost impossible to interpret cross-cultural evidence of this kind because of numerous cultural factors that have nothing to do with rule learning (see Downing, 1973a, and Gibson and Levin, 1975, pp. 517–538, for detailed discussions of the difficulties entailed in making cross-cultural comparisons in reading studies). This means that evidence of this kind would be subject to criticism whichever position it supported. In these circumstances the argument that the relationship has never been established does not appear to be a very compelling one. Venezky's second argument was based on the finding that complex rules are sometimes learnt faster than simpler ones (see Venezky and Johnson, 1973). However, as mentioned above, he himself explains this in terms of the number of exemplars encountered by the learner, and if this *is* a factor which influences learning rate then it is difficult to draw any conclusions about the *intrinsic* difficulty of acquiring simple and complex rules.

From the other camp, Downing (1973b) has argued that the effectiveness of teaching schemes based on reformed orthographies offers some support for the view that invariant rules are easier to learn. He cites evidence that children learn more rapidly using the initial teaching alphabet (i.t.a.) than with the conventional alphabet (see Section 8.7.1 for further details), and attributes this to the fact that the GPC rules are simpler in the former case. However, it is not clear that this result should be attributed to changes in the complexity of the regular correspondences since this is not the only factor which is changed in i.t.a. Other equally important modifications, such as the virtual elimination of exceptions, might equally well be responsible for the improvement.

Clearly, then, there is little consensus on the reasons why some GPC rules are easier to learn than others, and so there is no straightforward way of using these differences to throw light on the broader questions of how readers generally approach the problem of acquiring GPC rules. Indeed, very little seems to have been written about the acquisition of these rules from *any* point of view.

Like the process of learning to identify single letters, the acquisition of GPC rules can be regarded as a problem in discrimination learning (see Kintsch, 1970, for a detailed consideration of this topic). The subject is required to make appropriate responses to a variety of different spelling patterns. To do this he must first code the stimulus input in an appropriate way; that is, one that represents both the spelling pattern itself and the context in which it appears. In addition he must learn to associate the coded form of the stimulus with the required vocal (or subvocal) response.

In most psychological studies of rule learning the rules used in investigating the process of acquisition are much simpler than the GPC correspondences that occur in reading. In concept identification experiments the stimuli vary on a number of simple dimensions such as shape, size and colour, and in the simplest case the rule concerns only one of these dimensions. Thus the rule might be: make response *A* if the stimulus is *red* and make response *B* is it is *blue*. A closer approximation to GPC rules is the situation in which the response is determined by the *relationship* between the stimulus values on two different dimensions. Perhaps the most relevant example is the *conjunctive* rule (see Haygood and Bourne, 1965). Here the subject might be required to make one response if the stimulus is both red *and* square (say) and another response if either of these two conditions is not met. In this case the response to a red stimulus depends upon another characteristic of the stimulus (i.e. its shape). To some extent this is similar to the situation in learning GPC rules, where the response to a spelling pattern often depends on the context in which it appears. However, in other respects the similarity between GPC rules and conjunctive rules is not very great. Pronunciation rules are much more complex than the kinds of rules normally studied in psychological experiments. Rule-learning studies rarely call for the subject to make more than two different kinds of response whereas readers are required to distinguish between many responses and they normally have to combine several of them in pronouncing a single word. Another difference is that in experimental tasks the values of the relevant dimensions (e.g. their shapes, colours, etc.) are easily identified whereas in pronunciation the correct classification of values on one of the dimensions may itself depend on concept learning. For example, the pronunciation of the letter *c*, considered above, depends on whether it is followed by one class of letters (*i*, *y* or *e*) or another (any other letter), and this arbitrary partitioning of the alphabet has to be learned before the reader can learn to pronounce the letter *c* correctly. A third difference that almost certainly makes pronunciation much more difficult to learn is that many of the most common words in English do not conform to the rules at all. Thus a fair proportion of the 'learning trials' in normal reading must provide information which ultimately turns out to be misleading.

These important differences suggest that we are not likely to learn much about the acquisition of pronunciation rules by considering the kind of task that has been studied most intensively to date. It is essential to determine what is entailed in learning the main types of GPC rules themselves and then to investigate specifically how the various stages of the process are mastered. At the time of writing no one appears to have carried out such a detailed investigation of the process of learning pronunciation rules, and in the absence of such evidence it seems fruitless to speculate about the nature of the process.

Up to now we have concentrated on the problem of learning the pronunciation rules themselves. In addition to this it is necessary for a child to learn how to apply the rules efficiently when confronted with an unfamiliar word. There is some evidence that this may not be a trivial problem. Venezky (1978) reports a study in which a sample of poor readers were able to pronounce over 90 per cent of a set of invariant consonants when they appeared at the beginnings of words, but showed a dramatic fall in performance when the letters appeared in other positions. This pattern of behaviour suggests that while the subjects had mastered the GPC rules themselves, they were not always able to apply them properly.

One possible explanation of this finding is that the readers in question may have had difficulty in partitioning the string of letters into functional spelling units. This procedure, known as *graphemic parsing* (see Coltheart, 1978), is obviously an operation that has to be carried out before any GPC rules can be used to generate a phonemic representation of the word, and it is conceivable that subjects make mistakes or abandon their efforts to pronounce words when they are parsed incorrectly. If it is assumed that the assignment of phonemes takes place from left to right across the word, then the first letter is the least likely to be disrupted in this way, and this would account for the results described above.

If this interpretation of the results is correct it suggests that graphemic parsing procedures may be relatively difficult to learn and this raises the question of how the skill is acquired. Unfortunately, no work appears to have been carried out on this issue at the time of writing and so the question must remain unanswered.

8.6 MORE GENERAL ISSUES IN LEARNING TO READ

In the last two sections we have considered the problem of learning two of the more important subskills of reading. It seems likely that as soon as these skills are partially acquired they open the way to other kinds of learning. Thus the successful identification of a word using GPC rules may provide information that is required for filling up and developing the visual access file. In this case the acquisition of decoding skills would contribute directly to the learner's ability to recognize the word by direct access and ultimately this would help him to develop and extend his sight vocabulary.

Once a child has acquired the two basic skills much of his learning will probably involve applying these skills to an ever-increasing range of words. However, there may be developmental changes in the *process* of reading as well as developments in vocabulary. LaBerge and Samuels (1974) have suggested that certain aspects of the reading process require close attention during the early stages of learning but eventually become automatic after a certain (unspecified) amount of practice. As the demands of the individual subskills fall, the learner is able increasingly to devote his attention to those aspects of the task that have not yet become automatic. If changes of this kind do occur, they may have an important influence on the process of learning to read.

8.7 CONDITIONS THAT FACILITATE THE PROCESS OF LEARNING TO READ

The foregoing discussion of the learning process suggests a number of ways in which the learner's task might be simplified. In particular, we have argued that GPC rules may enable the reader to identify unfamiliar words and this might help him to extend his sight vocabulary. If this is correct, any reading scheme that concentrates on phonics should have a beneficial effect on the learning process. Similarly, benefits should accrue from schemes that allow readers to work out the identity of words by making use of prior contextual constraints or pictures.

The effects of these and other conditions on various aspects of reading achievement will be considered presently, but first it is necessary to mention briefly one or two methodological problems that may be encountered in studies that try to determine the effects that different learning conditions have on reading progress (see Chall, 1967, Chapter 4, for a more thorough analysis of these problems). Since they are concerned with changes that occur over periods of weeks or months, these studies normally have to be carried out in the classroom and this means that the conditions of learning cannot be controlled as precisely as the investigator might wish. The different teaching programmes often have to be administered by teachers whose primary concern is to help the individual child rather than to conduct a well-controlled scientific experiment. There will obviously be a tendency for teachers to deviate from reading schemes which they consider unhelpful or even detrimental to a child's development. In fact, in countries where there is a tradition of 'teacher freedom' it may be impossible to be sure that teachers follow any prescribed scheme at all.

A second problem with this kind of work is that it is subject to the Hawthorne effect. A teacher who is trying out a scheme which she favours may cause her class to produce good results not because the scheme is intrinsically any better than the alternatives but because her approach to teaching is somehow more conducive to learning.

In short, it is sometimes very difficult to interpret classroom studies. However, the problems are not insurmountable and in certain cases investigations have been conducted in such a way that reasonable conclusions can be drawn from them. In the summary that follows no attempt will be made to assess the advantages and disadvantages of individual reading schemes. Those who are concerned with the problem of selecting a suitable reading programme for a group of children are advised to refer to one of the many books that have been prepared specifically to instruct and advise the practising teacher (e.g. Southgate and Roberts, 1970; Moyle and Moyle, 1974; DeBoer and Dallman, 1970; Harris and Smith, 1976, and numerous others).

8.7.1   Training in phonic skills

Undoubtedly one of the more heated controversies in the reading literature concerns the value of training in phonic skills. In fact, for many decades this issue has been at the centre of 'The Great Debate' on ways of teaching children to read (see Chall, 1967).

As mentioned above, the work on individual differences in reading skill (see Sections 7.3.4 and 7.4) suggests that the ability to decode or pronounce words may be an important determinant of subsequent achievement in reading. It was suggested that the reason for this may be that it equips readers to work out the identity of words which they do not yet know by sight. If this argument is correct then training in phonic skills should facilitate the process of learning to read.

Does this actually happen? The most thorough and systematic review of the relevant research is that carried out by Chall (1967) and, as she pointed out, it transpires that the hypothesis is impossible to test as it stands because all reading programmes devote some time to phonic skills. However, she was able to provide a partial answer to the question by considering the results of nine studies which compared programmes that place a strong emphasis on phonics with others that assign a less important role to this aspect of training. Different tests of performance were used in each of the studies, but several of them included some kind of test of oral word recognition and a test of comprehension. In the case of word recognition, the majority of the studies showed that the advantage lay with phonic training. However, when it came to comprehension tests the results were less clear-cut. At the beginning of the 1st grade the children who received phonic training tended to obtain lower comprehension scores than the others, but the position was reversed by the end of the 2nd grade. Chall suggested that the early disadvantage of phonic training schemes could be attributed to the fact that the children acquired a habit of concentrating on the *pronunciation* of words rather than on their meanings. At a later stage, however, when they became more fluent at these decoding skills, they were able to pay more attention to the meaning of the passage. The fact that they were eventually able to outperform the children who received little phonics training suggests that an emphasis on decoding skills facilitates the process of learning to read.

Under what conditions are decoding skills most effectively learnt? Is it best for children to practise with individual letters and meaningless letter combinations or are they capable of picking up the rules by working with ordinary English words? Do children progress more rapidly if they are initially taught only those words that conform to the GPC rules? Is there any benefit to be gained by modifying the alphabet so that the irregularities in the GPC rules are minimized, making the child's learning task more systematic?

In an attempt to answer the first two questions Chall analysed 25 studies which compared reading schemes in which the phonic rules were taught by having children practise with subcomponents of words (she termed this 'systematic phonics training') and those in which phonics were taught with real words as part of the process of meaningful reading ('intrinsic phonics training'). The results of most of these studies showed that systematic phonics produced better results. Scores on comprehension tests and standardized vocabulary tests were generally better following this kind of training, and whenever it was tested oral word recognition performance was also found to be better. The results of experimental studies suggest that part of the advantage of training schemes based on units smaller than words may be that it is easier to make use of this kind of information when it comes to learning new words. Bishop (1964) conducted an experiment in which college students learned to pronounce either a set of Arabic characters or a list of words printed in Arabic characters. In each case there was a regular one-to-one correspondence between graphemes and phonemes. Following preliminary training, both groups of subjects were required to pronounce a new set of words constructed from the original characters and it was found that the level of performance on the new words was higher for the subjects who had learned to pronounce individual letters.

Jeffrey and Samuels (1967) carried out a similar study using kindergarten children and a specially constructed set of letters. As in Bishop's study, the results showed that the number of new words pronounced correctly was greater for the children who had learnt the sounds of the individual letters than for those whose training required them to pronounce whole words. Both groups of children went on to learn the intended pronunciation of the transfer words and it was found that the word group needed twice as many trials as the letter group before they were able to work through the list without error. Again the results suggest that detailed training on specific grapheme-to-phoneme correspondences may by one of the best ways of equipping the child to handle new words when he encounters them.

Apart from questions about the ideal size of the units employed in phonics training there has been some controversy about how the child should be introduced to the range of correspondences that occur in English. One suggestion, made, for example, by Bloomfield (1942), is that the GPC rules are most likely to be picked up rapidly if the reader is initially allowed to work only with those words that conform to the most general and powerful rules. This kind of training would minimize the potentially confusing effect of dealing with irregularities or minor variants of the GPC rules. According to this scheme the reader would only be exposed to regular words once he had mastered the main rules.

A possible disadvantage of this approach was pointed out by Levin and Watson (1963, cited in Singer and Ruddell, 1976). If all of the early vocabulary were based on regular GPC rules the children might come to expect an invariant relationship in all words and this could handicap them in their attempts to learn the more complex words in the second phase of Bloomfield's scheme. In other words, it might be important for children to learn that there are *variations* in the pronunciations of spelling units and to develop rule-learning techniques that take these variations into account. If this is true the best teaching strategy might be to introduce them to both regular and irregular words from the outset.

Levin and Watson (1963) conducted an experiment to determine which of these approaches is most effective. Third-grade children were required to associate strings of artificial characters with simple English words like *man*. The relationships between characters and phonemes were governed by rules, but not all of them were one-to-one correspondences. The learning trials were divided into two phases. In the first phase half of the subjects were presented with only one of two possible correspondences while the other half saw both possibilities. In the second part of the experiment both groups were required to learn materials which conformed to the variable rules. The results showed that the group who were introduced to the variations from the outset performed better in the second part of the experiment than the group who only dealt with one of the possibilities. Similar results were obtained in a study with 5th and 6th-grade children by Williams (1968).

On the basis of these studies the investigators suggest that it is probably best to introduce variability at an early stage and thus encourage the child to develop what they call a 'set for diversity'. However, there are reasons for treating this conclusion with reservation. First, it is not clear that the learning problems that occur in a brief experimental session are the same as those that occur over a period of months. For instance, it may be inappropriate to evaluate Bloomfield's recommendations on the basis of the level of performance during the period when the child first discovers the limitations of the rule he has been relying upon. It is quite possible that the performance of this group settles down at a higher level than that of the comparison group once they have made a few adjustments in their learning strategy. A second problem is that the optimal way of learning a variable rule may not be the same for every rule. It may be best to introduce both (or all) rules if they occur with equal frequency but to introduce only a single correspondence if this rule occurs in the overwhelming majority of relevant words. In the second situation it is easy to see that the strategy of introducing all of the rules could be counterproductive. In view of the limitations of the studies conducted so far it seems premature to try to reach any firm conclusions about which of these two approaches offers the most effective way of teaching phonic rules.

The final issue to be considered in the field of facilitating the acquisition of decoding skills concerns the effectiveness of avoiding the problems caused by GPC irregularities by modifying the teaching alphabet so that the relationship between graphemes and phonemes becomes a regular one. This has been attempted in three main ways. In the first, information about the pronunciation of letter patterns is conveyed by marks (known as *diacritical marks*) which are written or printed near the patterns to which they refer (e.g. Johnson, 1961; Fry, 1964). In the second, words are colour coded so that the pronunciation of each letter or letter combination is uniquely represented by the shade in which it is printed (e.g. Gattegno, 1962, 1969). The third, and most radical, modification of the alphabet is the *initial teaching alphabet* (i.t.a.) developed by Pitman (1959). In this case the alphabet is actually extended to include 44 different characters and this allows the vast majority of English words to be represented by letter strings which conform to one-to-one GPC rules.

It was argued earlier (see Section 8.1) that one of the main factors which influence a reader's progress during the first few years of schooling is the development of decoding skills. If this process is influenced by the complexity of the rules that have to be mastered in order to pronounce new words, then the use of reformed orthographies should facilitate the learning process.

The evidence available suggests that they do have this effect. Johnson, Jones, Cole and Walters (1972) compared the effects of teaching reading with traditional orthograhy and with a system of diacritical marks. Out of a total sample of 258 children, 30 pairs matched for age, sex, IQ and social class were selected for detailed investigation. The same reading schemes were used for each group. In the case of the group taught by the diacritical mark system the marks were added to the standard text. After several months of training the children were given a number of reading and spelling tests and the results showed, among other things, that the oral reading scores of the experimental group were significantly higher than those for children taught with traditional materials.

Similar advantages have been found with i.t.a. Downing (1967) compared the rate of progress of 873 children taught using i.t.a. with a control group of children using traditional orthography (t.o.). The pupils came from 82 classes from a large number of schools throughout Britain. An effort was made to match the i.t.a. and t.o. classes on the main institutional factors known to influence reading achievement (e.g. size of class, pupil/teacher ratio, urban or rural location, distribution of social classes in school intake, etc.). Teaching was based on a popular reading series (*Janet and John*) and equivalent materials were used in each of the alphabets. Reading progress was monitored on four different occasions—after 1 year, $1\frac{1}{2}$ years, 2 years and $2\frac{1}{2}$ years. The results showed that the experimental (i.t.a.) group progressed through the various stages of the reading scheme more rapidly than their controls. They also performed better on a test of oral word recognition (the Schonell Graded Word Reading Test) and on a comprehension test (part of the Neale Analysis of Reading Ability). These results support the view that the use of i.t.a. facilitates the early stages of learning to read, and similar results were obtained when i.t.a. was evaluated in America (Mazurkiewicz, 1964).

While the evidence just considered suggests that the process of learning to read may be aided by the use of special alphabets and reading materials, it does not necessarily follow that the benefits are retained when the child eventually transfers to normal text. In fact, it is sometimes argued that the experience is counterproductive because the learner might become dependent on cues that are not present in normal reading materials (see, for example, Samuels, 1968). However, this does not seem to be a serious problem since the evidence suggests that most children eventually transfer to t.o. quite successfully. In the evaluation of the diacritical mark system mentioned above, Johnson *et al.* (1972) found that the children who were taught with the modified alphabet performed better than the controls even when they were tested in t.o. In the i.t.a. experiment, Downing (1967) found that while the children trained in i.t.a. suffered a temporary setback when they first transferred to conventional script, their performance soon recovered. Indeed, it was found that the experimental group performed better than the controls on all of the main tests of reading in the 2-year and 2½-year follow-up studies even though the tests were administered exclusively in t.o. at this stage.

To summarize, there is a good deal of evidence that systematic training in phonics with small meaningless groups of letters helps the learner to develop his decoding skills. This in turn facilitates the process of learning to read. The research that has been conducted to date does not enable us to say with any confidence whether or not it is better to restrict the early reading vocabulary to words that conform to the major variants of the GPC rules. However, there is strong evidence that the process of learning to read is facilitated when regularity is created artificially by the use of a modified alphabet.

8.7.2 Effects of providing enriched context and training in the use of context

So far in the discussion of the conditions that facilitate learning we have considered the effects of training procedures which help the learner to identify new words by pronouncing them. Another way in which learners might be able to improve their performance is by making use of various kinds of contextual information, particularly linguistic constraints and the clues given by the illustrations that accompany the text. If these sources of information contribute significantly to the process of learning new words then it should be possible to speed up the learning process by training children to use contextual constraints or by providing additional information in the form of illustrations.

Some support for the first suggestion comes from the study carried out by Samuels, Dahl and Archwamety (1974). A group of children in the 3rd grade were trained in a variety of skills that could be of use in applying hypothesis-testing strategies in reading (e.g. using visual or oral context to anticipate a word with or without supplementary visual cues). Following training the children were given tests of comprehension and word recognition speed and, as predicted, they performed better on these tests than a group of control subjects who had received no special training in the use of context. Similar results were obtained in a study by Kennedy and Weener (1973). In this investigation a group of poor 3rd-grade readers were given training in anticipating a missing word in a visually presented cloze task. Another group received training in an auditory equivalent of the cloze task and there were two control groups which received no special training. After the training sessions each group was given a comprehension test (the Durrell Reading Comprehension Test) and the results of this test showed that the children who had practised with the visual cloze test performed better than those in any of the other three groups. As before, this finding suggests that training in the use of linguistic constraints may speed up the process of learning to read.

There is much less certainty about the effects of illustrations on learning to read. It was suggested that pictures might contribute to the process of building up sight vocabulary by helping readers to identify words when they come across them for the first time. Do they actually have this effect? Some of the research conducted so far tends to suggest that they may not and, in fact, there are even investigators who have argued that illustrations may *interfere* with the process of learning to read rather than facilitating it (Samuels, 1967, 1970; Singer, Samuels and Spiroff, 1973–1974).

Samuels (1967) based his conclusion on the results of a study in which 30 preschool children were required to learn to decode lists of simple words which they were initially unable to read. All of the stimuli were names of familiar objects, and for half of the subjects each word was accompanied by a picture of the object while for the other half the word was presented alone. If the subject failed to pronounce the word within a few seconds the experimenter prompted him by providing the desired response. After a learning session consisting of ten trials with the list as a whole, the subjects were given a test in which they were required to decode each of the words presented alone without any help from the experimenter. The results showed that the number of words responded to correctly was greater for the children who had not been presented with illustrations during the learning phase of the experiment. In other words, the presence of illustrations was, if anything, detrimental. A similar experiment using slightly older children was carried out by Singer *et al.* (1973–1974) and the results were essentially the same.

These results, together with others reviewed by Samuels (1970), suggest that in certain circumstances the presence of illustrations may interfere with the acquisition of sight vocabulary. The interpretation of the finding offered by Samuels (1967, 1970) was that the picture draws the child's attention away from the word with the result that word learning is impaired.

Does this mean that illustrations have detrimental effects in all circumstances? This seems unlikely. By prompting the subjects when they failed to identify the word it could be argued that the studies by Samuels and by Singer *et al.* neutralized one of the main potential advantages of illustrations—the fact that they provide a way of identifying words when other strategies fail. Given the way the experiments were conducted, the subject had an opportunity to learn the word whether or not he guessed it correctly. In the classroom where help may not be so readily available, the presence of a picture may be more critical since it might provide the subject's only useful clue to the identity of the word. Without this information successive presentations of the stimulus would evoke neither the meaning nor the pronunciation of the word and it seems unlikely that the reader would learn much in these circumstances. Recently, Austin (1980) carried out an experiment to determine whether pictures are helpful when other sources of information are not available. The procedure was similar to that used by Samuels (1967) except that the children were not given external feedback when they failed to identify the word. In these circumstances the pictures were found to have a beneficial effect and so it seems likely that they may sometimes play a useful role in the acquisition of sight vocabulary.

Whether or not pictures make a contribution at the level of word recognition, there is evidence to suggest that children can make good use of illustrations in identifying words and understanding connected prose. In an investigation conducted by Donald (1978), two groups of ten 7-year-old children were required to read two 66-word stories. In one group the first story was accompanied by an illustration and the second was presented alone, while in the second group it was the second story that was presented with a picture. The investigator monitored the initial oral reading of each story, taking note of all omissions, substitutions, insertions and corrections of words that occurred. After this the subject was asked to recall the story and to answer three simple comprehension questions. The results showed that in the presence of the illustration the subjects misread fewer words, and when they *did* make a mistake it was more likely to be semantically and syntactically consistent with the context than when the text was presented alone. Also, there was a greater tendency for subjects to correct themselves spontaneously when the picture was available. Finally, subjects were able to recall more of the basic ideas in the story and to answer the comprehension questions more adequately in the illustrated text condition. All of these findings suggest that children are capable of using pictures to improve their understanding of a passage and to help in the process of identifying unfamiliar words. If they do this in the school situation they may be able to work out the identity of words which they cannot recognize by themselves. Taken together with Austin's (1980) findings, these data suggest that the use of illustrations in children's books probably makes a material contribution to the process of learning to recognize words.

8.8 SUMMARY OF CHAPTER 8

Learning to read can be regarded as a process of mastering the individual subskills of reading and developing the capacities which allow these skills to work together in an efficient manner.

Two subprocesses in particular seem to be responsible for holding back a child's progress in learning to read. These are the skills underlying the direct recognition of words and the skills that enable the reader to identity new or unfamiliar words (i.e. word-attack skills). There is some evidence that difficulties with the first subprocess may stem from problems that the reader encounters in the process of reading unfamiliar or new words. The reason for this may be that a reader suffering from difficulties of the second kind may sometimes be unable to establish any link between the visual description of a word and its internal representation. If this connection is not made at some point then the direct recognition of a word using its visual features alone is obviously impossible.

The most effective way of identifying a novel word is almost certainly to pronounce the string of letters that make up the word and then use this phonological representation to identify the word indirectly. Unfortunately, while there is good reason to believe that pronunciation skills of this kind develop rapidly as the child learns to read and that they may be an important determinant of the child's progress in reading, there is little useful information on how the pronunciation rules themselves might be acquired or on how the child might learn to apply them to unfamiliar strings. It is conceivable that traditional work on discrimination learning and on concept or rule learning could be extended to provide an account of the acquisition of pronunciation skills. However, the empirical work in these fields has been concerned almost exclusively with learning tasks that are a great deal simpler than learning to pronounce letter strings. In particular, the experimental work has concentrated on the acquisition of relationships that are governed by a small number of rules with few variants and without any exceptions. None of these conditions applies to pronunciation rules and it seems unlikely that we shall learn much about how these rules are acquired until we develop experimental tasks which bear a closer resemblance to pronunciation itself.

Fortunately, it is possible to make one or two practical suggestions about the teaching of reading without knowing in any great detail how the skill is acquired. The central role of pronunciation skills in learning to read suggests that reading schemes which emphasize these skills should be particularly effective. This is generally confirmed by studies that compare the merits of different reading curricula. It also seems likely that the process of learning to read can be accelerated by the use of modified alphabets or other schemes designed to simplify the rules for decoding print.

Reading schemes of this kind may assist the reader by helping him to establish links between the appearance of words and their pronunciations or meanings. Another way in which these links can be made is by adopting the practice of introducing new words in an informative context so that the reader has a good chance of guessing the identity of an unfamiliar word. A particular variant of this approach is to accompany the words with pictures or diagrams, and while there is some disagreement in the literature about the effectiveness of this kind of technique, the evidence seems to suggest that it may make a useful contribution to the process of learning to read.

References

Aaronson, D., and Scarborough, H. S. (1976), Performance theories for sentence coding: Some quantitative evidence, *Journal of Experimental Psychology: Human Perception and Performance*, **2**, 56–70.

Abrams, S. G., and Zuber, B. L. (1972), Some temporal characteristics of information processing during reading, *Reading Research Quarterly*, **12**, 41–51.

Adams, M. J. (1979), Models of word recognition, *Cognitive Psychology*, **11**, 133–176.

Adelson, E. H. (1978), Iconic storage: The role of rods, *Science*, **201**, 544–546.

Aderman, D., and Smith, E. E. (1971), Expectancy as a determinant of functional units in perceptual recognition, *Cognitive Psychology*, **2**, 117–129.

Allport, D. A. (1971), Parallel encoding within and between elementary dimensions, *Perception and Psychophysics*, **10**, 104–108.

Anderson, A. H., and Garrod, S. (1979), The influence of textual features on comprehension. Paper presented to the spring meeting of the Experimental Psychology Society, York University, April.

Anderson, J. R. (1976), *Language, Memory and Thought*, Hillsdale, NJ, Lawrence Erlbaum Associates.

Anderson, J. R., and Bower, G. H. (1973), *Human Associative Memory*, Washington, DC, Winston.

Anderson, R. C., and Ortony, A. (1975), On putting apples into bottles—A problem of polysemy, *Cognitive Psychology*, **7**, 167–180.

Arnett, J. L., and Di Lollo, V. (1979), Visual information processing in relation to age and to reading ability, *Journal of Experimental Child Psychology*, **27**, 143–152.

Audley, R. J. (1976), Reading difficulties: The importance of basic research in solving practical problems. Presidential address to the meeting of the British Association for the Advancement of Science, Lancaster.

Austin, C. (1980), The effect of pictures on the acquisition of sight vocabulary in kindergarten children. Unpublished Honours project, University of Exeter.

Baddeley, A. D. (1964), Immediate memory and the 'perception' of letter sequences, *Quarterly Journal of Experimental Psychology*, **16**, 364–367.

Baddeley, A. D. (1978), The trouble with levels: A re-examination of Craik and Lockhart's framework for memory research, *Psychological Review*, **85**, 139–152.

Bakker, D. J. (1967) Temporal order, meaningfulness and reading ability, *Perceptual and Motor Skills*, **24**, 1027–1030.

Banks, W. P., and Barber, G. (1977), Color information in iconic memory, *Psychological Review*, **84**, 536–546.

Baron, J. (1973), Phonemic stage not necessary for reading, *Quarterly Journal of Experimental Psychology*, **25**, 241–246.

Baron, J. (1977), Mechanisms for pronouncing printed words: Use and acquisition. In D. LaBerge and S. Samuels (eds), *Basic Processes in Reading: Perception and Comprehension*, Hillsdale, NJ, Lawrence Erlbaum Associates.

Baron, J. (1979), Orthographic and word-specific mechanisms in children's reading of words, *Child Development*, **50**, 60–72.

Baron, J., and Strawson, C. (1976), Use of orthographic and word-specific knowledge in reading words aloud, *Journal of Experimental Psychology: Human Perception and Performance*, **2**, 386–393.

Baron, J., and Thurston, I. (1973), An analysis of the word superiority effect, *Cognitive Psychology*, **4**, 207–228.

Barron, R. W. (1978), Access to the meanings of printed words: Some implications for reading and learning to read. In F. B. Murray (ed.), *The Recognition of Words: IRA Series on the Development of the Reading Process*, Newark, Del., International Reading Association.

Barron. R. W. (1980), Visual-orthographic and phonological strategies in reading and spelling. In U. Frith (ed.), *Cognitive Processes in Spelling*, London, Academic Press.

Barron, R. W., and Baron, J. (1977), How children get meaning from printed words, *Child Development*, **48**, 587–594.

Barron, R. W., and Pittenger, J. B. (1974), The effect of orthographic structure and lexical meaning on same–different judgements, *Quarterly Journal of Experimental Psychology*, **26**, 566–581.

Beauvois, M-F., and Dérouesné, J. (1978), Phonological alexia: Study of a case of alexia without aphasia or agraphia, *Experimental Brain Research*, **32**, R5.

Becker, C. A. (1976), Allocation of attention during visual word recognition, *Journal of Experimental Psychology: Human Perception and Performance*, **2**, 556–566.

Becker, C. A. (1979), Semantic context and word frequency effects in visual word recognition, *Journal of Experimental Psychology: Human Perception and Performance*, **5**, 252–259.

Becker, C. A., and Killion, T. H. (1977), Interaction of visual and cognitive effects in word recognition, *Journal of Experimental Psychology: Human Perception and Performance*, **3**, 389–401.

Besner, D. (1980), *Visual Word Recognition: Codes and Procedures for Accessing the Internal Lexicon*, Unpublished doctoral dissertation, University of Reading, England.

Besner, D., Davies, J., and Daniels, S. (1981), Reading for meaning: Knowing a phonological code when you see one, *Quarterly Journal of Experimental Psychology: Human Experimental Psychology*, 33A, 415–437.

Bever, T. G. (1970), The cognitive basis of linguistic structures. In J. R. Hayes (ed.), *Cognition and the Development of Language*, New York, John Wiley & Sons.

Bishop, C. H. (1964), Transfer effects of word and letter training in reading, *Journal of Verbal Learning and Verbal Behavior*, **3**, 215–221.

Bloomfield, L. (1942), Linguistics and reading, *Elementary English Review*, **19**, 125–130, 183–186.

Bobrow, D., and Fraser, B. (1969), An augmented state transition network procedure. In D. Walker and L. Norton (eds), *Proceedings of the International Joint Conference on Artificial Intelligence*, Washington, DC.

Bobrow, S. A. (1970), Memory for words in sentences, *Journal of Verbal Learning and Verbal Behavior*, **9**, 363–372.

Bongartz, W., and Scheerer, E. (1976), Two visual stores and two processing operations in tachistoscopic partial report, *Quarterly Journal of Experimental Psychology*, **28**, 203–220.

Bouma, H. (1970), Interaction effects in parafoveal letter recognition, *Nature*, **226**, 177–178.

Bouma, H., and de Voogd, A. H. (1974), On the control of eye saccades in reading, *Vision Research*, **14**, 273–284.

Bowen, C., Gelabert, T., and Torgesen, J. (1978), Memorization processes involved in performance on the visual-sequential memory subtest of the Illinois Test of Psycholinguistic abilities, *Journal of Educational Psychology*, **70**, 887–893.

Bower, G. H., Black, J. B., and Turner, T. J. (1979), Scripts in memory for text, *Cognitive Psychology*, **11**, 177–220.

Bradley, L., and Bryant, P. E. (1978), Difficulties in auditory organisation as a possible cause of reading backwardness, *Nature*, **271**, 746–747.

Bransford, J. D., Barclay, J. R., and Franks, J. J. (1972), Sentence memory: A constructive versus interpretative approach, *Cognitive Psychology*, **3**, 193–209.

Bransford, J. D., and Johnson, M. K. (1973), Consideration of some problems of comprehension. In W. G. Chase (ed.), *Visual Information Processing*, New York, Academic Press.

Brewer, W. F. (1972), Is reading a letter-by-letter process? In J. F. Kavanagh and I. G. Mattingly (eds), *Language by Ear and by Eye*, Cambridge, Mass., MIT Press.

Briggs, G. G., and Kinsbourne, M. (1972), Visual persistence as measured by reaction time, *Quarterly Journal of Experimental Psychology*, **24**, 318–325.

Broadbent, D. E. (1967), Word-frequency effect and response bias, *Psychological Review*, **74**, 1–15.

Brown, R. (1973), *A First Language: The Early Stages*, Cambridge, Mass., Harvard University Press.

Bruce, D. J. (1964), The analysis of word sounds by children, *British Journal of Educational Psychology*, **34**, 158–170.

Bruder, G. A. (1978), Role of visual familiarity in the word-superiority effects obtained with the simultaneous matching task, *Journal of Experimental Psychology: Human Perception and Performance*, **4**, 88–100.

Bruner, J. S., and O'Dowd, D. (1958) A note on the informativeness of parts of words, *Language and Speech*, **1**, 98–101.

Buswell, G. T. (1922), Fundamental reading habits: A study of their development, *Supplementary Monographs no.* 21, Chicago, Chicago University Press.

Butler, B., and Hains, S. (1979), Individual differences in word recognition latency, *Memory and Cognition*, **7**, 68–76.

Cairns, H. S., and Kamerman, J. (1975), Lexical information processing during sentence comprehension, *Journal of Verbal Learning and Verbal Behavior*, **14**, 170–179.

Calfee, R. C. (1977), Assessment of independent reading skills: Basic research and practical applications. In A. S. Reber and D. L. Scarborough (eds), *Toward a Psychology of Reading: The Proceedings of the CUNY Conference*, Hillsdale, NJ, Lawrence Erlbaum Associates.

Calfee, R. C., Lindamood, P., and Lindamood, C. (1973), Acoustic-phonetic skills and reading in kindergarten through twelfth grade, *Journal of Educational Psychology*, **64**, 293–298.

Cermak, G. W. (1971), Short-term recognition memory for complex free-form figures, *Psychonomic Science*, **25**, 209–211.

Chafe, W. L. (1973), Language and memory, *Language*, **49**, 261–281.

Chall, J. (1967), *Learning to Read: The Great Debate,* New York, McGraw-Hill.

Chambers, S. M. (1979), Letter and order information in lexical access, *Journal of Verbal Learning and Verbal Behavior*, **18**, 225–241.

Chambers, S. M., and Forster, K. I. (1975), Evidence for lexical access in a simultaneous matching task, *Memory and Cognition*, **3**, 549–559.

Chomsky, C. (1969), *The Acquisition of Syntax in Children from 5 to 10*, Cambridge, Mass., MIT Press.

Ciuffreda, K. J., Bahill, A. T., Kenyon, R. V., and Stark, L. (1976), Eye movements during reading: Case reports, *American Journal of Optometry and Physiological Optics*, **53**, 389–395.

Clark, H. H. (1973), The language-as-fixed-effect fallacy. A critique of language statistics in psychological research, *Journal of Verbal Learning and Verbal Behavior*, **12**, 335–359.

Clark, H. H. (1978), Inferring what is meant. In W. J. M. Levelt and G. B. Flores d'Arcais (eds), *Studies in the Perception of Language*, Chichester, John Wiley & Sons.

Clark, H. H., and Clark, E. V. (1977), *Psychology and Language: An Introduction to*

Psycholinguistics, New York, Harcourt Brace Jovanovich.

Clark, H. H., and Sengul, C. J. (1979), In search of referents for nouns and pronouns, *Memory and Cognition*, **7**, 35–41.

Clayton, M. (1980), A test of morphological decomposition in prefixed words. Unpublished Honours project, University of Exeter.

Clifton-Everest, I. M. (1974), Immediate recognition of tachistoscopically presented visual patterns by backward readers, *Genetic Psychology Monographs*, **89**, 221–239.

Clifton-Everest, I. M. (1976), Dyslexia: Is there a disorder of visual perception? *Neuropsychologia*, **14**, 491–494.

Cohen, G., and Freeman, R. (1978), Individual differences in reading strategies in relation to handedness and cerebral asymmetry. In J. Requin (ed.), *Attention and Performance VII*, Hillsdale, NJ, Lawrence Erlbaum Associates.

Coltheart, M. (1972), Visual information-processing. In P. C. Dodwell (ed.), *New Horizons in Psychology 2*, Harmondsworth, Middlesex, Penguin Books.

Coltheart, M. (1975a), Iconic memory: A reply to Professor Holding, *Memory and Cognition*, **3**, 42–48.

Coltheart, M. (1975b), Doubts about iconic memory: A reply to Holding, *Quarterly Journal of Experimental Psychology*, **27**, 511–512.

Coltheart, M. (1977), Critical notice on E. J. Gibson and H. Levin (eds), *The psychology of reading, Quarterly Journal of Experimental Psychology*, **29**, 157–167.

Coltheart, M. (1978), Lexical access in simple reading tasks. In G. Underwood (ed.), *Strategies of Information-Processing*, London, Academic Press.

Coltheart, M. (1980), Iconic memory and visible persistence, *Perception and Psychophysics*, **27**, 183–228.

Coltheart, M., Besner, D., Jonasson, J. T., and Davelaar, E. (1979), Phonological encoding in the lexical decision task, *Quarterly Journal of Experimental Psychology*, **31**, 489–507.

Coltheart, M., Davelaar, E., Jonasson, J. T., and Besner, D. (1977), Access to the internal lexicon. S. Dornic (ed.), *Attention and Performance VI*, Hillsdale, NJ, Lawrence Erlbaum Associates.

Coltheart, M., and Freeman, R. (1974), Case alternation impairs word identification, *Bulletin of the Psychonomic Society*, **3**, 102–104.

Coltheart, M., Lea, C. D., and Thompson, K. (1974), In defense of iconic memory, *Quarterly Journal of Experimantal Psychology*, **26**, 633–641.

Coltheart, M., Patterson, K. E., and Marshall, J. C. (1980), *Deep Dyslexia*, London, Routledge & Kegan Paul.

Conrad, C. (1974), Context effects in sentence comprehension: A study of the subjective lexicon, *Memory and Cognition*, **2**, 130–138.

Corkin, S. (1974), Serial-ordering deficits in inferior readers, *Neuropsychologia*, **12**, 347–354.

Cosky, M. J. (1976), The role of letter recognition in word recognition, *Memory and Cognition*, **4**, 207–214.

Cromer, W. (1970), The Difference model: A new explanation for some reading difficulties, *Journal of Educational Psychology*, **61**, 471–483.

Cromer, W., and Wiener, M. (1966), Idiosyncratic response patterns among good and poor readers, *Journal of Consulting Psychology*, **30**, 1–10.

Crosby, R. M. N. (1968), *Reading and the Dyslexic Child*, London, Souvenir Press.

Cummings, E. M., and Faw, T. T. (1976), Short-term memory and equivalence judgements in normal and retarded readers, *Child Development*, **47**, 286–289.

Dale, H. C. A. (1973), Short-term memory for visual information, *British Journal of Psychology*, **64**, 1–8.

Daneman, M., and Carpenter, P. A. (1980), Individual differences in working memory and reading, *Journal of Verbal Learning and Verbal Behavior*, **19**, 450–466.

DeBoer, J. J., and Dallman, M. (1970), *The Teaching of Reading* (3rd edn), New York, Holt, Rinehart & Winston.

de Hirsch, K., Jansky, J. J., and Langford, W. S. (1966) *Predicting Reading Failure*, New York, Harper & Row.

Denckla, M. B., and Rudel, R. G. (1976a), Naming of object-drawings by dyslexic and other learning disabled children, *Brain and Language*, **3**, 1–15.

Denckla, M. B., and Rudel, R. G. (1976b), Rapid 'automatized' naming (R. A. N): Dyslexia differentiated from other learning disabilities, *Neuropsychologia*, **14**, 471–479.

de Villiers, P. A. (1974), Imagery and theme in recall of connected discourse, *Journal of Experimental Psychology*, **103**, 263–268.

Dick, A. O. (1971), On the problem of selection in short–term visual (iconic) memory, *Canadian Journal of Psychology*, **25**, 250–263.

Dick, A. O. (1974), Iconic memory and its relation to perceptual processing and other memory mechanisms, *Perception and Psychophysics*, **16**, 575–596.

Di Vesta, F. J., Hayward, K. G., and Orlando, V. P. (1979), Developmental trends in monitoring text for comprehension, *Child Development*, **50**, 97–105.

Doctor, E. A., and Coltheart, M. (1980), Children's use of phonological encoding when reading for meaning, *Memory and Cognition*, **8**, 195–209.

Doehring, D. G. (1968), *Patterns of Impairment in Specific Reading Disability*, Bloomington, Indiana University Press.

Donald, D. (1978), An analysis of the effects of contextually relevant illustrations on the learning to read strategies, performance and comprehension of 7-year-old average readers. Unpublished Master of Education thesis, University of Exeter.

Done, D. J., and Miles, T. R. (1978), Learning, memory and dyslexia. In M. M. Gruneberg, P. E. Morris and R. N. Sykes (eds), *Practical Aspects of Memory*, London, Academic Press.

Downing, J. (1973a), *Comparative Reading: Cross National Studies of Behavior and Processes in Reading and Writing*, New York, Macmillan.

Downing, J. (1973b), Linguistic Environments, II. In J. Downing (ed.), *Comparative Reading: Cross-national Studies of Behavior and Processes in Reading and Writing*, New York, Macmillan.

Downing, J. A. (1967), *The i.t.a. Symposium: Research Report on the British Experiment with i.t.a.*, Slough, National Foundation for Educational Research.

Dykstra, R. (1966), Auditory discrimination abilities and beginning reading achievement, *Reading Research Quarterly*, **1**, 5–34.

Edwards, D. C., and Goolaksian, P. A. (1974), Peripheral vision location and kinds of complex processing, *Journal of Experimental Psychology*, **102**, 244–249.

Efron, R. (1970), The relationship between the duration of a stimulus and the duration of a perception, *Neuropsychologia*, **8**, 37–55.

Egeth, H., Jonides, J., and Wall, S. (1972), Parallel processing of multi-element displays, *Cognitive Psychology*, **3**, 674–698.

Eichelman, W. H. (1970), Familiarity effects in the simultaneous matching task, *Journal of Experimental Psychology*, **86**, 275–282.

Ellis, N. C., and Miles, T. R. (1978a), Visual information processing as a determinant of reading speed, *Journal of Reading Research*, **1**, 108–120.

Ellis, N. C., and Miles, T. R. (1978b), Visual information processing in dyslexic children. In M. M. Gruneberg, P. E. Morris and R. N. Sykes (eds), *Practical Aspects of Memory*, London, Academic Press.

Ellis, N. C., and Miles, T. R. (1981), A lexical encoding deficiency I: Experimental evidence. In G. Th. Pavlidis and T. R. Miles (eds), *Dyslexia Research and its Applications to Education*, London, John Wiley & Sons.

Eriksen, C. W., and Collins, J. F. (1967), Some temporal characteristics of visual pattern perception, *Journal of Experimental Psychology*, **74**, 476–484.

Eriksen, C. W., and Collins, J. F. (1968), Sensory traces versus the psychological moment in the temporal organization of form, *Journal of Experimental Psychology*, 77, 376–382.

Farmer, A. R., Nixon, M., and White, R. T. (1976), Sound blending and learning to read: An experimental investigation, *British Journal of Educational Psychology*, 46, 155–163.

Fillenbaum, S. (1974), Syntactic factors in memory. In T. A. Sebeok (ed.), *Current Trends in Linguistics*, 12, The Hague, Mouton.

Fillmore, C. J. (1968), The case for case. In E. Bach and R. T. Harms (eds), *Universals in Linguistic Theory*, New York, Holt, Rinehart & Winston.

Fischler, I., and Bloom, P. A. (1979), Automatic and attentional processes in the effects of sentence contexts on word recognition, *Journal of Verbal Learning and Verbal Behavior*, 18, 1–20.

Fischler, I., and Goodman, G. O. (1978), Latency of associative activation in memory, *Journal of Experimental Psychology: Human Perception and Performance*, 4, 455–470.

Fisher, D. F. (1975), Reading and visual search, *Memory and Cognition*, 3, 188–196.

Fodor, J. A., Bever, T. G., and Garrett, M. F. (1974), *The Psychology of Language: An Introduction to Psycholinguistics and Generative Grammar*, New York, McGraw-Hill.

Fodor, J. A., and Garrett, M. F. (1967), Some syntactic determinants of sentential complexity, *Perception and Psychophysics*, 2, 289–296.

Fodor, J. A., Garrett, M. F., and Bever, T. G. (1968), Some syntactic determinants of sentential complexity, II: Verb structure, *Perception and Psychophysics*, 3, 453–461.

Forster, K. I. (1970), Visual perception of rapidly presented word sequences of varying complexity, *Perception and Psychophysics*, 8, 215–221.

Forster, K. I. (1976), Accessing the mental lexicon. In R. J. Wales and E. C. T. Walker (eds), *New Approaches to Language Mechanisms*, Amsterdam: North Holland.

Forster, K. I. (1979), Levels of processing and the structure of the language processor. In W. E. Cooper and E. C. T. Walker (eds), *Sentence Processing: Psycholinguistic Studies Presented to Merrill Garrett*, Hillsdale, NJ, Lawrence Erlbaum Associates.

Forster, K. I., and Bednall, E. S. (1976), Terminating and exhaustive search in lexical access, *Memory and Cognition*, 4, 53–61.

Forster, K. I., and Gartlan, G. (1975), Hash coding and search processes in lexical access. Paper delivered to Second Experimental Psychology Conference, University of Sydney.

Forster, K. I., and Olbrei, I. (1973), Semantic heuristics and syntactic analysis, *Cognition*, 2, 319–347.

Foss, D. J., and Hakes, D. T. (1978), *Psycholinguistics: An Introduction to the Psychology of Language*, Englewood Cuffs, NJ, Prentice-Hall.

Foss, D. J., and Jenkins, C. M. (1973), Some effects of context on the comprehension of ambiguous sentences, *Journal of Verbal Learning and Verbal Behavior*, 12, 577–589.

Foss, D. J., and Lynch, R. H. (1969), Decision processes during sentence comprehension: Effects of surface structure on decision times, *Perception and Psychophysics*, 5, 145–148.

Fox, B., and Routh, D. K. (1975), Analyzing spoken language into words, syllables and phonemes: A developmental study, *Journal of Psycholinguistic Research*, 4, 331–342.

Fox, B., and Routh, D. K. (1976), Phonemic analysis and synthesis as word-attack skills, *Journal of Educational Psychology*, 68, 70–74.

Fox, J. (1981), The effects of word similarity on recognition time. Unpublished Honours project, University of Exeter.

Frederiksen, C. H. (1975), Effects of context-induced processing operations on semantic information acquired from discourse, *Cognitive Psychology*, 7, 139–166.

Frederiksen, J. R., and Kroll, J. F. (1976), Spelling and sound: Approaches to the internal lexicon, *Journal of Experimental Psychology: Human Perception and Performance*, 2, 361–379.

Fry, E. (1964), A diacritical marking system to aid beginning reading instruction, *Elementary English*, 41, 526–529.

Gagné, R. M. (1965), *The Conditions of Learning*, New York, Holt, Rinehart & Winston.

Gagné, R. M. (1970), *The Conditions of Learning*, (2nd ed), New York, Holt, Rinehart & Winston.

Gardner, H., and Zurif, E. (1975), *Bee* but not *be*: Oral reading of single words in aphasia and alexia, *Neuropsychologia*, **13**, 181–190.

Gattegno, C. (1962), *Words in Colour*, Reading, Berks, Educational Explorers.

Gattegno, C. (1969), *Reading with Words in Colour: A Scientific Study of the Problem of Reading*, Reading, Berks., Educational Explorers.

Gentner, D. (1975), Evidence for the psychological reality of semantic components: The verbs of possession. In D. A. Norman, D. E. Rumelhart and the LNR research group, *Explorations in Cognition*, San Francisco, W. H. Freeman.

Gibson, E. J. (1965), Learning to read, *Science*, **148**, 1066–1072.

Gibson, E. J., and Levin, H. (1975), *The Psychology of Reading*, Cambridge, Mass, MIT Press.

Gibson, E. J., Pick, A. D., Osser, H. T., and Hammond, M. (1962), The role of grapheme-phoneme correspondences in the perception of words, *American Journal of Psychology*, **75**, 554–570.

Gibson, E. J., Shurcliff, A., and Yonas, A. (1970), Utilization of spelling patterns by deaf and hearing subjects. In H. Levin and J. P. Williams (eds), *Basic Studies in Reading*, New York, Basic Books.

Glanzer, M., and Ehrenreich, S. L. (1979), Structure and search of the internal lexicon, *Journal of Verbal Learning and Verbal Behavior*, **18**, 381–398.

Glushko, R. J. (1979), The organization and activation of orthographic knowledge in reading aloud, *Journal of Experimental Psychology: Human Perception and Performance*, **5**, 674–691.

Goins, J. T. (1958), *Visual Perceptual Abilities and Early Reading Progress*, Supplementary Educational Monograph no. 87, University of Chicago.

Golden, N. E., and Steiner, S. R. (1969), Auditory and visual functions in good and poor readers, *Journal of Learning Disabilities*, **2**, 476–481.

Golinkoff, R. M., and Rosinski, R. R. (1976), Decoding, semantic processing and reading comprehension skill, *Child Development*, **47**, 252–258.

Goodman, K. S. (1967), Reading: A psycholinguistic guessing game, *Journal of the Reading Specialist*, **6**, 126–135.

Goodman, K. S. (1970), Reading: A psycholinguistic guessing game. In H. Singer and R. B. Ruddell (eds), *Theoretical Models and Processes of Reading*, Newark, Del, International Reading Association.

Gough, P. B. (1972), One second of reading. In J. F. Kavanagh and I. G. Mattingly (eds), *Language by Ear and by Eye*, Cambridge, Mass., MIT Press.

Gough, P. B., Alford, J. A., and Holley-Wilcox, P. (1979), Words and contexts. In M. L. Kamil and A. J. Moe (eds), *Reading Research: Studies and Applications* (28th yearbook of the National Reading Conference), Clemson, SC, National Reading Conference.

Green, D. W. (1975), The effects of task on the representation of sentences, *Journal of Verbal Learning and Verbal Behavior*, **14**, 275–283.

Gupta, R., Ceci, S. J., and Slater, A. M. (1978), Visual discrimination in good and poor readers, *Journal of Special Education*, **12**, 409–416.

Guthrie, J. T. (1973a), Reading comprehension and syntactic responses in good and poor readers, *Journal of Educational Psychology*, **65**, 294–299.

Guthrie, J. T. (1973b), Models of reading and reading disability, *Journal of Educational Psychology*, **65**, 9–18.

Guthrie, J. T., and Goldberg, H. K. (1972), Visual sequential memory in reading disability, *Journal of Learning Disabilities*, **5**, 41–46.

Guthrie, J. T., and Seifert, M. (1977), Letter-sound complexity in learning to identify words, *Journal of Educational Psychology*, **69**, 686–696.

Guttentag, R. E., and Haith, M. M. (1978), Automatic processing as a function of age and reading ability, *Child Development*, **49**, 707–716.

Haber, R. N. (1976), Control of eye movements during reading. In R. A. Monty and J. W. Senders (eds), *Eye Movements and Psychological procsses*, Hillsdale, NJ, Lawrence Erlbaum Associates.

Haber, R. N., and Hershenson, M. (1973), *The Psychology of Visual Perception*, New York, Holt, Rinehart & Winston.

Haber, R. N., and Standing, L. G. (1969), Direct measures of short-term visual persistence, *Quarterly Journal of Experimental Psychology*, **21**, 43–54.

Haber, R. N., and Standing, L. G. (1970), Direct estimates of the apparent duration of a flash, *Canadian Journal of Psychology*, **24**, 216–229.

Haberlandt, K., and Bingham, G. (1978), Verbs contribute to the coherence of brief narratives: Reading related and unrelated sentence triples, *Journal of Verbal Learning and Verbal Behavior*, **17**, 419–426.

Hakes, D. T. (1971), Does verb structure affect comprehension? *Perception and Psychophysics*, **10**, 229–232.

Hakes, D. T., and Cairns, H. S. (1970), Sentence comprehension and relative pronouns, *Perception and Psychophysics*, **8**, 5–8.

Hakes, D. T., Evans, J. S., and Brannon, L. L. (1976), Understanding sentences with relative clauses, *Memory and Cognition*, **4**, 283–290.

Hakes, D. T., and Foss., D. J. (1970), Decision processes during sentence comprehension: Effects of surface structure reconsidered, *Perception and Psychophysics*, **8**, 413–416.

Halliday, M. A. K., and Hasan, R. (1976), *Cohesion in English*, London, Longman.

Harris, L. A., and Smith, C. B. (1976), *Reading Instruction: Diagnostic Teaching in the Classroom* (2nd eds), New York, Holt, Rinehart & Winston.

Haviland, S. E., and Clark, H. H. (1974), What's New? Acquiring new information as a process in comprehension, *Journal of Verbal Learning and Verbal Behavior*, **13**, 512–521.

Haygood, R. C., and Bourne, L. E., Jr (1965), Attribution and rule-learning aspects of conceptual behavior, *Psychological Review*, **72**, 175–195.

Healy, A. F. (1976), Detection errors on the word *the*: Evidence for reading units larger than letters, *Journal of Experimental Psychology: Human Perception and Performance*, **2**, 235–242.

Henderson, L., (1972), Visual and verbal codes: Spatial information survives the icon, *Quarterly Journal of Experimental Psychology*, **24**, 439–447.

Hicks, C. (1980), The ITPA visual sequential memory task: An alternative interpretation and the implications for good and poor readers, *British Journal of Educational Psychology*, **50**, 16–25.

Hochberg, J. (1970), Components of literacy: Speculations and exploratory research. In H. Levin and J. P. Williams (eds), *Basic Studies in Reading*, New York, Basic Books.

Hogaboam, T. W., and Perfetti, C. A. (1975), Lexical ambiguity and sentence comprehension, *Journal of Verbal Learning and Verbal Behavior*, **14**, 265–274.

Hogaboam, T. W., and Perfetti, C. A. (1978), Reading skill and the role of verbal experience, *Journal of Educational Psychology*, **70**, 717–729.

Holding, D. H. (1970), Guessing behaviour and the Sperling store, *Quarterly Journal of Experimental Psychology*, **22**, 248–256.

Holding, D. H. (1975a), Sensory storage reconsidered, *Memory and Cognition*, **3**, 31–41.

Holding, D. H. (1975b), Doubts about iconic memory: A reply to Coltheart, Lea and Thompson, *Quarterly Journal of Experimental Psychology*, **27**, 507–509.

Holmes, V. M., and Forster, K. I. (1972), Perceptual complexity and underlying sentence structure, *Journal of Verbal Learning and Verbal Behavior*, **11**, 148–156.

Hornby, P. A. (1971), Surface structure and topic-comment distinction: A developmental study, *Child Development*, **42**, 1975–1988.

Hornby, P. A. (1974), Surface structure and presupposition, *Journal of Verbal Learning and Verbal Behavior*, **13**, 530–538.

Hubel, D. H., and Wiesel, T. N. (1959), Receptive fields of single neurons in the cat's striate cortex, *Journal of Physiology*, **148**, 574–591.

Huey, E. B. (1908), *The Psychology and Pedagogy of Reading*, New York, Macmillan (republished by MIT Press, 1968).

Ikeda, M., and Saida, S. (1978), Span of recognition in reading, *Vision Research*, **18**, 83–88.

Isakson, R. L., and Miller, J. W. (1976), Sensitivity to syntactic and semantic cues in good and poor comprehenders, *Journal of Educational Psychology*, **68**, 787–792.

Jackson, M. D. (1980), Further evidence for a relationship between memory access and reading ability, *Journal of Verbal Learning and Verbal Behavior*, **19**, 683–694.

Jackson, M. D., and McClelland, J. L. (1975), Sensory and cognitive determinants of reading speed, *Journal of Verbal Learning and Verbal Behavior*, **14**, 565–574.

Jackson, M. D., and McClelland, J. L. (1979), Processing determinants of reading speed, *Journal of Experimental Psychology: General*, **108**, 151–181.

Jarvella, R. J., and Collas, J. G. (1974), Memory for the intentions of sentences, *Memory and Cognition*, **2**, 185–188.

Javal, L. E. (1878), Essai sur la physiologie de la lecture, *Annales d'Oculistique*, **82**, 242–253.

Jeffrey, W. E., and Samuels, S. J. (1967), Effect of method of reading training on initial learning and transfer, *Journal of Verbal Learning and Verbal Behavior*, **6**, 354–358.

Johnson, H. (1961), *The Sound Way to Correct Spelling* (Three graded spelling books based on a phonic approach), London. Longman.

Johnson, H., Jones, D. R., Cole, A. C., and Walters, M. B. (1972), The use of diacritical marks in teaching beginners to read, *British Journal of Educational Psychology*, **42**, 120–126.

Johnson, M. K., Bransford, J. D., and Solomon, S. K. (1973), Memory for tacit implications of sentences, *Journal of Experimental Psychology*, **98**, 203–205.

Johnson, N. F. (1975), On the function of letters in word identification: Some data and a preliminary model, *Journal of Verbal Learning and Verbal Behavior*, **14**, 17–29.

Johnson-Laird, P. N. (1974). Experimental psycholinguistics, *Annual Review of Psychology*, **25**, 135–160.

Johnson-Laird, P. N., and Stevenson, R. (1970), Memory for syntax, *Nature*, **227**, 412–413.

Johnston, J. C., and McClelland, J. L. (1973), Visual factors in word perception, *Perception and Psychophysics*, **14**, 365–370.

Jorm, A. F. (1979), The cognitive and neurological basis of developmental dyslexia: A theoretical framework and review, *Cognition*, **7**, 19–33.

Juola, J. F., Leavitt, D. D., and Choe, C. S. (1974), Letter identification in word, nonword and single-letter displays, *Bulletin of the Psychonomic Society*, **4**, 278–280.

Just, M. A., and Carpenter, P. A. (1980), A theory of reading: From eye fixations to comprehension, *Psychological Review*, **87**, 329–354.

Kahneman, D. (1968), Method, findings and theory in studies of visual masking, *Psychological Bulletin*, **70**, 404–425.

Kaplan, R. (1972), Augmented transition networks as psychological models of sentence comprehension, *Artificial Intelligence*, **3**, 77–100.

Kaplan, R. M. (1974), *Transient processing load in relative clauses*. Unpublished doctoral dissertation, Harvard University.

Kaplan, R. M. (1975), On process models for sentence analysis. In D. A. Norman, D. E. Rumelhart, and the LNR research group, *Explorations in Cognition*, San Francisco, W. H. Freeman.

Katz, L. (1977), Reading ability and single-letter orthographic redundancy, *Journal of Educational Psychology*, **69**, 653–659.

Katz, L., and Wicklund, D. A. (1972), Letter scanning rate for good and poor readers in grades two and six, *Journal of Educational Psychology*, **63**, 363–367.

Kennedy, A. (1978), Eye movements and the integration of semantic information during reading. In M. M. Gruneberg, P. E. Morris and R. N. Sykes (eds), *Practical Aspects of Memory*, London Academic Press.

Kennedy, D. K., and Weener, P. (1973), Visual and auditory training with the cloze procedure to improve reading and listening comprehension, *Reading Research Quarterly*, **8**, 524–541.

Kimball, J. (1973), Seven principles of surface structure parsing in natural language, *Cognition*, **2**, 15–47.

Kinsbourne, M., and Warrington, E. K. (1962), A disorder of simultaneous form perception, *Brain*, **85**, 461–486.

Kintsch, W. (1970), *Learning, Memory and Conceptual Processes*, New York, John Wiley & Sons.

Kintsch, W. (1974), *The Representation of Meaning in Memory*. Hillsdale, NJ, Lawrence Erlbaum Associates.

Kintsch, W. (1977), On recalling stories. In M. A. Just and P. A. Carpenter (eds), *Cognitive Processes in Comprehension*, Hillsdale, NJ, Lawrence Erlbaum Associates.

Kintsch, W., and Keenan, J. (1973), Reading rate and retention as a function of the number of propositions in the base structure of sentences, *Cognitive Psychology*, **5**, 257–274.

Kintsch, W., Kozminsky, E., Streby, W. J., McKoon, G., and Keenan, J. M. (1975), Comprehension and recall of text as a function of a content variable, *Journal of Verbal Learning and Verbal Behavior*, **14**, 196–214.

Kintsch, W., and van Dijk, T. A. (1978), Toward a model of discourse comprehension and production, *Psychological Review*, **85**, 363–394.

Klapp, S. T., Anderson, W. G., and Berrian, R. W. (1973), Implicit speech in reading, reconsidered, *Journal of Experimental Psychology*, **100**, 368–374.

Kleiman, G. M. (1980), Sentence frame contexts and lexical decisions: Sentence acceptability and word-relatedness effects, *Memory and Cognition*, **8**, 336–344.

Klein, H. A., Klein, G. A., and Bertino, M. (1974), Utilization of context for word identification in children, *Journal of Experimental Child Psychology*, **17**, 79–86.

Kolers, P. A. (1970), Three stages of reading. In H. Levin and J. P. Williams (eds), *Basic Studies on Reading*, New York, Basic Books.

Koppitz, E. M. (1958), The Bender Gestalt test and learning disturbances in young children, *Journal of Clinical Psychology*, **14**, 292–295.

Kroll, N. E. A., Parks, T., Parkinson, S. R., Bieber, S. L., and Johnson, A. (1970), Short-term memory while shadowing: Recall of visually and of aurally presented letters, *Journal of Experimental Psychology*, **85**, 220–224.

Krueger, L. E. (1970), Search time in a redundant visual display, *Journal of Experimental Psychology*, **83**, 391–399.

Krueger, L. E. (1975), Familiarity effects in visual information processing, *Psychological Bulletin*, **82**, 949–974.

LaBerge, D., and Samuels, S. J. (1974), Toward a theory of automatic information processing in reading, *Cognitive Psychology*, **6**, 293–323.

Lachmann, F. M. (1960), Perceptual-motor development in children retarded in reading ability, *Journal of Consulting Psychology*, **24**, 427–431.

Lahey, B. B., and Lefton, L. A. (1976), Discrimination of letter combinations in good and poor readers, *Journal of Special Education*, **10**, 205–210.

Lahey, B. B., and McNees, M. P. (1975), Letter discrimination errors in kindergarten through third-grade: Assessment and operant training, *Journal of Special Education*, **9**, 191–199.

Larsen, S. C., Rogers, D., and Sowell, V. (1976), The use of selected perceptual tests in differentiating between normal and learning disabled children, *Journal of Learning Disabilities*, **9**. 85–90.

Latour, P. L. (1962), Visual threshold during eye movements, *Vision Research*, **2**, 261–262.

Lefton, L. A. (1978), Eye movements in reading disabled children. In Senders, J. W., Fisher, D. F., and Monty, R. A. (eds), *Eye Movements and the Higher Psychological Functions*, Hillsdale, NJ, Lawrence Erlbaum Associates.

Lefton, L. A., Spragins, A. B., and Byrnes, J. (1973), English orthography: Relation to reading experience, *Bulletin of the Psychonomic Society*, **2**, 281–282.

Lesgold, A. M. (1972), Pronominalizations: A device for unifying sentences in memory, *Journal of Verbal Learning and Verbal Behavior*, **11**, 316–323.

Lesgold, A. M., Roth, S. F., and Curtis, M. E. (1979), Foregrounding effects in discourse comprehension, *Journal of Verbal Learning and Verbal Behavior*, **18**, 291–308.

Leslie, R., and Calfee, R. C. (1971), Visual search through word lists as a function of grade level, reading ability and target repetition, *Perception and Psychophysics*, **10**, 169–171.

Levelt, W. J. M. (1978), A survey of studies in sentence perception: 1970–1976. In W. J. M. Levelt and G. B. Flores d'Arcais (eds), *Studies in the Perception of Language*, Chichester, John Wiley & Sons.

Levin, H., and Kaplan, E. L. (1970), Grammatical structure and reading. In H. Levin and J. P. Williams (eds), *Basic Studies in Reading*, New York, Harper & Row.

Levin, H., and Watson, J. (1963), The learning of variable grapheme-to-phoneme correspondences: Variations in the initial consonant position. In *A Basic Research Program on Reading*, US Office of Education Cooperative Research Project no. 639, Ithaca, NY, Cornell University.

Liberman, I. Y. (1973), Segmentation of the spoken word and reading acquisition, *Bulletin of the Orton Society*, **23**, 65–77.

Liberman, I. Y., Shankweiler, D., Liberman, A. M., Fowler, C., and Fischer, F. W. (1977), Phonetic segmentation and recoding in the beginning reader. In A. S. Reber and D. L. Scarborugh (eds), *Toward a Psychology of Reading*, Hillsdale, NJ, Lawrence Erlbaum Associates.

Lovell, K., and Gorton, A. (1968), A study of some differences between backward and normal readers of average intelligence, *British Journal of Educational Psychology*, **38**, 240–248.

Lunzer, E. A., Dolan, T., and Wilkinson, J. E. (1976), The effectiveness of measures of operativity, language and short-term memory in the prediction of reading and mathematical understanding, *British Journal of Educational Psychology*, **46**, 295–305.

Lyle, J. G. (1968a), Performance of retarded readers on the memory-for-designs test, *Perceptual and Motor Skills*, **26**, 851–854.

Lyle, J.G. (1968b), Errors of retarded readers on block designs, *Perceptual and Motor Skills*, **26**, 1222.

Lyle, J. G. and Goyen, J. (1968), Visual recognition, developmental lag and strephosymbolia in reading retardation, *Journal of Abnormal Psychology*, **73**, 25–29.

McClelland, J. L. (1976), Preliminary letter identification in the perception of words and nonwords, *Journal of Experimental Psychology: Human Perception and Performance*, **2**, 80–91.

McClelland, J. L., and Johnston, J. C. (1977), The role of familiar units in perception of words and nonwords, *Perception and Psychophysics*, **22**, 249–261.

McClelland, J. L., and O'Regan, J. K. (1981), Expectations increase the benefit derived from parafoveal visual information in reading, *Journal of Experimental Psychology: Human Perception and Performance*, **7**, 634–644.

McCloskey, M., and Watkins, M. J. (1978), The seeing—more-than-is-there phenomenon; Implications for the locus of iconic storage, *Journal of Experimental Psychology: Human Perception and Performance*, **4**, 553–564.

McConkie, G. W., and Rayner, K. (1975), The span of the effective stimulus during a fixation in reading, *Perception and Psychophysics*, **17**, 578–586.

McConkie, G. W., and Rayner, K. (1976), Asymmetry of the perceptual span in reading, *Bulletin of the Psychonomic Society*, **8**, 365–368.

McConkie, G. W., and Zola, D. (1979), Is visual information integrated across successive fixations in reading? *Perception and Psychophysics*, **25**, 221–224.

McConkie, G. W., and Zola, D. (1981), Language constraints and the functional stimulus in reading. In A. M. Lesgold and C. A. Perfetti (eds), *Interactive Processes in Reading*, Hillsdale, NJ, Lawrence Erlbaum Associates.

McFarland, C. E., and Rhodes, D. D. (1978), Memory for meaning in skilled and unskilled readers, *Journal of Experimental Child Psychology*, **25**, 199–207.

MacKay, D. G. (1973), Aspects of the theory of comprehension, memory and attention, *Quarterly Journal of Experimental Psychology*, **25**, 22–40.

Mackworth, J. F. (1965), Visual noise causes tunnel vision, *Psychonomic Science*, **3**, 67–68.

Mackworth, J. F. (1972), Some models of the reading process: Learners and skilled readers, *Reading Research Quarterly*, **7**, 701–733.

McNinch, G. (1971), Auditory perceptual factors and measured first-grade reading achievement, *Reading Research Quarterly*, **6**, 472–492.

Mandler, J. M., and Johnson, N. S. (1977), Remembrance of things parsed: Story structure and recall, *Cognitive Psychology*, **9**, 111–151.

Manelis, L. (1974), The effect of meaningfulness in tachistoscopic word perception, *Perception and Psychophysics*, **16**, 182–192.

Manelis, L., and Tharp, D. A. (1977), The processing of affixed words, *Memory and Cognition*, **5**, 690–695.

Marcel, A. J. (in press), Conscious and unconscious reading. The effects of visual masking on word perception, *Cognitive Psychology*.

Marcel, A. J., and Patterson, K. (1978), Word recognition and production: Reciprocity in clinical and normal studies. In J. Requin (ed.), *Attention and Performance VII*, Hillsdale, NJ, Lawrence Erlbaum Associates.

Marcel, T. (1974), The effective visual field and the use of context in fast slow readers of two ages, *British Journal of Psychology*, **65**, 479–492.

Marmurek, H. C. (1977), Processing letters in words at different levels, *Memory and Cognition*, **5**, 67–72.

Marsh, G., Desberg, P., and Cooper, J. (1977), Developmental changes in reading strategies, *Journal of Reading Behavior*, **9**, 391–394.

Marshall, J. C., and Newcombe, F. (1966), Syntactic and semantic errors in paralexia, *Neuropsychologia*, **4**, 169–176.

Marshall, J. C., and Newcombe, F. (1973), Patterns of paralexia: A psycholinguistic approach, *Journal of Psycholinguistic Research*, **2**, 175–199.

Martin, J. P. (1954), Pure word blindness considered as a disturbance of visual space perception, *Proceedings of the Royal Society of Medicine*, **47**, 293.

Mason, J. M. (1976), The roles of orthographic, phonological and word-frequency variables on word-nonword decisions, *American Educational Research Journal*, **13**, 199–206.

Mason, M. (1975), Reading ability and letter search time: Effects of orthographic structure defined by single-letter positional frequency, *Journal of Experimental Psychology: General*, **104**, 146–166.

Mason, M. (1978), From print to sound in mature readers as a function of reader ability and two forms of orthographic, *Memory and Cognition*, **6**, 568–581.

Mason, M., and Katz, L. (1976), Visual processing of nonlinguistic strings: Redundancy effects and reading ability, *Journal of Experimental Psychology: General*, **105**, 338–348.

Mason, M., Katz, L., and Wicklund, D. A. (1975), Immediate spatial order memory and item memory in sixth-grade children as a function of reader ability, *Journal of Educational Psychology*, **67**, 610–616.

Massaro, D. W. (1973), Perception of letters, words and nonwords, *Journal of Experimental Psychology*, **100**, 349–353.

Massaro, D.W. (1975), (ed.), *Understanding Language: An Information Processing Analysis of Speech Perception, Reading and Psycholinguistics*, New York, Academic Press.

Massaro, D. W. (1976), Review of *The Psychology of Reading* by E. J. Gibson and H. Levin, *American Journal of Psychology*, **89**, 161–172.

Massaro, D. W., and Klitzke, D. (1977), Letters are functional in word identification, *Memory and Cognition*, **5**, 292–298.

Matin, E. (1974), Saccadic suppression: A review and an analysis, *Psychological Bulletin*, **81**, 899–917.

Mazurkiewicz, A. J. (1964), Teaching reading in America using the Initial Teaching Alphabet, *Elementary English*, **41**, 766–772.

Mehler, J., Segui, J., and Carey, P. (1978), Tails of words: Monitoring ambiguity, *Journal of Verbal Learning and Verbal Behavior*, **17**, 29–35.

Merikle, P. M. (1976), On the disruption of visual memory: Interference produced by visual report cues, *Quarterly Journal of Experimental Psychology*, **28**, 193–202.

Merikle, P. M., Coltheart, M., and Lowe, D. G. (1971), On the selective effects of a patterned masking stimulus, *Canadian Journal of Psychology*, **25**, 264–279.

Meyer, D. E., and Gutschera, F. (1975), Orthographic versus phonemic processing of printed words. Paper presented at meeting of the Psychonomic Society, Denver, Colorado, November.

Meyer, D. E., and Schvaneveldt, R. W. (1971), Facilitation in recognizing pairs of words: Evidence of a dependence between retrieval operations, *Journal of Experimental Psychology*, **90**, 227–234.

Meyer, D. E., Schvaneveldt, R. W., and Ruddy, M. G. (1974), Functions of graphemic and phonemic codes in visual word recognition, *Memory and Cognition*, **2**, 309–321.

Meyer, D. E., Schvaneveldt, R. W., and Ruddy, M. G. (1975), Loci of contextual effects in visual word recognition. In P. Rabbitt and S. Dornic (Eds), *Attention and Performance V*, New York, Academic Press.

Meyer, G. E., and Maguire, W. M. (1977), Spatial frequency and the mediation of short-term visual storage, *Science*, **198**, 524–525.

Mezrich, J. J. (1973), The word superiority effect in brief visual displays: Elimination by vocalization, *Perception and Psychophysics*, **13**, 45–48.

Miles, T. R., and Wheeler, T. J. (1974), Towards a new theory of dyslexia, *Dyslexia Review*, **11**, 9–11.

Mitchell, D. C. (1972a), *Visual memory in tachistoscopic recognition*. Unpublished doctoral dissertation, University of London.

Mitchell, D. C. (1972b), Short-term visual memory and pattern masking, *Quarterly Journal of Experimental Psychology*, **24**, 394–405.

Mitchell, D. C. (1976), Buffer storage modality and identification time in tachistoscopic recognition, *Quarterly Journal of Experimental Psychology*, **28**, 325–337.

Mitchell, D. C. (1979), The locus of the experimental effects in the rapid serial visual presentation (RSVP) task, *Perception and Psychophysics*, **25**, 143–149.

Mitchell, D. C., and Green, D. W. (1978), The effects of context and content on immediate processing in reading, *Quarterly Journal of Experimental Psychology*, **30**, 609–636.

Mitchell, D. C., and Green, D. W. (1980), Contextual effects in continuous reading. Paper presented to the British Psychology Society Conference on Reading, Exeter University, 22–23 March.

Morton, J. (1964), The effects of context on the visual duration threshold for words, *British Journal of Psychology*, **55**, 165–180.

Morton, J. (1969), Interaction of information in word recognition, *Psychological Review*, **76**, 165–178.

Morton, J. (1970), A functional model for memory. In D. A. Norman (ed.), *Models of Human Memory*, New York, Academic Press.

Morton, J. (1980), Disintegrating the lexicon: An information processing approach. Paper delivered at CNRS Conference on Cognitive Psychology at l'Abbeye de Royaumont, 15 June.

Moyle, D., and Moyle, L. M. (1974), *Modern Innovations in the Teaching of Reading* (2nd edn), London, University of London Press for the United Kingdom Reading Association.

Neisser, U. (1967), *Cognitive Psychology*, New York, Appleton-Century-Crofts.

Nelson, H. E., and Warrington, E. K. (1980), An investigation of memory functions in dyslexic children, *British Journal of Psychology*, **71**, 487–503.

Neville, M. H., and Pugh, A. K. (1976–1977), Context in reading and listening: Variations in approach to cloze tasks, *Reading Research Quarterly*, **12**, 13–31.

Newell, A. (1973), Production systems: Models of control structures. In W. G. Chase (ed.), *Visual Information Processing*, New York, Academic Press.

Newell, A., and Simon, H. A. (1972), *Human Problem Solving*, Englewood Cliffs, NJ, Prentice-Hall.

Newman, J. E., and Dell, G. S. (1978), The phonological nature of phoneme monitoring: A critique of some ambiguity studies, *Journal of Verbal Learning and Verbal Behavior*, **17**, 359–374.

Nodine, C. F., and Lang, N. J. (1971), The development of visual scanning strategies for differentiating words, *Developmental Psychology*, **5**, 221–232.

Nodine, C. F., and Simmons, F. G. (1974), Processing distinctive features in the differentiation of letterlike symbols, *Journal of Experimental Psychology*, **103**, 21–28.

Nodine, C. F., and Steurle, N. L. (1973), Development of perceptual and cognitive strategies for differentiating graphemes, *Journal of Experimental Psychology*, **97**, 158–166.

Norman, D. A. (1976), *Memory and Attention: An Introduction to Human Information Processing* (2nd edn), New York, John Wiley & Sons.

Norman, D. A., and Bobrow, D. G. (1975), On data-limited and resource-limited processes, *Cognitive Psychology*, **7**, 44–64.

Norman, D. A., and Rumelhart, D. E. (1975) (eds), *Explorations in Cognition*, San Francisco, W. H. Freeman.

Oaken, R., Wiener, M., and Cromer, W. (1971), Identification, organization and reading comprehension for good and poor readers, *Journal of Educational Psychology*, **62**, 71–78.

Olson, D. R. (1972), Language use for communicating, instructing and thinking. In J. B. Carroll and R. O. Freedle (eds), *Language Comprehension and the Acquisition of Knowledge*, New York, John Wiley & Sons.

O'Neill, G., and Stanley, G. (1976), Visual processing of straight lines in dyslexic and normal children, *British Journal of Educational Psychology*, **46**, 323–327.

O'Regan, J. K. (1975), *Structural and contextual constraints on eye movements in reading*. Unpublished doctoral dissertation, University of Cambridge.

O'Regan, K. (1979), Saccade size control in reading: Evidence for the linguistic control hypothesis, *Perception and Psychophysics*, **25**, 501–509.

Owen, F. W., Adams, P. A., Forrest, T., Stolz, L. M., and Fisher, S. (1971), Learning disorders in children: Sibling study, *Monographs of the Society for Research in Child Development*, **36**, no. 4.

Pace, A. J., and Golinkoff, R. M. (1976), Relationship between word difficulty and access of single-word meaning by skilled and less skilled readers, *Journal of Educational Psychology*, **68**, 760–767.

Paris, S. G., and Lindauer, B. K. (1976), The role of inference in children's comprehension and memory for sentences, *Cognitive Psychology*, **8**, 217–227.

Paris, S. G., and Upton, L. R. (1976), Children's memory for inferential relationships in prose, *Child Development*, **47**, 660–668.

Patterson, K. E. (1978), Phonemic dyslexia: Errors of meaning and the meaning of errors, *Quarterly Journal of Experimental Psychology*, **30**, 587–607.

Patterson, K. E., and Marcel, A. J. (1977), Aphasia, dyslexia, and the phonological coding of written words, *Quarterly Journal of Experimental Psychology*, **29**, 307–318.

Pavlidis, G. (1978), The dyslexics' erratic eye movements: Case studies, *Dyslexia Review*, **1**, 22–28.

Pavlidis, G. Th. (1979), How can dyslexia be objectively diagnosed? *Reading*, **13**, 3–15.

Perfetti, C. A., Finger, E., and Hogaboam, T. W. (1978), Sources of vocalization latency differences between skilled and less skilled young readers, *Journal of Educational Psychology*, **70**, 730–739.

Perfetti, C. A., Goldman, S. R., and Hogaboam, T. W. (1979), Reading skill and the identification of words in discourse context, *Memory and Cognition*, **7**, 273–282.

Perfetti, C. A., and Hogaboam, T. (1975), The relationship between simple word decoding and reading comprehension skill, *Journal of Educational Psychology*, **67**, 461–469.

Perfetti, C. A., and Roth, S. (1981), Some of the interactive processes in reading and their role in reading skill. In A. M. Lesgold and C. A. Perfetti (eds), *Interactive Processes in Reading*, Hillsdale, NJ, Lawrence Erlbaum Associates.

Phillips, W. A. (1971), Does familiarity affect transfer from iconic to short-term memory? *Perception and Psychophysics*, **10**, 153–157.

Phillips, W. A. (1974), On the distinction between sensory storage and short-term visual memory, *Perception and Psychophysics*, **16**, 283–290.

Phillips, W. A., and Baddeley, A. D. (1971), Reaction time and visual short-term memory, *Psychonomic Science*, **22**, 73–74.

Phillips, W. A., and Christie, D. F. M. (1977), Components of visual memory, *Quarterly Journal of Experimental Psychology*, **29**, 117–133.

Pick, A. D. (1965), Improvement of visual and tactual form discrimination, *Journal of Experimental Psychology*, **69**, 331–339.

Pickering, J. A. (1975), Frequency and lexical access in visual word recognition. Unpublished paper available from the author at Warwick University.

Pirenne, M. H. (1967), *Vision and the Eye*, (2nd edn), London, Chapman & Hall.

Pirozzolo, F. J., and Rayner, K. (1978), Disorders of oculomotor scanning and graphic orientation in Developmental Gerstmann Syndrome, *Brain and Language*, **5**, 119–126.

Pitman, J. (1959), *The Ernhardt Augmented (40-sound 42-character) Lower-case Roman Alphabet*, London: Pitman.

Pollatsek, A., Well, A. D., and Schindler, R. M. (1975), Familiarity affects visual processing of words, *Journal of Experimental Psychology: Human Perception and Performance*, **1**, 328–338.

Posner, M. I., and Boies, S. J. (1971), Components of attention, *Psychological Review*, **78**, 391–408.

Posner, M. I., Boies, S. J., Eichelman, W. H., and Taylor, R. L. (1969), Retention of visual and name codes of single letters, *Journal of Experimental Psychology, Monograph* **79** (1, part 2).

Posner, M. I., and Snyder, C. R. (1975), Attention and cognitive control. In R. L. Solso (ed.), *Information Processing and Cognition: The Loyola Symposium*, Hillsdale, NJ, Lawrence Erlbaum Associates.

Purcell, D. G., Stanovich, K. E., and Spector, A. (1978), Visual angle and the word superiority effect, *Memory and Cognition*, **6**, 3–8.

Pylyshyn, Z. W. (1973), What the mind's eye tells the mind's brain: A critique of mental imagery, *Psychological Bulletin*, **80**, 1–24.

Ratcliff, R., and Mckoon, G. (1978), Priming in item recognition: Evidence for the propositional structure of sentences, *Journal of Verbal Learning and Verbal Behavior*, **17**, 403–417.

Rayner, K. (1975a), The perceptual span and peripheral cues in reading, *Cognitive Psychology*, **7**, 65–81.

Rayner, K. (1975b), Parafoveal identification during a fixation in reading, *Acta Psychologica*, **39**, 271–282.

Rayner, K. (1977), Visual attention in reading: Eye movements reflect cognitive processes, *Memory and Cognition*, **4**, 443–448.

Rayner, K. (1978), Eye movements in reading: Eye guidance and integration. In P. A. Kolers, M. E. Wrolstad and H. Bouma (eds), *Processing of Visible Language*, New York, Plenum Press.

Rayner, K. (1979), Eye guidance in reading: Fixation locations within words, *Perception*, **8**, 21–30.

Rayner, K., and McConkie, G. W. (1976), What guides a reader's eye movements? *Vision Research*, **16**, 829–837.

Rayner, K., McConkie, G. W., and Ehrlich, S. (1978), Eye movements and integrating information across fixations, *Journal of Experimental Psychology: Human Perception and Performance*, **4**, 529–544.

Rayner, K., Well, A. D., and Pollatsek, A. (1980), Asymmetry of the effective visual field in reading, *Perception and Psychophysics*, **27**, 537–544.

Reicher, G. M. (1969), Perceptual recognition as a function of meaningfulness of stimulus material, *Journal of Experimental Psychology*, **81**, 275–280.

Richardson, E., DiBenedetto, B., and Bradley, C. M. (1977), The relationship of sound blending to reading achievement, *Review of Educational Research*, **47**, 319–333.

Richardson, J. T. E. (1975), The effect of word imageability on acquired dyslexia, *Neuropsychologia*, **13**, 281–288.

Riding, R. J., and Pugh, J. C. (1977), Iconic memory and reading performance in 9-year-old children, *British Journal of Educational Psychology*, **47**, 132–137.

Riggs, L. A., (1965), Light as a stimulus for vision. In C. H. Graham (ed.), *Vision and Visual Perception*, New York, John Wiley & Sons.

Riggs, L. A. (1976), Saccadic suppression of phospheres: Proof of a neural basis for saccadic suppression. In R. A. Monty, and J. W. Senders (eds), *Eye Movements in Psychological Processes*, Hillsdale, NJ, Lawrence Erlbaum Associates

Rosner, J., and Simon, D. P. (1971), The auditory analysis test: An initial report, *Journal of Learning Disabilities*, **41**, 384–392.

Roth, S. F., Perfetti, C. A., and Lesgold, A. M. (1979), Reading ability and children's word identification processes. Paper presented at the annual meeting of the Midwestern Psychological Association, Chicago, May.

Rozin, P., and Gleitman, L. R. (1977), The structure and acquisition of reading II: The reading process and the acquisition of the alphabetic principle. In A. S. Reber and D. L. Scarborough (eds), *Toward a Psychology of Reading: Proceedings of the CUNY Conferences*, Hillsdale, NJ, Lawrence Erlbaum Associates.

Rubenstein, H., Garfield, L., and Millikan, J. A. (1970), Homographic entries in the internal lexicon, *Journal of Verbal Learning and Verbal Behavior*, **9**, 487–494.

Rubenstein, H., Lewis, S. S., and Rubenstein, M. A. (1971), Evidence for phonemic recoding in visual word recognition, *Journal of Verbal Learning and Verbal Behavior*, **10**, 645–657.

Rubenstein, H., Richter, M. L., and Kay, E. J. (1975), Pronounceability and the visual recognition of nonsense words, *Journal of Verbal Learning and Verbal Behavior*, **14**, 651–657.

Rumelhart, D. E. (1975), Notes on a schema for stories. In D. G. Bobrow and A. M.

Collins (eds), *Representations and Understanding: Studies in Cognitive Science*, New York, Academic Press.

Rumelhart, D. E. (1977), Toward an interactive model of reading. In S. Dornic (ed.), *Attention and Performance VI*, Hillsdale, NJ, Lawrence Erlbaum Associates.

Rumelhart, D. E. (1977b), *Introduction to human information processing*, New York, John Wiley & Sons.

Rumelhart, D. E., and Siple, P. (1974), Process of recognizing tachistoscopically presented words, *Psychological Review*, **81**, 99–118.

Sabol, M. A., and DeRosa, D. V. (1976), Semantic encoding of isolated words, *Journal of Experimental Psychology: Human Learning and Memory*, **2**, 58–68.

Sachs, J. S. (1967), Recognition memory for syntactic and semantic aspects of connected discourse, *Perception and Psychophysics*, **2**, 437–442.

Sachs, J. S. (1974), Memory in reading and listening to discourse, *Memory and Cognition*, **2**, 95–100.

Saffran, E. M., and Marin, O. S. M. (1977), Reading without phonology: Evidence from aphasia, *Quarterly Journal of Experimental Psychology*, **29**, 515–525.

Sakitt, B. (1976a), Iconic memory, *Psychological Review*, **83**, 257–276.

Sakitt, B. (1976b), Psychophysical correlates of photoreceptor activity, *Vision Research*, **16**, 129–140.

Sakitt, B., and Appelman, J. B. (1978), The effects of memory load and the contrast of the rod signal on partial report superiority in a Sperling task, *Memory and Cognition*, **6**, 562–567.

Samuels, S. J. (1967), Attentional process in reading: The effect of pictures on the acquisition of reading responses, *Journal of Educational Psychology*, **58**, 337–342.

Samuels, S. J. (1968), Relationship between formal intralist similarity and the von Restorff effect, *Journal of Educational Psychology*, **59**, 432–437.

Samuels, S. J. (1970), Effects of pictures on learning to read, comprehension and attitudes, *Review of Educational Research*, **40**, 397–407.

Samuels, S. J., and Anderson, R. H. (1973), Visual recognition memory, paired-associate learning and reading achievement, *Journal of Educational Psychology*, **65**, 160–167.

Samuels, S. J., Dahl, P., and Archwamety, T. (1974), Effect of hypothesis/test training on reading skill, *Journal of Educational Psychology*, **66**, 835–844.

Sanford, A. J., and Garrod, S. C. (1981), *Understanding Written Language: Explorations of Comprehension Beyond the Sentence*, Chichester, John Wiley & Sons.

Savin, H. B. (1972), What the child knows about speech when he starts to learn to read. In J. F. Kavanagh and I. G. Mattingly (eds), *Language by Ear and by Eye*, Cambridge, Mass., MIT Press.

Scarborough, D. L. (1972), Memory for brief visual displays of symbols, *Cognitive Psychology*, **3**, 408–429.

Schank, R. C. (1975), *Conceptual Information Processing*, Amsterdam, North Holland.

Schank, R. C., and Abelson, R. P. (1977), *Scripts, Plans, Goals and Understanding*, Hillsdale, NJ, Lawrence Erlbaum Associates.

Scheerer, E. (1973), Integration, interruption and processing rate in visual backward masking: I. Review, *Psychologische Forschung*, **36**, 71–93.

Schuberth, R. E., and Eimas, P. D. (1977), Effects of context on the classification of words and nonwords, *Journal of Experimental Psychology: Human Perception and Performance*, **3**, 27–36.

Schuberth, R. E., Spoehr, K. T., and Lane, D. M. (1981), Effects of stimulus and contextual information on the lexical decision process, *Memory and Cognition*, **9**, 68–77.

Schvaneveldt, R. W., Meyer, D. E., and Becker, C. A. (1976), Lexical ambiguity, semantic context and visual word recognition, *Journal of Experimental Psychology: Human Perception and Performance*, **2**, 243–256.

Selfridge, O. G. (1959), Pandemonium: A paradigm for learning. In *The Mechanisation of the Thought Process*, London, Her Majesty's Stationery Office.

Selfridge, O. G., and Neisser, U. (1960), Pattern recognition by machine, *Scientific American*, **203**, 60–68.

Seymour, P. H. K., and Porpodas, C. D. (1980), Lexical and non-lexical processing of spelling in dyslexia. In U. Frith (ed.), *Cognitive Processes in Spelling*, London, Academic Press.

Shallice, T., and Warrington, E. K. (1975), Word recognition in a phonemic dyslexic patient, *Quarterly Journal of Experimental Psychology*, **27**, 187–199.

Shallice, T., and Warrington, E. K. (1977), The possible role of selective attention in acquired dyslexia, *Neuropsychologia*, **15**, 31–41.

Shallice, T., and Warrington, E. K. (1980), Single and multiple component central dyslexic syndromes. In M. Coltheart, K. E. Patterson and J. Marshall (eds), *Deep Dyslexia*, London, Routledge & Kegan Paul.

Shebilske, W. (1975), Reading eye movements from an information-processing point of view. In D. W. Massaro (ed.), *Understanding Language: An Information-processing Analysis of Speech Perception, Reading and Psycholinguistics*, New York, Academic Press.

Shebilske, W. L. (1978), Reading eye movements, macro-structure and comprehension processes. In P. A. Kolers, M. E. Wrolstad and H. Bouma (eds), *Processing of Visible Language*, New York, Plenum Press.

Shiffrin, R. M., and Gardner, G. T. (1972), Visual processing capacity and attentional control, *Journal of Experimental Psychology*, **93**, 72–82.

Shiffrin, R. M., and Schneider, W. (1977), Controlled and automatic human information processing: II. Perceptual learning, automatic attending and a general theory, *Psychological Review*, **84**, 127–190.

Singer, H., and Ruddell, R. B. (1976), *Theoretical Models and Processes of Reading* (2nd edn), Newark, Del, International Reading Association.

Singer, H., Samuels, S. J., and Spiroff, J. (1973–1974), The effect of pictures and contextual conditions on learning responses to printed words, *Reading Research Quarterly*, **9**, 555–567.

Sloboda, J. A. (1976), Decision times for word and letter search: A holistic word identification model examined, *Journal of Verbal Learning and Verbal Behavior*, **15**, 93–101.

Smiley, S. S., Oakley, D. D., Worthen, D., Campione, J. C., and Brown, A. L. (1977), Recall of thematically relevant material by adolescent good and poor readers as a function of written versus oral presentation, *Journal of Educational Psychology*, **69**, 381–387.

Smith, C. E., and Keogh, B. K. (1962), The group Bender-Gestalt as a reading readiness screening instrument, *Perceptual and Motor Skills*, **15**, 639–645.

Smith, E. E., and Haviland, S. E. (1972), Why words are perceived more accurately than nonwords: Inference versus unitization, *Journal of Experimental Psychology*, **92**, 59–64.

Smith, E. E., and Spoehr, K. T. (1974), The perception of printed English: A theoretical perspective. In B. H. Kantowitz (ed.), *Human Information Processing: Tutorials in Performance and Cognition*. Hillsdale, NJ, Lawrence Erlbaum Associates.

Smith, F. (1971), *Understanding Reading: A Psycholinguistic Analysis of Reading and Learning to Read*, New York, Holt, Rinehart & Winston.

Smith, F., Lott, D., and Cronnell, B. (1969), The effect of type size and case alternation on word identification, *American Journal of Psychology*, **82**, 248–253.

Snowling, M. J. (1980), Development of grapheme-phoneme correspondence in normal and dyslexic readers, *Journal of Experimental Child Psychology*, **29**, 294–305.

Southgate, V., and Roberts, G. R. (1970), *Reading—Which Approach?* London, University of London Press.

Sperling, G. (1960), The information available in brief visual presentations, *Psychological Monographs*, **74** (whole no. 498).

Sperling, G. (1963), A model for visual memory tasks, *Human Factors*, **5**, 19–31.

Sperling, G. (1967), Successive approximations to a model for short-term memory, *Acta Psychologica*, **27**, 285–292.

Spoehr, K. T. (1978), Phonological encoding in visual word recognition, *Journal of Verbal Learning and Verbal Behavior*, **17**, 127–141.

Spoehr, K. T., and Smith, E. E. (1973), The role of syllables in perceptual processing, *Cognitive Psychology*, **5**, 71–89.

Spoehr, K. T., and Smith, E. E. (1975), The role of orthographic and phonotactic rules in perceiving letter patterns, *Journal of Experimental Psychology: Human Perception and Performance*, **1**, 21–34.

Spring, C. (1971), Perceptual speed in poor readers, *Journal of Educational Psychology*, **62**, 492–500.

Spring, C., and Capps, C. (1974a), Encoding speed and memory span in dyslexic children, *Journal of Special Education*, **10**, 35–46.

Spring, C., and Capps, C. (1974b), Encoding speed, rehearsal and probed recall of dyslexic boys, *Journal of Educational Psychology*, **66**, 780–786.

Stanley, G. (1977), Visual-information processing and specific reading disability (dyslexia). In R. H. Day and G. Stanley (eds), *Studies in Perception*, Perth, University of Western Australia Press.

Stanley, G. (1978), Eye movements in dyslexic children. In G. Stanley and K. W. Walsh (eds), *Brain Impairment: Proceedings of the 1977 Brain Impairment Workshop*, Victoria, The Dominion Press.

Stanley, G., and Hall, R. (1973a), A comparison of dyslexics and normals in recalling letter arrays after brief presentation, *British Journal of Educational Psychology*, **43**, 301–304.

Stanley, G., and Hall, R. (1973b), Short-term visual information processing in dyslexics, *Child Development*, **44**, 841–844.

Stanners, R. F., and Forbach, G. B. (1973), Analysis of letter strings in word recognition, *Journal of Experimental Psychology*, **98**, 31–35.

Stanners, R. F., Forbach, G. B., and Headley, D. B. (1971), Decision and search processes in word–nonword classification, *Journal of Experimental Psychology*, **90**, 45–50.

Stanners, R. F., Jastrzembski, J. E., and Westbrook, A. (1975), Frequency and visual quality in a word–nonword classification task, *Journal of Verbal Learning and Verbal Behavior*, **14**, 259–264.

Stanovich, K. E. (1980), Toward an interactive-compensatory model of individual differences in reading fluency, *Reading Research Quarterly*, **16**, 32–71.

Stanovich, K. E. (1981), Attentional and automatic context effects in reading. In A. M. Lesgold and C. A. Perfetti (eds), *Interactive Processes in Reading*, Hillsdale, NJ, Lawrence Erlbaum Associates.

Stanovich, K. E. (in press), Relationships between word decoding speed and reading progress, *Journal of Educational Psychology*.

Stanovich, K. E., and Bauer, D. W. (1978), Experiments on the spelling-to-sound regularity effect in word recognition, *Memory and Cognition*, **6**, 410–415.

Stanovich, K. E., and West, R. F. (1979), Mechanisms of sentence context effects in reading: Automatic activation and conscious attention, *Memory and Cognition*, **7**, 77–85.

Stanovich, K. E., and West, R. F. (1981), The effect of sentence context on ongoing word recognition: Tests of a two-process theory, *Journal of Experimental Psychology: Human Perception and Performance*, **7**, 658–672.

Sternberg, S. (1967), Two operations in character recognition: Some evidence from reaction time measurements, *Perception and Psychophysics*, **2**, 45–53.

Sternberg, S. (1969), The discovery of processing stages: Extensions of Donder's method, *Acta Psychologica*, **30**, 276–315.

Stevens, A. L., and Rumelhart, D. E. (1975), Errors in reading: Analysis using an augmented transition network model of grammar. In D. A. Norman and D. E. Rumelhart, *Explorations in Cognition*, San Francisco, W. H. Freeman.

Swinney, D. A. (1979), Lexical access during sentence comprehension: (Re) consideration of context effects, *Journal of Verbal Learning and Verbal Behavior*, **18**, 645–659.

Taft, M., and Forster, K. I. (1975), Lexical storage and retrieval of prefixed words, *Journal of Verbal Learning and Verbal Behavior*, **14**, 638–647.

Taft, M., and Forster, K. I. (1976), Lexical storage and retrieval of polymorphic and polysyllabic words, *Journal of Verbal Learning and Verbal Behavior*, **15**, 607–620.

Tanenhaus, M. K., Leiman, J. M., and Seidenberg, R. W. (1979), Evidence for multiple stages in the processing of ambiguous words in syntactic contexts, *Journal of Verbal Learning and Verbal Behavior*, **18**, 427–440.

Taylor, G. A., Miller, T. J., and Juola, J. F. (1977), Isolating visual units in the perception of words and nonwords, *Perception and Psychophysics*, **21**, 377–386.

Taylor, S. E., Franckenpohl, H., and Pette, J. L. (1960), Grade level norms for the components of the fundamental reading skill, *EDL Information and Research Bulletin No. 3*, Huntington, NY, Educational Developmental Laboratories.

Terry, P., Samuels, S. J., and LaBerge, D. (1976), The effects of letter degradation and letter spacing on word recognition, *Journal of Verbal Learning and Verbal Behavior*, **15**, 577–585.

Terry, P. R. (1976–1977), Effect of orthographic transformations upon speed and accuracy of semantic categorizations, *Reading Research Quarterly*, **12**, 166–175.

Thompson, M. C., and Massaro, D. W. (1973), Visual information and redundancy in reading, *Journal of Experimental Psychology*, **98**, 49–54.

Thorndyke, P. W. (1977), Cognitive structures in comprehension and memory of narrative discourse, *Cognitive Psychology*, **9**, 77–110.

Thorne, J. P., Bratley, P., and Dewar, H. (1968), The syntactic analysis of English by machine. In D. Michie (ed.), *Machine Intelligence 3*, New York, American Elsevier.

Tieman, D. G. (1972), Recognition memory for comparative sentences. Unpublished doctoral dissertation, Stanford University.

Tinker, M. A. (1936), Eye movement, perception and legibility in reading, *Psychological Bulletin*, **33**, 275–290.

Tinker, M. A. (1946), The study of eye movements in reading, *Psychological Bulletin*, **43**, 93–120.

Tinker, M. A. (1958), Recent studies of eye movements in reading, *Psychological Bulletin*, **55**, 215–231.

Torgesen, J., and Goldman, T. (1977), Verbal rehearsal and short-term memory in reading-disabled children, *Child Development*, **48**, 56–60.

Trieschmann, R. B. (1968), Undifferentiated handedness and perceptual development in children with reading problems, *Perceptual and Motors Skills*, **27**, 1123–1134.

Tulving, E., and Gold, C. (1963), Stimulus information and contextual information as determinants of tachistoscopic recognition of words, *Journal of Experimental Psychology*, **66**, 319–327.

Tulving, E., Mandler, G., and Baumal, R. (1964), Interaction of two sources of information in tachistoscopic word recognition, *Canadian Journal of Psychology*, **18**, 62–71.

Turvey, M. T. (1973), On peripheral and central processes in vision: Inferences from an information processing analysis of masking with patterned stimuli, *Psychological Review*, **80**, 1–52.

Vellutino, F. R. (1977), Alternative conceptualizations of dyslexia: Evidence in support of a verbal-deficit hypothesis, *Harvard Educational Review*, **47**, 334–354.

Vellutino, F. R., Pruzek, R., Steger, J. A., and Meshoulam, U. (1973), Immediate visual recall in poor and normal readers as a function of orthographic-linguistic familiarity, *Cortex*, **9**, 368–384.

Vellutino, F. R., Smith, H., Steger, J. A., and Kaman, M. (1975), Reading disability: Age differences and the perceptual-deficit hypothesis, *Child Development*, **46**, 487–493.

Vellutino, F. R., Steger, J. A., DeSetto, L., and Phillips, F. (1975), Immediate and delayed recognition of visual stimuli in poor and normal readers, *Journal of Experimental Child Psychology*, **19**, 223–232.

Vellutino, F. R., Steger, J. A., Kaman, M., and DeSetto, L. (1975), Visual form perception in deficient and normal readers as a function of age and orthographic linguistic familiarity, *Cortex*, **11**, 22–30.

Vellutino, F. R., Steger, J. A., and Kandel, G. (1972), Reading disability: An investigation of the perceptual deficit hypothesis, *Cortex*, **8**, 106–118.

Vellutino, F. R., Steger, B. M., Moyer, S. C., Harding, C. J., and Niles, J. A. (1977), Has the perceptual deficit dypothesis led us astray? *Journal of Learning Disabilities*, **10**, 375–385.

Venezky, R. L. (1970), *The Structure of English Orthography*, The Hague, Mouton.

Venezky, R. L. (1974), Theoretical and experimental bases for teaching reading. In T, A. Sebeok (ed.), *Current Trends in Linguistics*, vol. 12, The Hague, Mouton.

Venezky, R. L. (1978), Reading acquisition: The occult and the obscure. In F. B. Murray and J. J. Pikulski (eds), *The Acquisition of Reading: Cognitive, Linguistic and Perceptual Prerequisites*, Baltimore, University Park Press.

Venezky, R. L., and Johnson, D. (1973), Development of two letter-sound patterns in grades one through three, *Journal of Educational Psychology*, **64**, 109–115.

Vernon, M. D. (1971), *Reading and its Difficulties*, Cambridge, Cambridge University Press.

Vernon, M. D. (1977), Varieties of deficiency in the reading progress, *Harvard Educational Review*, **47**, 396–410.

Volkmann, F. C. (1962), Vision during voluntary saccadic eye movements, *Journal of the Optical Society of America*, **52**, 571–578.

Volkmann, F. C. (1976), Saccadic suppression: A brief review. In R. A. Monty and J. W. Senders (eds), *Eye Movements and Psychological Processes*, Hillsdale, NJ, Lawrence Erlbaum Associates.

Volkmann, F. C., Schick, A. M. L., and Riggs, L. A. (1968), Time course of visual inhibition during voluntary saccades, *Journal of the Optical Society of America*, **58**, 562–569.

von Wright, J. M. (1972), On the problem of selection in iconic memory, *Scandinavian Journal of Psychology*, **13**, 159–171.

Wallach, L., Wallach, M. A., Dozier, M. G., and Kaplan, N. E. (1977), Poor children learning to read do not have trouble with auditory discrimination but do have trouble with phoneme recognition, *Journal of Educational Psychology*, **69**, 36–39.

Wanner, E. (1974), *On Remembering, Forgetting and Understanding Sentences: A Study of the Deep Structure Hypothesis*, The Hague, Mouton.

Wanner, E., and Maratsos, M. (1974), An augmented transition network model of relative clause comprehension. Unpublished paper available from the authors.

Warrington, E. K. (1979), Varieties of acquired dyslexia. Paper presented to the London meeting of the Experimental Psychology Society, January.

Warrington, E. K., and Shallice, T. (1979), Semantic access dyslexia, *Brain*, **102**, 43–63.

Weber, R. M. (1970), First graders' use of grammatical context in reading. In H. Levin and J. P. Williams (eds), *Basic Studies in Reading*, New York, Basic Books.

Werner, E. E., Simonian, K., and Smith, R. S. (1967), Reading achievement, language functioning and perceptual-motor development of 10- and 11-year-olds, *Perceptual and Motor Skills*, **25**, 409–420.

West, R. F., and Stanovich, K. E. (1978), Automatic contextual facilitation in readers of three ages, *Child Development*, **49**, 717–727.

Wheeler, D. D. (1970), Processes in word recognition, *Cognitive Psychology*, **1**, 59–85.

Whipple, C. I., and Kodman, F. J. (1969), A study of discrimination and perceptual learning with retarded readers, *Journal of Educational Psychology*, **60**, 1–5.

Wiener, M., and Cromer, W. (1967), Reading and reading difficulty: A conceptual analysis, *Harvard Educational Review*, **37**, no. 4.

Williams, J. P. (1968), Successive versus concurrent presentation of multiple grapheme–phoneme correspondences, *Journal of Educational Psychology*, **59**, 309–314.

Williams, P. (1976), Early reading: Some unexplained aspects. In J. E. Merritt (ed.), *New Horizons in Reading: Proceedings of the Fifth IRA Conference on Reading, Vienna, Austria*, Newark, Del., International Reading Association.

Willows, D. (1980), Utilization of graphic, syntactic and semantic cues in normal reading development. Paper presented to the British Psychology Society (Cognitive Section) Conference on Reading, Exeter University, March.

Woods, W. A. (1970), Transition network grammars for natural language analysis, *Communications of the ACM*, **13**, 591–606.

Woods, W. A. (1973), An experimental parsing system for augmented transition network grammars. In R. Rustin (ed.), *Natural Language Processing*, Englewood Cliffs, NJ, Prentice-Hall.

Woodworth, R. S. (1938), *Experimental Psychology*, New York, Henry Holt.

Zach, L., and Kaufman, J. (1972), How adequate is the concept of perceptual deficit for education? *Journal of Learning Disabilities*, **5**, 351–356.

Zangwill, O. L., and Blakemore, C. (1972), Dyslexia: Reversal of eye-movements during reading, *Neuropsychologia*, **10**, 371–373.

Zurif, E. B., and Carson, G. (1970), Dyslexia in relation to cerebral dominance and temporal analysis, *Neuropsychologia*, **8**, 351–361.

Author Index

232

Subject Index